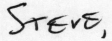

Steve,

Enjoy the read!

Keep this with your

Eagles flag.

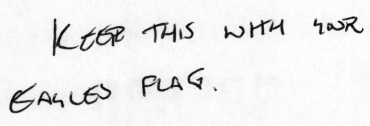

UNDERDOGS

THE PHILADELPHIA EAGLES' EMOTIONAL ROAD TO SUPER BOWL VICTORY

ZACH BERMAN

RUNNING PRESS

PHILADELPHIA

Running Press
Hachette Book Group
1290 Avenue of the Americas, New York, NY 10104
www.runningpress.com
@Running_Press

Printed in the United States of America

First Edition: October 2018

Published by Running Press, an imprint of Perseus Books, LLC, a subsidiary of Hachette Book
Group, Inc. The Running Press name and logo is a trademark of the Hachette Book Group.

The Hachette Speakers Bureau provides a wide range of authors for speaking events.
To find out more, go to www.hachettespeakersbureau.com or call (866) 376-6591.

The publisher is not responsible for websites (or their content)
that are not owned by the publisher.

Cover Image: © Getty Images. Photo Insert: © Getty Images and © AP Images

Print book cover and interior design by Josh McDonnell.

Library of Congress Control Number: 2018949119

ISBNs: 978-0-7624-9354-8 (hardcover), 978-0-7624-9352-4 (ebook)

LSC-C

10 9 8 7 6 5 4 3 2 1

To my father, who read everything I wrote.

I wish he could read this.

CONTENTS

FOREWORD

It took months to fully sink in. The Philadelphia Eagles are Super Bowl Champions! The day after the game we climbed aboard our charter flight home and each of us had a cardboard sign taped to our seats with our names and the words "Super Bowl Champion." Even that didn't prevent me from waking up some mornings and reassuring myself that this wasn't just some wild, wonderful dream.

I've had this theory for years that if you take the most talented team in the league and subtract three key players as the result of injuries, a potentially 13–3 team could end up 9–7 or even 8–8. I entered the 2017 season with the belief that this Eagles team was pretty good—good enough to win nine or ten games and make the playoffs if they stayed healthy in key areas. Super Bowl contention, however, was at least a year or two away. If you had told me that the Eagles would lose their great left tackle Jason Peters, their most talented linebacker Jordan Hicks, their all-around offensive weapon Darren Sproles, their kicker Caleb Sturgis, their special teams captain Chris Maragos, and ultimately, their MVP-caliber quarterback Carson Wentz, I would have predicted a four- or five-win season. To this day, what they achieved is absolutely unfathomable.

In the days that passed since Super Bowl LII, I've given a lot of thought as to what actually made this historic victory possible, and I realized it started with the head coach. The hiring of Doug Pederson was huge. I've known Doug for eighteen years and I was excited when I heard that he was the Eagles' choice. This former quarterback knows football and paid his dues as an assistant coach and coordinator. But most importantly, Doug is an excellent communicator. That's a must for success. He looks you in the eyes when he speaks. He listens, really listens. Players are comfortable in his presence and are encouraged to share their thoughts. None of this means that he lacks authority. While fans see a very affable man who treats everyone with warmth and respect, he can also be as tough and critical as the situation requires.

Former Eagles coach Dick Vermeil once told me that successful head coaches are surrounded by people who are good enough to take their jobs. Offensive Coordinator Frank Reich has already left to become head coach of the Indianapolis Colts, while Jim Schwartz was the former head coach of the Detroit Lions. I have no doubt that Jim will be a head coach again in the near future.

The most important personnel move in modern Eagles history occurred when the Eagles selected Carson Wentz with the second overall pick in the 2016 NFL Draft. I have always believed that a franchise quarterback is a key to a championship team. Not only is Carson Wentz a great athlete, he also embodies every attribute that great quarterbacks possess. He loves football and is totally dedicated to getting better every day. He's also a born leader. Every member of the organization, not just the team, likes and respects him. What an impact he's had on the Eagles! Even when he went down in the Rams game on December 10, he refused to disappear. He remained a contributor in the Eagles' quarterback meetings and was there to support Nick Foles in every possible way. Nick finished the job with some key wins, a great playoff run, and an MVP Super Bowl performance.

The Eagles' personnel department did an excellent job both before and during the season. Adding free agents Chris Long and LeGarrette Blount, among others, paid big dividends. Not only did both men make significant on-field contributions, they were key figures in the locker room. It's no accident that both were members of the 2016 Super Bowl Champion New England Patriots. They knew what it took to win it all, and this feeling was absorbed by their teammates. After the draft, the Eagles signed the undrafted Corey Clement, a Glassboro, New Jersey, native who was a productive back at the University of Wisconsin. He was impressive from day one.

They also signed the most talented free agent wide receiver on the market in Alshon Jeffery. He started out slow, but his impact increased during the season and right through the Super Bowl. Acquiring running back Jay Ajayi from the Miami Dolphins at the trade deadline certainly paid off, too.

Perhaps this season was saved when the Eagles plucked kicker Jake Elliott off the Bengals' practice squad after Caleb Sturgis was injured. Jake was clutch all the way and his 61-yarder—the longest field goal in Eagles history—won the first Giants game at the gun and provided enormous momentum going forward.

In recent years people have been telling me how much they would like to see me add a Super Bowl victory to my Eagles résumé. Believe me, it was everything I dreamed of and more. But I wanted it for the fans first and foremost. Eagles fans are amazing. Some take out second mortgages to buy season tickets. Some spend their last dollars to buy Eagles jerseys as Christmas gifts for their children. All remain dedicated through thick and thin.

I never prepared what I would say when that magic moment occurred. What came out of my mouth was completely spontaneous and from my heart. "Eagles fans everywhere—this is for you! Let the celebration begin!"

And what a celebration it was. I remember the Flyers Stanley Cup parades and certainly the Phillies World Series parades, but this one exceeded anything I could have imagined. The ride down Broad Street, the scene at the Art Museum—all memories that will live forever.

I'm glad Zach Berman has written this book chronicling a magical season. No journalist is better qualified to examine this incredible trip to the title. Zach is present every day, sitting in the front row at media conferences. His questions are always well thought out and professionally presented. In an age when too many writers and broadcasters simply throw rumors up against a wall with the hope that something sticks, Zach is thorough and factual in all that he writes. I'm certain that this publication will be referenced for years to come when people look back on the remarkable 2017 NFL season and the Eagles' triumph as the Champions of Super Bowl LII.

—Merrill Reese
May 30, 2018

PREFACE

The first time it occurred to me that this could be a special Eagles team came in a Charlotte hotel room in the minutes after midnight on October 12. The Eagles had just beaten the Carolina Panthers on a short week to advance to 5–1. They played without some of their key players on the road against one of the NFL's best teams on three days' rest. When they won, it sunk in that there was something different about this team.

Before that, though? This was a book I never expected to write. I wish I could say I stood on the sideline during those early-morning training camp practices in August and saw the makings of a Super Bowl team. They looked like they would be improved in 2017, and I expected a playoff contender, but certainly not the best team in the NFL.

That was also what made the Eagles' ride so magical. There wasn't the same "this is the year!" excitement that reaches a crescendo in Philadelphia most Septembers. 2017 was viewed as another year to build—Year 2 with the Doug Pederson–Carson Wentz partnership, the second year of Howie Roseman's renewal. Owner Jeffrey Lurie emphasized the team's long-term plan. It wasn't a Super Bowl–or–bust campaign.

But there was a unique, intangible quality about this team. When building a team, so much attention goes to the quantifiable elements—the height, weight, speed; how well a player passes, runs, catches, blocks, tackles, or covers; all the factors that lead to "talent." And the Eagles had as much or more talent than just about any team they played. In fact, going into the Super Bowl, they had the superior roster—even though they were the "underdogs."

But what made this team special was its personality and resiliency, a certain mental toughness and chemistry that was different than anything I had seen in my six years covering the Eagles. It's hard to identify what leads to those qualities—they're intangible, after all—but it was the right mix at the right time. The players were motivated and competitive, embracing and embodying the underdog mentality that had galvanized the fan base.

The injuries accumulated throughout the season, but they never caused an implosion. When Wentz injured his knee in Los Angeles, I figured it was one injury too many. Wentz seemed to be the reason the Eagles overcame all the injuries throughout the year. But the team was always more than one player—even their most valuable player.

There was a confidence that was not manufactured, that belied what odd-smakers suggested. I stood by Malcolm Jenkins's locker after the Eagles lost to the Dallas Cowboys in a meaningless season finale. They were still the top seed in the playoffs, but Nick Foles had struggled and many were left wondering whether the Eagles could beat the NFC's heavyweights.

"Why should fans be confident during the next two weeks in this team?" I asked Jenkins.

"Why wouldn't they be?" he responded.

I mentioned the way the offense played in the final two weeks of the season. Jenkins did not want to hear it. And it wasn't false confidence. He genuinely disagreed.

"We still won thirteen games," he answered. "Number one seed. Everyone's got to come through Philly. I don't care if you were starting at quarterback. . . . We win one game, we're in the NFC championship at home in Philly. So yeah, I don't care who we have at quarterback, who we have at offense, we'd take those odds."

He was right, except for one part. They wouldn't have won if I played quarterback. Foles, who had excelled at times throughout his career, thrived on the biggest stage. He was every bit the star quarterback that the franchise had once hoped for a few years earlier.

Jenkins saw something in his team that others might have missed, and I thought about that while driving home after the Eagles beat the Minnesota Vikings in the NFC Championship Game to advance to the Super Bowl. The

Philadelphia streets flooded with fans that night celebrating the NFC title. But inside the Eagles' locker room that night, they weren't surprised. And they weren't finished. They expected to go to the Super Bowl to win.

Throughout the week in Minnesota, they were not the "happy-to-be-here" team. That confidence that was present all season? It only intensified leading up to the Super Bowl. I predicted them to win that game because when putting aside the "Patriots mystique" and analyzing the matchups, I thought the Eagles had the advantage. However, I must admit, when Tom Brady took the ball down five points in the fourth quarter, I thought there was too much time on the clock and the Patriots would win. I had seen that movie before. Then Brandon Graham came through with the biggest sack in Eagles history and gave Philadelphia a memory decades in the making.

The scene in the postgame locker room revealed a joy that I had never seen before. Some players danced. Others cried. And when Doug Pederson gathered the team to speak, it could have come straight out of a sports movie. But this was as real as could be, and better than any script that could have been written.

The team was a privilege to cover—a journey ripe with rich storylines, compelling characters, and drama that made the Eagles' story unique.

My hope is that comes across in the following pages. As a beat reporter for the team, I'm provided a unique, behind-the-scenes view of the team. I'm in the locker room just about every day, conversing with the principle characters and seeing the story unfold in front of me. This book gave me the opportunity to take a step back from my day-to-day coverage of the team, to widen my lens to examine how this team and this unprecedented victory came to be. I was able to connect the dots of how the roster was assembled, how the team improved, and the qualities that inspired and made possible the team's Super Bowl run. I've also had the privilege of getting to know the team, and by the end of this book, you, too, should have a better understanding of the backstories of some of the players, coaches, and executives who made this season so special.

The reporting in this book is a compilation of what I've written and observed during my six years in the trenches with the team. Most of the quotes were said directly to me or in a press conference or group interview session.

If the quote or information was given directly to someone else, the source is identified in the text. The in-game dialogue comes from players who wore a microphone for videos released by NFL Films or the Eagles' official website. This was all weaved together into a narrative of the season. It's their story—not mine, so this is the only time you'll hear my voice in these pages.

• • •

The best part of every morning as a kid in the Philadelphia area was reading the sports page. I'd digest the *Philadelphia Inquirer*'s Eagles coverage instead of breakfast. I'd often read the *Philadelphia Daily News* during lunch. I learned about the Eagles through the words of their writers.

For that reason, covering the Eagles' first Super Bowl for those very publications—and now in this book—was deeply personal. In my daily reporting, I try not to lose sight of that eager, passionate teenager waking up today in Philly looking for the latest news on the Eagles (even if they're looking for that news on their phone). In many ways, my daily coverage is written for him or her. So is this book.

—Zach Berman
May 15, 2018

INTRODUCTION

FINALLY!

The wildest Super Bowl party wasn't the one going on in the overfilled streets of Philadelphia on February 4, 2018. It was unfolding in the Eagles' locker room at U.S. Bank Stadium.

After defeating the New England Patriots—the NFL's ultimate Goliath—Eagles players, coaches, and executives all gathered in the U.S. Bank Stadium locker room for a long-awaited, surreal celebration. They had answered the decades-long prayers of their city, and it was time to party. The players hadn't yet changed out of their uniforms when the music started and the champagne sprayed. But when Doug Pederson, the Eagles head coach, walked to the middle of the locker room and called everyone together under a purple banner that read "Super Bowl LII Champions," the celebration halted so Pederson could speak. After each of the team's wins throughout an improbable postseason run, Pederson would start off, "We're not done . . ."

And after every game, they'd shout back, "Yet!"

On this night, after their miraculous victory, Pederson started his postgame speech with a question.

"Are we done?"

"Yes!" the players responded in unison.

"We're done, baby!" Pederson said. "I'm so happy for every one of you—coaches, players, [owner Jeffrey] Lurie, the organization—for everything you guys have put yourself through from day one . . . [and battling] through the injuries. Guys, I can't tell you how happy I am. I really am. You're world champions, men!"

His players, euphoric from victory and the flowing libations, hung on every word. They shouted back in unison, "World champions!"

"World champions!" Pederson repeated. "Just look around! Look around. OK? This is what you guys have done. This is what you've accomplished. You guys get on me a lot about dress code and the way we practice and do things. Well, guess what? It's for this moment right here. For this moment! Because [that's] the discipline it takes to win this game. And this is a team game. We said before: An individual can make a difference. But . . ."

"A team makes a miracle!" The players finished Pederson's sentence, affirming what he told them throughout their playoff campaign.

"Goddamn! We made a miracle, dog!" one player shouted from the back.

"Philly's gonna burn!" another player hollered.

"Tonight, you did it. *We* did it!" Pederson said. "Against a fine football team. When you're asked, you're complimentary. But at the same time, we're going to party!"

Who was Pederson kidding? The party had already started—one look around the room would tell you that. Of course, the postgame locker room was only prologue for what would come next—a team-wide bonanza in Minneapolis that night, more celebrations in the days that followed, a parade up Broad Street that will long live in Philadelphia lore, and a lifetime of glory. They were the ultimate underdogs who had just won the Super Bowl with a backup quarterback as MVP. Pederson wasn't going to tame their fun.

"I don't know how or where we're going [tonight]," Pederson said. "But we'll figure it out!"

"All bottles on Mr. Lurie!" one player shouted to no one and everyone at the same time.

Then, all the players dropped to one knee and prayed. After the prayer, safety Malcolm Jenkins came to the middle of the group. A vocal leader of the team, he followed Pederson's speech after every game to address his teammates. Jenkins is a polished communicator when in front of the camera, but he's unplugged when riding the high of a victory. His candid rallying cry after quarterback Carson Wentz's season-ending knee injury eight weeks earlier set the tone for the Eagles' postseason response thereafter. When the Eagles reached the pinnacle of the NFL, what remained for Jenkins to say?

"Real talk, I don't got nothing for you, man!" Jenkins said. "I'm so proud to be a part of this team, man. I'm telling you, I've been in the league for f—ing nine years. I ain't never been a part of nothing like this and [never] seen nothing like this! First time we're bringing this thing back to Philly. I said it a few weeks ago, 'Be legendary!' That s— is etched in stone!"

Jenkins called for and was handed the Lombardi Trophy, the iconic twenty-two-inch, seven-pound sterling silver prize that had never seen the inside of the Eagles' South Philadelphia headquarters. Jenkins's teammates crowded him, sticking their hands up to touch the trophy.

"Every single person in this room is on this, man!" Jenkins said. "It took every single drop from every single one of y'all! And we did it! Despite what anybody said, man. We believed in each other every time something came, and we fought harder, we loved more, we grinded harder, and this is it. And we had more fun doing it than anybody. We started on family, and we end it on family. One, two, three: Family!"

With that, the party could resume. The players chewed cigars, sipped scotch, and sprayed champagne. Jenkins walked over to his locker, took off his jersey, and reached for the top shelf, where a bottle of Johnny Walker Blue awaited him. He took a big swig straight from the top before passing it around. This is how to celebrate a miracle. Back home in Philadelphia, fans poured into the streets, climbed greased light poles, and prepared to party until dawn. But inside the locker room, where players posed with the elusive Lombardi Trophy, there was an ecstasy that could only be understood by the fifty-one other teams that had won a Super Bowl before.

There were hugs and long embraces all around, with no teammate spared from the joy. The soundtrack ranged from Queen's "We Are the Champions" to Drake's "Big Rings" to Meek Mill's "Dreams and Nightmares," a song that had become an anthem for the Eagles during their playoff run. When the Philadelphia rapper's music pulsated throughout the locker room speakers, a dance party broke out. Players jumped up and down, singing along while holding their cell phones high into the air to document the moment. It was the type of raw emotion that is seldom witnessed, even after a dramatic victory.

There's always another week, a reason to try to stay humble, some controversy to avoid. Win the Super Bowl, though, and the cloak of decorum can come off. It's a feeling of pure joy few have experienced, and it was sweeter than the team could have imagined.

"This trumps everything," said linebacker Mychal Kendricks, who had played in Philadelphia since 2012. "Nothing else even matters. . . . There's a point in time where you just don't give a damn. And [this] was that time. . . . Do you understand what we just did, bro? First time in Philly history!"

PART 1

BUILDING THE MIRACLE TEAM

AN OBSESSIVE OWNER,
A DESPERATE CITY

Jeffrey Lurie waited almost twenty-four years to become a world champion. Throughout his time owning the Eagles, Lurie often used the word "obsession" when discussing his quest for the Super Bowl, and once said that winning a Super Bowl is "what I think about every single day of the year."

Lurie is not a Philadelphia native; he moved to the city in 1994 after purchasing the Eagles. But he felt like he had waited a lifetime for this. He acquired a franchise that was almost like a civic trust, the city's fandom an inheritance from generation to generation. There is no better indicator of the Eagles' role in Philadelphia and its suburbs than to sample the mood in the region the day after an Eagles win compared to an Eagles loss. And whenever the season concluded—whether it was after the last regular season game, a playoff game, or the Super Bowl in 1981 and 2005—there was always that irksome feeling of an unfulfilled dream. When that dream was finally realized, Lurie basked in his ability to deliver on a longstanding pledge.

"I can't tell you how many times people come up to me wherever it is— there's always Eagles fans everywhere—and they just . . . start crying," Lurie said of his experience after the Super Bowl. "They . . . start hyperventilating. The stories they have with their mothers, their fathers, who they got to experience it with. I don't know if you could explain it to fans everywhere in the country, but those of us who know the passion and the love for this football team, and how much they've wanted the Eagles to win a Super Bowl, it's like it gets played out every day in a real emotional, personal way."

Lurie never expected it to take so long. On May 6, 1994, he spent a then-record $185 million to purchase the Eagles, a team with a rabid fan base, a decrepit stadium, and little history of success in the Super Bowl era. In the thirty years before Lurie purchased the team, the Eagles totaled only ten winning seasons and one Super Bowl appearance. The *Wall Street Journal* panned the purchase, and Lurie wondered if he'd made the wrong decision. But he wanted into the NFL badly after a failed attempt to buy the New England Patriots, and the well-known passion of Philadelphia sports fans appealed to him. Lurie did not want to be an absentee owner, vowing that wherever he bought a team he would move there from Los Angeles. He's now in his twenty-fifth year in the Philadelphia area, where he's raised his two children and met his now-wife, Tina.

But when he bought the team, Lurie was an outsider (a Boston native) vowing to deliver to Eagles fans what had always eluded them. On May 17, 1994, the city hosted a celebration for the new owner. Among the thousand or so in attendance were Mayor Ed Rendell, Eagles players, Mummers, cheerleaders, season-ticket holders, and the Keystone Jazz Band.

"If I were to describe myself as any particular type of owner," Lurie said that day, according to the *Philadelphia Inquirer*, "it would be a fans' owner, because you really get great satisfaction when you can go out on the streets and scream you're number one and you're world champions."

LURIE'S LIST

Early in Jeffrey Lurie's ownership, he jotted down a list of what he thought were the essential tenets to a winning organization. Those included a first-class practice facility and a state-of-the-art stadium dedicated to the football team; a dynamic head coach with a strong staff of assistant coaches; a smart, creative football executive; and a franchise quarterback. The Eagles upgraded their facilities during Lurie's first decade of ownership, checking off the first two items on the list. The other parts were more uncertain.

His first coaching hire came in 1995 when he tabbed Ray Rhodes to lead the team. The Eagles achieved early success, reaching the playoffs in Rhodes's first two seasons and going 1–2 in the postseason. Then came two substandard seasons that forced Lurie to examine his next move. Lurie would later realize why Rhodes failed to produce a championship. "We didn't have a franchise quarterback, so it was not sustainable," he would say. But at the time, the failure to deliver cost the coach his job.

After the 1998 season, Rhodes was dismissed and the Eagles made a bold decision to hire Green Bay Packers Quarterbacks Coach Andy Reid, who had no coordinator experience and did not top any lists of hot coaching prospects. But Lurie and team president Joe Banner were sold on Reid's long-term vision, a sign of his organizational skills and leadership qualities. Reid didn't find much need to explain his plan to the public; he had the support of his bosses. The first step was picking their franchise quarterback. The Eagles chose Donovan McNabb with the No. 2 overall pick in the 1999 draft—the same selection the Eagles used on Carson Wentz seventeen years later—even though it was not met with universal approval. McNabb was famously booed on his draft day by a bus full of Eagles fans who trekked up the New Jersey Turnpike to New York City because they wanted running back Ricky Williams. The McNabb pick proved to be the right one, and together with Reid he led the Eagles to one of the most successful periods in franchise history. From 2001 to 2004, the Eagles made the NFC championship game every year. They lost in three consecutive Januarys before finally breaking through to reach Super Bowl XXXIX—where they faced the New England Patriots, Lurie's childhood team and the franchise he once tried to purchase. The Patriots beat the Eagles that evening, spoiling the Eagles' chance at a Super Bowl and solidifying a Patriots dynasty that would continue for years to come.

In 2008, Reid and McNabb would reach one more NFC Championship game together, but again, they went no further. A couple years later the Eagles tried loading up for another run with Michael Vick at quarterback, but lost in the first round of the playoffs two seasons in a row. After fourteen years, Reid's tenure in Philadelphia had run its course. The Eagles parted ways with Reid after he posted a 4–12 record in 2012, then hired Chip Kelly, the University of Oregon's innovative head coach who represented a significant shift from Reid. Kelly brought an up-tempo offense, a devotion to sports science, and—as it later turned out—an abrasive personality leading to internal griping about his interpersonal skills. Still, the Eagles reached the playoffs in Kelly's first year, and optimism grew in Philadelphia.

AN ELUSIVE SUPER BOWL

By 2014, twenty years had passed since Lurie bought the team. There was one Super Bowl appearance, five NFC championship games, and zero parades up Broad Street. While the fans had grown restless, Lurie explained that he felt the sting more than anyone else. That did not assuage the Lincoln Financial Field tailgaters, though, and they let him know it whenever they could. But Jeffrey Lurie remained resolute about his core beliefs. The faces changed, the facilities were updated, yet Lurie still sought the right combination of quarterback, coach, and personnel executive. He was convinced it would eventually materialize.

"I anticipated it being difficult, but I thought if you can get to four, five, six championship games, or get to the playoffs the majority of the years, as we have, then you'd have the luck that would transcend whatever strengths or weaknesses you have," Lurie said. "Other teams have had that. We haven't. If you keep the same values and the same passion to do the best you can, that'll right itself over time."

It didn't happen with Kelly. The team collapsed in the final month of the 2014 season to miss the playoffs. Then throughout the 2015 season, after major front-office and roster upheaval orchestrated by Kelly, Kelly's ship sank as trust in him had eroded. Lurie fired Kelly during the final week of the season, not even waiting until after the finale. Disappointed that the locker room and organization were muddled in low morale, he now sought a coach with "emotional intelligence," one who realized the fragility of a locker room and who could help rebuild the organizational culture. Lurie began the process of hiring his fourth coach, seemingly no closer to the Super Bowl than he was in 1994.

The hope from the fan base renewed every summer, but patience thinned and skepticism mushroomed.

After firing Kelly, Lurie took out the checklist he keeps in the top drawer next to his bed and added a new requirement for a successful franchise: chemistry. That elusive, immeasurable, all-important element in the locker room and the organization that breeds real success. Lurie had come to embrace the value of culture in a franchise's success, both among the players and between the coaches and the executives in the front office. In fact, one of Lurie's prevailing lessons between the Eagles' two Super Bowl appearances was the "absolutely paramount importance of collaboration and a selfless locker room culture."

It would be easy to confuse that motive with seeking what's comfortable and finding someone who can placate those in charge. That perception only became more pronounced when Lurie hired Doug Pederson as head coach in January 2016. Critics of the decision charged the Eagles with trying to recreate the Andy Reid era, since Pederson was the first quarterback Reid signed and was later his assistant coach in both Philadelphia and Kansas City. (Of course, with nine playoff appearances in fourteen years, there could have been worse eras to emulate.) Pederson was an unheralded hire—no other team interviewed him for a head coaching position—but Lurie said he "checked the box on everything." In Pederson, who was forty-seven at the time, Lurie saw a "smart, strategic thinker" with "unparalleled" communication skills, and found him "comfortable in [his] own skin." Lurie seemed unworried about how the hire would sell. After two decades, he had learned the standings sell more than the sizzle.

"The fans just want to win," Lurie said. "In picking a new head coach, it's not about winning the press conference. It's just about picking the best leader, and it was very clear to us that was the way to go."

The Eagles' search had started with two thousand pages of information on twenty-five candidates. That list was soon pared down to six available coaches. The Eagles spoke to two internal candidates and four from outside the organization. Multiple reports suggested the Eagles were trying in earnest to hire Giants offensive coordinator Ben McAdoo, but then the Giants swooped in and offered him their head coaching job. That created the perception that Pederson was not the top choice. Lurie insisted otherwise.

"At the end of the search," Lurie said, "this was an easy call."

• • •

After Pederson's hire, Lurie once again consulted his list. He had picked his new head coach and felt good about his staff. The facilities, with continued investment in renovations, were in great shape. He thought he had made strides toward creating the culture of collaboration required to win. But he still needed a franchise quarterback. He also needed someone who could figure out how to get one. Fortunately, that man was already in the building.

THE REDEMPTION
OF HOWIE ROSEMAN

Howie Roseman walked through the locker room after the Super Bowl with his shirt untucked under his suit, a Super Bowl Champions cap on his head, and the type of satisfied smile that could only belong to someone who lost his dream job only to be handed it back again.

"Nobody can ever say we're not world champions. Ever!" Roseman shouted in a moment of glee.

Two years prior to the Eagles' Super Bowl win—before he played a pivotal role in building the championship team—Roseman was in exile. Now he was back in a big way, and his smile showed it.

• • •

Growing up in Marlboro, New Jersey, Roseman didn't want to be the quarterback—he wanted to *pick* the quarterback. NFL draft day was like a holiday for Roseman. Take the 1995 draft. Roseman, then a nineteen-year-old at the University of Florida, sat on the couch of his off-campus apartment in Gainesville with stacks of handwritten notes, rankings of players, and a board broken down by areas of need and potential prospects for every team. This was before draft analysis became a cottage industry on the internet, too—it's not as if Roseman could just search Google for the information and the NFL rosters.

The New York Jets picked No. 9 that year. The Jets were Roseman's childhood team. When they selected Penn State tight end Kyle Brady, Roseman's roommate remembered him shouting with outrage. It was not the pick Roseman would have made if he were the Jets general manager.

But the lack of a traditional background as a football player himself also meant Roseman wasn't restrained by conventional wisdom. He once sat in his living room in college watching ESPN with his roommate, Justin Gordon, when a news report surfaced about a team releasing a player for no compensation.

"Justin, there's not enough trades in the NFL," Roseman said then. "They don't know how to value people and picks, and once I get there, I'm going to make more trades than you've ever seen."

Roseman and Gordon used to watch the Gators' practices from the fourth floor of a parking garage overlooking their practice field. Roseman once turned to Gordon and pointed out a young running back wearing No. 21, saying that player would become the next Herschel Walker. That player was Fred Taylor, who now ranks seventeenth on the NFL's all-time rushing list. Their other roommate at the time was Jedd Fisch, who later became an NFL assistant coach. Like Roseman, Fisch had lacked the background as a player that most coaches had, but still managed to fulfill his dream of breaking into professional football. Their nonplaying backgrounds created a stigma they both needed to overcome—something Roseman did not believe was valid.

"Do you want the heart surgeon who had bypass surgery, or do you want the one who has studied it the longest?" Roseman said. "When all those guys were playing in the NFL or at a high level in college, I was studying everything."

Roseman started sending letters to every NFL team while he was in high school. He chose Florida for his undergraduate studies because he wanted to be part of a big football school. He then studied law at Fordham so he could better understand NFL contracts. Roseman proved unrelenting trying to break into the NFL. He received a call back from Jets executive Mike Tannenbaum in 1999 after Roseman sent him twenty letters seeking an interview. "And every time I send you a rejection, you'd send a thank you for the rejection," Tannenbaum said in a 2010 *Philadelphia Inquirer* article, addressing Roseman.

Roseman had received an earlier rejection from Eagles President Joe Banner, but a more recent outreach proved successful. In 2000, after Roseman had finished law school and completed the bar exam as a backup plan, Banner offered him an unpaid internship with the Eagles examining the salary cap. Roseman took the job without skipping a beat. He arrived wearing a shirt and tie but without anywhere to sit, so Banner offered him a sliver of space on an administrative assistant's desk. To Roseman, it might as well have been the corner office; he now had access to an NFL organization, and he was going to make the most of it. He learned from scouts after hours. He developed relationships with agents. He interacted with players. He wrote scouting reports on his own time—just like he did in college—except now he could submit them to the Eagles' decision-makers. He quickly went from unpaid intern to full-on employee, and, in fact, needed new business cards often, going from director of football administration in 2003 to vice president of football administration in 2006 to vice president of player personnel in 2008. Finally, in 2010, Roseman's childhood dream came true when the Eagles named him the eleventh general manager in franchise history, choosing him over other candidates with more experience. At age thirty-four, he was the youngest GM in NFL history.

When he was first promoted to GM, Roseman did not have final say on personnel decisions; Head Coach Andy Reid retained those responsibilities. The Eagles reached the postseason in his first season as GM, losing in the first round to the Green Bay Packers. But Michael Vick had reestablished himself as a top quarterback, and Roseman helped set into motion the plan to go all in on a championship run in 2011 through the draft and by acquiring top free agents. However, what was initially dubbed the "Dream Team" turned out to be a nightmare group remembered for gross underachievement. The Eagles' top two draft picks were such bad fits that neither lasted beyond two seasons. And many of the high-profile free-agent signings backfired, highlighted by disappointing cornerback Nnamdi Asomugha. Reid was in charge of personnel, but the Eagles were regressing during Roseman's tenure as general manager and he took a share of the blame. The boat finally sank in 2012 when the Eagles finished 4–12, prompting Jeffrey Lurie to fire Reid after fourteen years.

Roseman, however, managed to keep his job as general manager, and, in fact, would now have more power than ever in assembling the roster. He was also a key part of the next coaching search. The owner did not hold the Eagles' sub-.500 record during Roseman's three years as general manager, along with a few questionable draft picks, against him. Lurie kept "voluminous notes" of the Eagles' decision-makers and "came to the conclusion that the person that was providing by far the best talent evaluation in the building was Howie Roseman."

The Eagles targeted college coaching sensation Chip Kelly at the start of their 2013 search for a new head coach. Kelly had just brought Oregon to the National Championship Game and had leverage in negotiations. He sent signals that he wasn't sure he wanted to leave college football for the NFL, and there was speculation that if he did, he would want personnel control. Kelly initially turned down the Eagles job, forcing the team to reroute their search. However, when Kelly's interest rekindled, he was offered the job and ultimately given final decision-making power over the 53-man roster, leaving control of the 90-man roster with Roseman. The person who controls the 90-man maintains final say on draft picks and free-agent acquisitions during the off-season, while the person who controls the 53-man determines which players take the field during the season.

"I'm a football coach. I'm not a general manager," Kelly said when he was hired. "I'm not a salary cap guy. I coach football. I need people who can go out there and say, 'Hey this is what you want. These are the people.'"

The marriage remained amicable in public, yet the Roseman-Kelly partnership splintered behind the scenes, coming to a head after the 2014 season. That year, the Eagles finished 10–6 for the second consecutive year, yet they failed to make the playoffs. Talking to the press after the season finale, Lurie offered an emphatic endorsement for Roseman and said he would "absolutely" return as general manager. He seemed almost taken aback by the question.

One day later, when Kelly was asked about his relationship with Roseman, he said their relationship was "good" and focused his answer on Roseman's work with the salary cap, calling that "his training." Kelly's praise was higher for Tom Gamble, the team's vice president of player personnel at the time, who was considered Kelly's closest confidant in the front office. Kelly called Gamble "a heck of a football guy" and lauded the work he did with the Eagles. It might not have been explicit, but it didn't take much decoding to realize who Kelly preferred picking the players.

Three days later, on December 31, 2014, Gamble was unceremoniously fired. Then, after forty-eight hours of mystery from the Eagles' front office, more big changes were announced. Lurie had stripped Roseman of personnel responsibilities and handed all football decisions to Kelly, believing that change was needed to maximize Kelly's effectiveness. He also wanted to let Kelly sink or swim with his own decisions. "I think it was much more Chip's requirement to sort of have a football guy that he was comfortable with in terms of helping him day to day and minute by minute," Lurie said at the time.

Lurie did not want to fire Roseman, though. The owner had long been fond of Roseman, and so he offered a contract extension, a raise, and new title as executive vice president of football operations. But it was still clear to all that Roseman had lost a power struggle to Kelly. Roseman's responsibilities were now limited to contract negotiations, salary cap management, and overseeing the team's medical and equipment staffs. His office was also moved to a different part of the team's facilities, far away from the "football people." Fancy title aside, Roseman was now less involved in personnel decisions than he was before he became the Eagles general manager. There was a rush in the media to figure out what had happened with Roseman: How could someone who rose so quickly crash so suddenly? One insider suggested that the attributes that allowed Roseman to rise so quickly hurt him when he reached the top because the relentless drive that fueled his motivation to reach the top created unrest around him.

The irony seemed to be that Roseman's crowning achievement as general manager was landing Kelly as head coach, and it was Kelly who contributed more than anyone to his downfall. It was unknown at the time how long Roseman would be away from football decisions, or if he would ever regain them. As it turned out, the interregnum would last just one year, and it was an invaluable year at that.

Roseman spent his gap year learning. With Lurie's blessing, Roseman studied management structures elsewhere in sports and business. He had worked in Philadelphia ever since Joe Banner gave him that sliver of office space, so this was his chance to see what happened beyond the Eagles headquarters at One NovaCare Way in South Philadelphia. He reached out to and learned from different executives throughout professional sports. The lessons he learned forced him to examine his own philosophies, and to consider what he would do if presented with the personnel role again.

"When you get an opportunity at a really young age and the arrow's pointing up and you don't really get a chance to step back, and [then] something like this happens, there's humility in it," Roseman said.

Roseman has often said the year away taught him the value of a franchise quarterback, although it doesn't take travel and research to reach that determination. More than anything, it allowed him to grasp the big-picture nature of the job and how so many people throughout the organization play a role in a team's success. Roseman did not need to micromanage; he needed to view the football operations from a macro perspective.

"I think during that year, when you have the opportunity to talk to people in Major League Baseball, in the NBA, in the NHL, in the EPL, and even working outside sports, you see that it's hard to have one person who just makes every single decision and runs every single department," Roseman said. "Sometimes we forget . . . it's big business. We're managing payroll, we have a bunch of resources, and we're trying to hire a lot of good people. Really, I think maybe we're the last sport that doesn't do [splitting up the jobs] as much."

Lurie observed the football executive role evolve during his ownership, indicating that the job requires "so much more than simply what has been [done] in the past decades with scouting." It requires big-picture strategic thinking.

"There's not a day that goes by where I'm just sitting in my office and I go, 'What are we doing with the roster?'" Roseman said, echoing his boss's observation. "That's why running the department is so big. There's not enough time in the day."

As Roseman was learning and growing throughout the 2015 season, Chip Kelly's fortunes were headed in the opposite direction. After two straight 10–6 campaigns, Kelly's Eagles went 6–9 through the first fifteen games, prompting Lurie to fire him before the final contest. Days later, Lurie revealed in a press conference that Roseman would retain his title of executive vice president of football operations, but that he would once again be involved in player personnel, sharing those duties with newly promoted Senior Director of Player Personnel Tom Donahoe, who had been a team advisor since 2012. A search would later commence for a new executive to work with Roseman, but that hire would not be made for a few months. Instead, Lurie indicated that Roseman, Donahoe, and the new head coach would collaborate in personnel matters.

• • •

F. Scott Fitzgerald wrote that "there are no second acts in American lives." Roseman proved otherwise with the Eagles. He once feared that his chance would never come again. But when he reclaimed his dream job, Roseman performed better than he did during his first act. The free-agent signings were sounder. There were fewer reaches in the draft. And when the Eagles finished with the best record in the NFL in 2017—in large part because they had the league's deepest roster—Roseman was named Executive of the Year. During Super Bowl Week, fans chanted his name from the stands as if he were a football hero himself. It was the redemption of Howie Roseman.

"It was a tough situation that he went through," team president Don Smolenski said. "He put his nose to the ground and he took some time to reflect, and it's nice to sort of see . . . him be able to enjoy this moment."

THE RIGHT STAFF

Jeffrey Lurie's plans for the post–Chip Kelly Eagles went beyond reinstalling Roseman to run the football operations department and hiring Pederson as head coach. Lurie also paid attention to the staff that would report to them.

After firing Kelly, the Eagles put Tom Donahoe in charge of personnel, though that would only be temporary. Donahoe, who had run personnel for the Pittsburgh Steelers and Buffalo Bills, would help Roseman until the Eagles found a new player personnel executive. Lurie emphasized the importance of that position, and after the 2016 draft, the Eagles hired Joe Douglas away from the Chicago Bears, where he had been in charge of college scouting.

Douglas took a much different path to his position than Roseman did. Whereas Roseman's break came on the business side of the football operations before adding scouting responsibilities, Douglas made his mark in the NFL as a grizzled scout.

He joined the Baltimore Ravens in 2000 as part of their "20/20 club," which is a title the Ravens gave the twentysomethings making around $20,000 per year, entering the organization learning departments ranging from scouting to coaching to equipment to training. His responsibilities included providing the "van grade." Douglas needed to make airports runs to pick up players, and he was tasked with observing how the prospect acted and communicated in the van. This taught him one way to learn about a player's character. It wasn't just how they acted in front of the head coach. How did they act when they were tired from a long flight and in the van with a low-level grunt?

Douglas tracked his career progression by the areas he visited. When he started as a regional scout, his superiors assigned him to find every prospect from Maine to Virginia. Then, Virginia stretched to North Carolina. He soon crossed the border to South Carolina. When he pumped gasoline in Georgia, Douglas realized the progress he made. He would arrive at one school at 7 a.m., learn everything he could about the player until 4 p.m., and then drive six hours before checking into a roadside hotel room. At night, he typed his report on the school he attended. He repeated this routine at a different school the next day.

Douglas's most important scouting find came in the fall of 2007. He was the Northeast area scout and became enthralled by a tall quarterback at the University of Delaware named Joe Flacco who had not yet become a household name. Douglas visited Flacco's practices. He went to Flacco's games. Delaware doesn't have a major college football program—someone sitting at home watching ESPN wouldn't know how good Flacco could become. Douglas called assistant general manager Eric DeCosta and implored DeCosta to watch Flacco.

"He had an enthusiasm in his voice that, knowing Joe [Douglas], he's not the type of guy who is going to get real excited about anything," DeCosta said. "But I knew Joe, and I knew Joe was excited about this quarterback."

DeCosta attended a Delaware-Navy game in October 2007 and watched Flacco throw four touchdowns. When the coaching staff became involved after the season, they realized why Douglas was enthusiastic. The Ravens drafted Flacco with the No. 18 overall pick in 2008. Flacco led Baltimore to the Super Bowl five years later and won Super Bowl MVP. His journey to Baltimore could be traced back to an unknown area scout watching him at Delaware.

"It's a tribute to Joe Douglas," said DeCosta, who called Douglas a "scout's scout."

Take a look at Douglas watching an Eagles practice, and you can tell why he works in football. He is still built like an offensive lineman, with his big frame and shaved head making him appear like he came out of central casting for the position. (In fact, Douglas had a bit role in the 2000 film *The Replacements*. He played, of course, an offensive lineman.)

After working his way up the scouting ladder, Douglas's biggest position came with the Eagles, where he was given oversight of the scouting staff and helped assemble the Super Bowl roster. Roseman still had final say on football decisions, but Douglas was in charge of the entire scouting department. He set the draft board and the free agent board. He brought a new language and grading system for the scouts and has significant input in all personnel decisions.

In March 2017, Lurie called hiring Douglas "the pivotal moment of the last year"—an overstatement considering it came the same year the Eagles acquired Wentz, but nonetheless stressing how critical Douglas was for the team's roster construction.

CRUCIAL DEFENSIVE ACCUMEN

During Pederson's introductory news conferences as Eagles head coach, Jim Schwartz stood on the side watching questions peppered toward the coach. Schwartz could empathize. He had been there before.

The most important assistant coaching hire for Pederson would be his defensive coordinator. Considering all of Pederson's coaching experience came on the offensive side of the ball, he needed a strong coach to lead the defense—this mirrored how important Jim Johnson's defensive expertise was to Andy Reid. Enter Schwartz, who spent five seasons as the Detroit Lions head coach from 2009 to 2013 and had been a defensive coordinator in Tennessee and Buffalo. Pederson announced Schwartz as the defensive coordinator in that opening news conference, which was an indication of just how significant the hire was for Pederson and the Eagles. He was part of the package being sold to Eagles fans that day.

Pederson and Schwartz did not have a relationship before 2016, and Schwartz was selective about where he would work. During the job interview, Pederson wanted to know how Schwartz would function in the assistant role. Schwartz's résumé, after all, was more extensive than Pederson's. Schwartz broke into the NFL in 1993 as unpaid intern on Bill Belichick's staff in Cleveland fetching cigarettes for assistant coaches and making airport runs. A Georgetown alum with an economics degree, Schwartz was recognized in a 2008 *New York Times* article as one of the NFL's leading practitioners in the use of statistical analysis, a characteristic that aided his teams' preparedness—including the 2017 Eagles defense. Schwartz worked his way up from position coach to a defensive coordinator with the Tennessee Titans before becoming the Lions head coach in 2009. Schwartz inherited a 0–16 team and brought them to the playoffs in three years, but he was fired after back-to-back losing seasons in 2012 and 2013. Even though he's believed to want to be a head coach again, he has proven to be one of the NFL's most credentialed defensive coordinators, offering the bona fides and the acumen needed for Pederson's staff.

The Eagles defensive coordinator position was an attractive opening for Schwartz. Pederson offered a job that was as close to a head coach as Schwartz could get at the time. Pederson called Schwartz the "head coach on defense," giving Schwartz rare autonomy. Schwartz could install the attacking, 4–3 defensive scheme that he had used throughout his career, a departure from what the Eagles used under Kelly and even from what Pederson was exposed to while he was an assistant coach with the Kansas City Chiefs. That formation promoted more reacting and less thinking on defense and was not overly complicated for players to learn. Schwartz called it "very easy in theory, difficult in execution."

"He's the professional on that side," Pederson said in 2016. "My expertise is on offense. His is over there on defense. So whether I have suggestions or not, it's our defense. But at the same time, he's the master. He's done it for 100 years. It's proven. Just like the offense that I've been in is proven. I wouldn't expect him to come over on the offensive side and make suggestions, whether it be on personnel or plays or the calling or any of that. So I kind of leave [the defense] up to him."

• • •

The Eagles were committed to making the quarterback paramount in the organization, and they had created a quarterback incubator with their coaching staff. Pederson brought experience as an NFL quarterback, quarterbacks coach, and offensive coordinator. Offensive coordinator Frank Reich offered the same background. And though John DeFilippo never played quarterback in the NFL, he was once a college quarterback who had also been a quarterbacks coach and offensive coordinator in the pros before becoming the QB coach in Philadelphia. In fact, both Reich and DeFilippo had called plays in the NFL. This quarterback-centric staff was a part of how Lurie envisioned the post-Kelly Eagles.

One other key part of Pederson's coaching staff were the holdovers from Kelly's regime. There were key assistants that the Eagles wanted to retain. Duce Staley, the fifth all-time leading rusher in Eagles history, remained the running backs coach. Jeff Stoutland stayed on as offensive line coach, a key hire considering the Eagles returned top-tier linemen such as Jason Peters, Jason Kelce, and Lane Johnson. Justin Peelle stayed on board as tight ends coach and Cory Undlin returned as defensive backs coach. This allowed for continuity.

"My personal evaluation of the coaching staff that he put together, or inherited, but was open to inherit, is outstanding," Lurie said in September 2017. "I mean, really outstanding. That's a huge credit because quarterback analysis, locker room chemistry, and the ability to put together a top-notch coaching staff, those are three real key ingredients. I think he aced them all."

The Eagles brought back almost the entire staff for the 2017 season. The one change came at wide receivers coach. After the receivers underachieved in 2016, the Eagles replaced Greg Lewis with Mike Groh. Another former quarterback, Groh had experience coaching high-profile wide receivers and was brought in to develop a critical position. DeFilippo's stock rose during his first year in Philadelphia and he became attractive to teams seeking an offensive coordinator. But the Eagles exercised their option to refuse an under-contract assistant coach from interviewing elsewhere. They did not want to disrupt the infrastructure created for Wentz, even if it could stymie DeFilippo's career advancement. The move was consistent with everything else the Eagles exhibited at the start of the off-season. Every decision was made with Carson Wentz in mind.

THE PURSUIT OF THE SAVIOR

January 2016 marked the beginning of a new era for the Eagles. Howie Roseman would oversee the attainment of personnel, and Doug Pederson and his staff would coach them. Their first step was finding a franchise quarterback, as discussed during Pederson's initial job interview. For all the hours of talk-radio debate about what kind of coach, general manager, defensive scheme, or offensive playing style it would take for the Eagles to win their first Super Bowl, all factors paled in comparison to the importance of the quarterback.

"You can then rationalize any structure you want," Lurie said. "Number one, you have to start with getting that quarterback."

During a four-month process in 2016, the Eagles identified Carson Wentz as the QB who would give them their best chance of a parade down Broad Street.

Much of the Eagles' brass first watched Wentz in person at the 2016 Senior Bowl in Mobile, Alabama, where the top senior college football prospects spend a week in January practicing for an all-star game in front of coaches, scouts, and executives from NFL teams.

Even Jeffrey Lurie attended practice—uncommon for an owner—which signaled the Eagles were gathering intel on Wentz. Lurie joined Roseman, who led the personnel team; Pederson, still in his first week as head coach; and a contingency of scouting staff and coaches. Wentz excelled during Senior Bowl practices, catching the eye of the entire group from Philadelphia. However, the Eagles' brass realized that they would not be able to select Wentz if they could not move near the top of the draft. As it stood, they were nowhere near the top.

"That was really the start of the process to try and move up, was here, in Mobile," Roseman said at the same event one year later. "The first thing [we noticed about Wentz] was the physical ability. Just seeing the ball come out of his hand, and the size and the athleticism, and the leadership. He had juice with his teammates inside and outside of the huddle."

The Eagles then met with Wentz at the Renaissance hotel in Mobile. Roseman witnessed Wentz's "photographic memory," discussing offensive plays and concepts as if they were happening on the screen. The Eagles also took to Wentz's personality, which they could see would sell in Philadelphia.

"He reminded us of Brent Celek," Roseman said, referring to the popular Eagles tight end. "Kind of Midwestern roots and the tough-guy persona."

The infatuation with Wentz continued at the annual scouting combine in Indianapolis, where all the draft prospects gather in a centralized location for on-field workouts, intelligence testing, medical examinations, and interviews. The Eagles conducted a fifteen-minute formal interview with Wentz, with team officials peppering him with questions. One question was about the freedom his coaches afforded him at the line of scrimmage. Quarterbacks coach John DeFilippo wondered what Wentz would say about the criticism that he's not as prepared for the NFL as someone from a bigger college football program.

They watched game film from Wentz's senior season at North Dakota State and asked him why he made specific decisions regarding a number of particular plays. Wentz shared exactly what he was thinking in those moments that occurred months earlier, and could easily recall each play and explain his process in making each decision. DeFilippo quizzed him on the route of a given wide receiver and asked how Wentz would react against coverage he might see in the NFL, and Wentz didn't hesitate in giving his answer. For casual football fans, it might sound like listening to a foreign language. For football fanatics, it was like listening to Mozart conduct an orchestra.

"Good job, man!" DeFilippo said at the end of the interview, as captured on the team website.

On the day Wentz threw passes at the combine, Eagles officials watched from a suite at Lucas Oil Stadium. Two doors down, the Miami Dolphins' front office set up shop. The two teams started to lay the framework of a trade that would move the Eagles into the top ten of the upcoming draft. They packaged the No. 13 pick along with starting defensive players Byron Maxwell and Kiko Alonso to receive the Dolphins' No. 8 pick. That put the Eagles in striking distance for a quarterback, but they were not there yet.

"We were trying to get to one or two to get a quarterback," Roseman said.

After the combine, the Eagles' commitment to drafting a quarterback only intensified. Lurie, Pederson, Roseman, DeFilippo, Reich, and Donahoe were all part of the Eagles' traveling contingent that arrived at North Dakota State's campus on March 30, 2016, to meet with Carson Wentz. They gathered in a meeting room and witnessed the same football acumen from the college senior that they had encountered in Indianapolis. Lurie wondered if the evaluators had ever seen anything like it, and their comparisons put Wentz in exclusive company. On the field, Wentz showed athleticism rare for a 6-foot-5, 237-pound quarterback. He made all the throws the Eagles needed to see. He continued checking all the boxes.

Later that night, they all went to dinner at Mezzaluna, a restaurant in downtown Fargo located just behind the iconic Fargo Theatre. There was an ovation when Wentz entered the restaurant, with patrons snapping photos on their cell phones. The television above the bar was tuned to ESPN, which happened to be showing Wentz's college highlights. The local hero's appearance even interrupted a date in the restaurant when a woman admonished her companion for gawking at Wentz.

Fargo is fourteen hundred miles from Philadelphia and is not exactly a destination for many from back East. But on that night, twenty-eight-year-old John Pisula, an Eagles fan from Willow Grove, Pennsylvania, a Philadelphia suburb, happened to be in Fargo for business and had taken clients out for a nice dinner. Pisula spotted the Eagles officials sitting around a table and his face started to flush. His dinner guests wondered what he had observed.

Wentz sat at the head of the table, flanked by Lurie to his left and Pederson to his right. Roseman sat next to Lurie with Reich on the other side. DeFilippo sat next to Pederson with Donahoe on the other side. They shared a toast. Wentz raised a glass of water.

Pisula realized it was a business dinner on a scouting trip and vacillated between whether to interrupt or not. He also wondered what stroke of serendipity brought him to an upscale eatery in Fargo, of all places, where the owner, head coach, and top executives of his favorite sports team were seated with their potential franchise quarterback. It would be one thing if this was in Center City, Philadelphia. But this was not Broad Street; this was Fargo's version of Broadway. Pisula decided to approach the table and ask for photos.

"I didn't want to blow up their spot, but this was like the coolest thing I'd ever done," Pisula said. "It's something I can tell my kids about . . . especially if Carson is the quarterback who leads us to a few Super Bowls."

Pisula posted the photos on Twitter and they went viral within minutes, circulating via media outlets to Eagles fans everywhere. There was no more mystery—the Eagles were serious about Wentz, their interest available for anyone with a social media account to see. Roseman received a text message from another Eagles executive revealing that the dinner had become news. It offered the Eagles' brass a lesson about how social media affected scouting.

When Pederson was later asked what he remembered about the dinner, he joked, "Too many selfies."

"Yeah," Roseman said, "Eagles Nation is everywhere!"

At one point, Roseman stepped outside to answer a call. When he walked back into the restaurant, he considered the way Wentz treated all the onlookers as part of the scouting report. He even overheard the manager and hostess discussing Wentz.

"Carson is just the greatest guy," Roseman remembered them saying. "He's always so humble, and he's always so appreciative of all of us here."

On the flight home, there wasn't much debate. Wentz fit what they wanted. He was the highest-rated quarterback prospect they had evaluated since Indianapolis Colts quarterback Andrew Luck in 2012.

"We came to the unanimous conclusion, and I rely on the football people more than myself, but what I heard from all the football people in there is they thought Carson Wentz had the chance to be a very special QB," Lurie said. "Checked every box from personality to talent to motivation, every box possible."

After the Fargo trip, the Eagles were convinced they needed to surrender whatever it took to move up to acquire Wentz. The team later hosted Wentz in Philadelphia for a predraft visit, solidifying their interest. It was his first visit to

Philadelphia and only lasted twenty-four hours, but it was long enough for the Eagles to share with Wentz that they wanted him on their team.

The Eagles accumulated an eighty-page report on Wentz ranging from his psychological makeup to his medical history. They thought they needed a top-two pick to get him, and at the moment the Tennessee Titans held the top selection and the Cleveland Browns were at No. 2. The Titans didn't need a quarterback and were considered a likely candidate to trade their pick, but as it turned out, that trade wouldn't be with the Eagles.

On April 14, 2016, the Los Angeles Rams worked out a deal with the Titans to acquire the No. 1 pick. Although the Rams showed interest in both University of California quarterback Jared Goff and Wentz, they intended to pick Goff. On the day that trade was made, Goff was actually visiting the Eagles' headquarters for a get-to-know-you session. During that meeting, Goff's phone buzzed with a message about the Rams-Titans deal.

The Eagles, who preferred Wentz over Goff anyway, now knew that they absolutely had to acquire the No. 2 pick from the Browns to get their man. Fortunately for the Eagles, Cleveland, which was just as desperate for a franchise quarterback, was not sold on Wentz and was more inclined to stockpile draft picks by trading No. 2. In an interview with an ESPN affiliate, a Browns official indicated that the organization did not believe Wentz would become a top-twenty quarterback in the NFL. The Eagles offered a bounty of draft picks, including two first-rounder picks, a second-round pick, a third-round pick, and a fourth-round pick, and Cleveland accepted the deal. The Eagles were now in position to select Wentz.

"We made a decision to not go in that direction," Browns coach Hue Jackson said of Wentz before Week 1 of the 2016 season. "A lot of things are going to be written and said because we didn't, but it's going to take a little time before that decision of what we did or what anyone else did will come to fruition."

Wentz went to Chicago on April 28, 2016, to attend the draft along with a number of other top prospects. He ate at a Fargo restaurant called Maxwell's on the night before, giving him one last chance at normalcy before his life forever changed. The draft event inself might have been a formality at that point, but once the Eagles picked him, there was no going back to his North Dakota cocoon. Wentz sat in the green room of the Auditorium Theatre and, after the Rams took Goff with the first overall pick, he heard his phone ring and saw a number with a 215 area code.

"Carson, Howie Roseman, how we doing, bud?" Roseman said into the phone, as captured by the team website.

"Doing great, how are you?" Wentz responded.

"Ready to be an Eagle?" Roseman asked.

"Yes, sir!" Wentz answered.

"We're really excited to get you, man," Roseman said. "It's going to be great. We're going to have a lot of fun."

"Most definitely," Wentz responded. "I'm excited."

"Enjoy the moment with your family, can't wait to see you when you get here," Roseman finished before giving the phone to Jeffrey Lurie.

"Hey, Carson," Lurie said. "Congratulations. You ready to join our Eagles family?"

"Yes, I am! Real excited," Wentz answered.

"Great! Can't wait to see you tomorrow," Lurie said. "Long time leading up to this. I know you've been waiting. I can't tell you, we can't be more excited . . . . Enjoy this moment. We'll keep it quiet until we hand it in. Can't wait to work with you."

Pederson then took the phone. After initial pleasantries, the coach told Wentz that he seemed "a little calm" through the draft night hysteria.

"You gotta be!" Wentz said.

"How's it feel to be an Eagle?" Pederson asked.

"Feels terrific," Wentz responded. "You guys sold me when I was there. I'm ready to go!"

"We tried to sell it hard!" Pederson said.

Wentz then spoke with Reich and DeFilippo, who both had personalized messages for their new quarterback.

"All I was thinking about today was when you were here in the building and the way we finished our meeting," Reich said, "and we were like, 'We'd love to have you in this room,' and you looked at us and said, 'Hey, make it happen!' So Mr. Lurie and Howie, they made it happen. So excited. So excited. Can't even tell you. And it's all in on your toughness and competitiveness. That's what it's all about!"

DeFilippo spoke about how they were ready to issue Wentz his playbook and reminded him that the Eagles said they would make the deal, and they did.

After the phone call, all that was left was the Eagles submitting their draft card to the league and NFL commissioner Roger Goodell announcing Wentz's name. At 8:22 p.m. Philadelphia time, Carson Wentz was introduced as the No. 2 overall pick by the Eagles. He shook Goodell's hand and put on an Eagles hat to compliment his gray suit, gold tie, and green pocket square. He held up an Eagles jersey and smiled. There were chants of "E-A-G-L-E-S, Eagles!" from fans who made the trip to the Midwest. Wentz chose the song "Flyover States" by country singer Jason Aldean to play over the auditorium's speakers. He went through the requisite media and promotional activities before finally celebrating with his family.

The next morning, Wentz flew to Philadelphia, arriving at 2:10 p.m. to a throng of autograph seekers waiting at the airport. Dom DiSandro, the Eagles' vice president of team security, scurried Wentz to a van that waited outside the airport. One autograph seeker booed the young QB for not stopping to sign, despite the fact that security wouldn't let him. Welcome to Philadelphia!

Wentz traveled with his older brother and sister-in-law, Zach and Andrea Wentz, showing them the Eagles facility and their new hometown, as they planned to move from North Dakota to offer a support system to help with the transition.

It took a series of trades and extensive scouting, but the player the Eagles targeted to bring them their first Lombardi Trophy was officially their quarterback.

"It was a very detailed, involved process," Lurie said. "Some day we can write a book about it if it all works out."

THE START OF FREE AGENCY

On January 2, 2017, just hours after the Eagles completed their 2016 season with seven wins and nine losses, Roseman and the front office gathered to formalize a plan for what would prove to be a Super Bowl campaign. And it would all start with the opening of free agency when the new NFL year officially began in early March.

Their biggest objective was upgrading the offensive weapons around quarterback Carson Wentz, who started all sixteen games during his rookie season. The Eagles had one of the NFL's worst collections of skill-position players, which includes wide receivers, tight ends, and running backs. A great quarterback can enhance the productivity of the players around him, but he cannot draw water from a rock.

Roseman remembered a time a few years earlier when the Eagles led the NFL in plays that produced 20 yards or more, a sign of the type of explosive playmakers that could spur a young quarterback's development. Those players, headlined by running back LeSean McCoy and wide receiver DeSean Jackson, were sent packing by former coach Chip Kelly. When Roseman regained the reins, he saw an offense that needed an infusion of skill-position talent. "I don't have a DeLorean time machine to go back in time and get some of those guys back," Roseman said after the season.

It was not the first time a promising young quarterback in Philadelphia lacked offensive weapons. Nearly two decades earlier, Donovan McNabb was the player who carried the fan base's Super Bowl hopes. The Eagles waited until McNabb's sixth season to give him a top receiver in Terrell Owens, and that pairing helped McNabb reach his only Super Bowl. The front office had learned from the experience and refused to waste Wentz's early years.

Their problem was that they entered the free agency period with salary-cap limitations based on burdensome contracts that already filled their payroll. To pave the way to make a big splash when free agency opened, they released some expensive veterans, including popular defensive end Connor Barwin who had played four seasons in Philadelphia.

On day one of free agency, March 10, 2017, the Eagles set their first target on Alshon Jeffery, a former Pro Bowler who had played five seasons for the Bears and was the top wide receiver on the open market but had his previous two seasons marred by injury and suspension. With their cap situation tight as it was, seeing the Eagles make a play for Jeffery was like watching a budget-conscious shopper eyeing up a luxury sports car. Initially, the Eagles did not think they could afford Jeffery. At the scouting combine in February, Roseman heard rumors about what it might cost to lure Jeffery, and unfortunately, it seemed too high a price. But when free agency opened and Jeffery did not get the type of offer he wanted, his agent phoned the Eagles, according to the *Chicago Tribune*, and inquired about their interest in detail. Jeffery already had relationships in the Eagles building, including wide receivers coach Mike Groh, who had the same position when Jeffery starred in Chicago; two executives with ties to the Bears; and fellow University of South Carolina product Duce Staley, who was the Eagles' running backs coach. Jeffery was willing to gamble on himself with a short-term contract that would allow him to reset his value if he performed well. Jake Rosenberg, the Eagles' director of football administration, structured a one-year, $9.5 million contract that could swell up to $14 million with earned incentives. It satisfied the desire of both sides.

"I wouldn't necessarily say it was something that we wanted," Roseman said of the one-year deal. "But from our perspective it was a win-win situation . . . . For us, we thought it was a great opportunity to get a player who's extremely talented and has something to prove and wanted to be here. So it worked out, and obviously you always like to have guys on longer deals, but we also have to look at the opportunities. We said all along that we're going to try to be aggressive if the opportunity made sense, and we just thought the contract made a lot of sense."

It was a good sign for the Eagles that Jeffery *wanted* to come to Philadelphia to play with Wentz, considering he had options elsewhere. This wasn't a money grab, but rather a player who saw the Eagles as a chance to improve his value and to experience a winning season, something he hadn't done since he was a rookie five years prior. After agreeing to the deal, Jeffery sent a text message to Wentz.

"I told him my job is to help him win the MVP, which I truly believe," Jeffery said.

"I don't really care about MVP," Wentz responded. "I want to win championships."

The front office viewed Jeffery as a player that could remain in Philadelphia beyond the one-year contract, so he could grow with Wentz. That was part of the appeal. Jeffery wasn't, in their eyes, a Band-Aid to help bridge Wentz to his next receiver. The Eagles didn't know how far away they were from the Super Bowl, but they wanted Jeffery to help them reach it—even if it was not in the 2017 season.

"If Alshon were thirty-three or something, we probably would have had very little interest in doing a one-year deal like that," Lurie said. "This was a twenty-seven-year-old, very good, young receiver that we thought could be someone that we would potentially be able to re-sign. We never signed anybody that we couldn't potentially re-sign going forward. That was the standard. . . . Why give up assets or give up significant cap room or something like that?"

Jeffery was not the only wide receiver the Eagles signed in free agency. They also reached a deal with Torrey Smith, who had played six years in the NFL and won a Super Bowl in Baltimore. Two years earlier, Smith left the Ravens to sign a five-year, $40 million contract in San Francisco, but his production dipped with the 49ers. The Eagles offered quarterback stability, a chance to return to the East Coast, and familiarity with ex-Ravens executives in the Eagles' front office. It didn't hurt that Smith's wife was from suburban Philadelphia, either. Smith could provide the Eagles a deep threat and veteran leadership, with a personality that would fit in with the Eagles' burgeoning socially conscious locker room. In Jeffery and Smith, the Eagles revamped their receiving corps by adding two proven players in their twenties.

The Eagles' other off-season priority was to fortify their offensive line depth. So in the same week they signed Jeffery and Smith, the Eagles signed guard Chance Warmack and re-signed offensive lineman Stefen Wisniewski. Wisniewski eventually developed into the Eagles' starting left guard, but at the time he was brought on for insurance. A year earlier, Roseman watched a promising start to the 2016 season fall apart when standout offensive tackle Lane Johnson was suspended ten games for violating the league's performance-enhancing-drug policy. The Eagles needed to deepen their bench with experienced players to withstand such absences should they arise, in order to ensure solid protection for Wentz throughout the 2017 season.

"It would be a disservice for us to not also talk about our offensive line because it starts up front, and if [Wentz] doesn't have time to throw, it doesn't matter who we have on the outside [at wide receiver]," Roseman said.

The Eagles relied on more than the first week of free agency to build their roster. They made other moves between then and the draft that proved critical to their upcoming season. In fact, when Douglas discussed the lessons learned from the Eagles' Super Bowl roster building, he pointed to the transactions that went beyond these two pressure points on the off-season calendar. The Eagles made more than 130 roster moves and issued more than $160 million in salary obligations to improve the 2017 roster, and most of these transactions remained below the radar at the time they made them.

"The interesting thing about our year is some teams view the upgrading of the team in two phases—unrestricted free agency and the draft—and then there's a certain timeline in the league year. . . . But when you look at our player acquisitions, it's been a year-long process," Douglas said. "We brought in guys at different levels of free agency at different times of the year. They've all been the type of [people], type of player[s] that we target."

The first two moves occurred while the Eagles were at the NFL Annual Meeting at the Arizona Biltmore, a plush resort in Phoenix influenced by Frank Lloyd Wright's architecture. If the scouting combine is the NFL's version of convention, then the annual meeting is their version of vacation. There are important league issues discussed, but it's only attended by the owner, top executives, and head coaches from each team, and many bring their families and enjoy a more casual atmosphere compared to other off-season events.

It's not often a busy time for transactions, either. It usually transitions teams from free agency to the draft. But at the 2017 meeting, the Eagles were more active than expected. They signed veteran defensive end Chris Long and cornerback Patrick Robinson on the same day. Long and Robinson had fewer years ahead of them than behind them, and neither contract punished the Eagles' salary cap. Long was signed to provide depth on the defensive line. Robinson came as a veteran among a group of young cornerbacks. Both players fit a certain profile. The Eagles had attempted these low-risk, veteran contracts before. They're like lottery tickets—if they work, they can strike big. Most don't work, but the contracts don't tend to put a dent in the team's long-term planning. Long and Robinson arrived as respected veterans, former first-round picks whose personalities and professionalism could go a long way in the locker room. The Eagles paid more attention than ever before to chemistry, understanding that a roster cannot be painted by the numbers. It's not just a "player X" at "salary Z," but how does that player function within the locker room? During the season, both Long and Robinson proved to be valuable players on the field and respected teammates off it. This was by design. After the 2016 season, when the Eagles were disappointed about the 7–9 finish, management spent time thinking about the "type of person" they want to acquire more than just the player for a position.

The Eagles returned from the league meeting with notable holes in the starting lineup at running back and defensive tackle. They solved defensive tackle by trading for Tim Jernigan, a twenty-four-year-old from the Ravens—another player whom Douglas knew from Baltimore. The Eagles dropped twenty-five spots in the third round of the draft to acquire Jernigan. They considered it a small price to pay for a starting defensive tackle, and they rewarded Jernigan with a lucrative $48 million contract extension seven months later.

The first player to call Jernigan after the trade was Fletcher Cox, the Eagles' highest-paid player, who would line up next to Jernigan. "We keep you here, we have a chance to be really special," Cox said. For the previous four seasons, Cox played next to Bennie Logan, who the Eagles let leave in free agency. Jernigan wasn't just a cheaper option for 2017, but also a player the Eagles believed was a better fit in defensive coordinator Jim Schwartz's scheme—especially playing next to Cox. Their thinking was that in order to maximize Cox, who was their foundational piece on defense, they needed a player who could take advantage of the double-teams that Cox draws as well as alleviate the attention offensive linemen pay to him. "Last year when Fletch had such a good start, that first month, teams adjusted," Schwartz said, referencing the 2016 season. "They started taking him away, and we didn't win enough one-on ones away from him because that other tackle got the one-on-ones."

• • •

The most important free agent signing for the Eagles, though, was also the most unexpected.

NICK FOLES'S
PHILADELPHIA REUNION

When Nick Foles first came to Philadelphia in 2012, the Eagles picked him. When he returned in March 2017, Foles picked the Eagles.

"I have nothing but great things to say about the city, the fans," Foles said upon re-signing. "I miss running out at the Linc and being a part of that on game day. Crazy enough, you miss the boos from time to time. I laugh just thinking about playing and getting booed, and going back and throwing a touchdown and hearing the eruption. It's the only place that you get something like that."

The Eagles drafted Nick Foles in the third round of the 2012 draft, although it was not as if he was their targeted choice. The Eagles also had their eye on eventual Super Bowl–winning quarterback Russell Wilson, but the Seattle Seahawks selected him thirteen picks before the Eagles' spot.

Such things happen on draft day, and the Eagles were nonetheless bullish on Foles, too, who stood 6-foot-6 and 243 pounds with massive 10⅜-inch hands. He wore long, shaggy blond hair that flowed out of his helmet. He's trimmed his hair throughout the years, but in 2012 he looked like he could have been cast as the main character in the 2004 film *Napoleon Dynamite*—straight down to the glasses Foles wore after practice.

Looks aside, Foles possessed the size and tools that the Eagles wanted to mold. The team was determined to select a quarterback that year, and Foles stood out early in the process. They met him at the scouting combine, made him one of the thirty players they invited to the team's complex before the draft, and even sent Doug Pederson, then the quarterbacks coach, to Foles's hometown of Austin, Texas, before the draft. Pederson was the only NFL coach who put Foles through a private workout.

The Eagles started seeing Foles's potential in his first summer with the team. Andy Reid said during the 2012 preseason that he could not remember a quarterback having Foles's success in exhibition games, going 24–38 for 361 yards and four touchdowns in his first two games. Reid attributed this to the evolution of the passing game in college football that better prepared quarterbacks for the NFL. Foles usurped Mike Kafka as the Eagles' No. 2 quarterback by the end of the preseason, and replaced starter Michael Vick in the lineup after Vick suffered an injury in mid-November.

The win-loss record didn't show it, but Foles turned heads in the Eagles' building. He started six games and totaled 1,699 yards while completing 60.8 percent of his passes for six touchdowns and five interceptions. The highlight of Foles's season came in a December 9, 2012, game over the Tampa Bay Buccaneers when he threw for 381 yards and threw a game-winning touchdown on the final play. Veteran players on the field shared a similar observation about Foles: The moment was not too big for Foles. Former Eagles wide receiver Jeremy Maclin said "he can be special," in part because of "intangibles [that] are off the chart."

Despite Foles's promising rookie campaign, his role in the organization remained uncertain after Reid's dismissal at the end of the season. Lurie said at the time that Foles will have "every opportunity, and everyone in the building thinks the world of him in terms of his promise and potential," but insisted that Foles's role would be determined by the new coach, not the owner. When that new coach was Chip Kelly, whose college football coaching success included mobile quarterbacks, there was skepticism about how the not-so-mobile Foles would contribute. However, Kelly stayed open-minded and was complimentary from the outset about Foles, insisting that he wanted a chance to coach Foles and expressing his admiration for Foles's skill, toughness, and accuracy. Foles thought he could fit in Kelly's offense, even if he wasn't necessarily described as mobile.

"I wouldn't be right here right now if I didn't," Foles said during the spring of 2013. "I want to be here. I love this team, and I love this city."

During training camp, Kelly kept an open competition for the starting job between Foles and Michael Vick. Vick outplayed Foles and earned the job, although Vick's injury history suggested Foles would be needed eventually.

By Week 5, it happened. After Vick injured his hamstring late in the second quarter, Foles entered the lineup and led the Eagles to a victory over the Giants to end a three-game losing skid, then started the following week against Tampa Bay and collected his second-straight victory. Just when it appeared there might be a quarterback controversy in Philadelphia, Foles followed with a dreadful Week 7 performance against the Dallas Cowboys, passing for only 80 yards before leaving the game with a concussion. It seemed like maybe that's the type of career Foles would have—promising one week, putrid the next—and this pendulum would prevent him from becoming a franchise quarterback. The Eagles were inconsistent, and there was reason to start speculating that neither Foles nor Vick would be their starting quarterback in 2014 and beyond.

Then came the game that changed the trajectory of Foles's career, turning him into the Eagles' clear starting quarterback and bringing his approval rating higher than it would reach at any point in his career until the Eagles' Super Bowl run.

In Week 9, Foles tied an NFL record with seven touchdown passes in a game against the Oakland Raiders. He completed 22 of 28 pass attempts for 406 yards, and had Kelly not removed him in the fourth quarter because the Eagles were winning by a big margin, Foles could have broken that record. Still, the league recognized the feat and his cleats were shipped to the Pro Football Hall of Fame in Canton, Ohio.

"I look back at that day as the day we put everything together, sort of that aha moment where, 'We can do this, we know who we are, we can be explosive,'" Foles remembered. "And we sort of took off from that point."

Former Eagles running back LeSean McCoy said Foles "just seemed so focused" against the Raiders, playing "like he had something to prove." And he did—from that point forward, Foles was the Eagles' starter. Vick never took the job back, although Kelly waited until the end of the month to make it official. However, it was still unclear whether Kelly would commit to Foles as the team's long-term franchise quarterback beyond that season.

"He is the starting quarterback for the next thousand years here," Kelly responded after further prodding by the media. "If I'm wrong next week, then

I'm wrong next week."

The win over the Raiders was the start of a five-game winning streak and a stretch of seven wins in eight games that clinched the NFC East for the Eagles. Foles finished the season with twenty-seven touchdowns and two interceptions, the second-best touchdown-to-interception ratio in NFL history. He led the NFL in passer rating, earned a Pro Bowl invitation (where he won MVP), and brought the Eagles back to the playoffs. Reaching the postseason required a Week 17 victory over the Dallas Cowboys that played on national television, then the biggest stage on which Foles had ever played.

Foles's first-ever postseason game came on January 4, 2014, against the New Orleans Saints and future Hall of Fame quarterback Drew Brees, who shares the same high school alma mater as Foles: Austin Westlake. They were born ten years apart, and Brees was a legend in their hometown. As a senior at Westlake, Foles watched the school celebrate the ten-year anniversary of the 1996 state championship team that Brees led as quarterback.

Brees bested Foles that night in Philadelphia, yet it wasn't because of the way Foles played. He completed 23 of 33 pass attempts for 195 yards and two touchdowns and left the field in the fourth quarter with a lead, but the Eagles defense could not prevent Brees from leading a game-winning drive. It was only two weeks shy of his twenty-fifth birthday, and he finished one of the best statistical seasons in Philadelphia history. The future appeared bright for Foles, who was the unquestioned Eagles starter. He couldn't have expected 2014 to be his exit year in Philadelphia.

• • •

There was a story on Foles's mind after the magical 2013 campaign. His father, Larry, built a restaurant empire that he eventually sold for $59 million, and despite his great success he had always put on an apron to fulfill whatever tasks were needed on a given day, from cleaning dishes to filling in for an absent employee. Foles remembered his father coming home at nights covered by the stench of kitchen grease. Those memories resonated with Foles because he never wanted to forget where he started—even after throwing for twenty-seven touchdowns in the NFL.

"I want to remember my core values," Foles said that summer.

In April 2014, Foles married his girlfriend, Tori, whom he met while both were students at the University of Arizona (she played volleyball) and started dating after college. They enjoyed lounging at home together, cooking and playing card games that rotated between "Palace" and "Speed." He had spent the prior NFL season living with G. J. Kinne, a quarterback on the practice squad, and they'd often talk shop while at home. He found that married life offered an outlet away from football.

"When I'm done here, I go home and I spend time with Tori and I get away from this," Foles said in the summer of 2014. "That has helped me keep my sanity. That juices me [up] to come back the next day and get after it, because I'm not taking it home with me."

But Foles could not escape the spotlight. It was brighter than it had ever been, and expectations only elevated. During a quiet moment before the 2014 season opener, Foles considered what question he would ask if he shared a table with former Eagles quarterbacks. He wanted to know how those players reacted to a bad game.

"And the emotions that go with it, just how we're a unique profession," Foles said. "If you have one bad game, it's really going to be talked about. . . . I would ask them how they dealt with it when they had that bad game, when everybody was down on them, what they do. Because that's what I want to learn. That's what shows me a lot about people. When bad things happen in your life, how are you going to react?"

He started to learn about Philadelphia. Two years provided him enough time to learn just how much the Eagles meant to their fans. In 2012, when he first entered the lineup, he realized how depressing losing could be in Philadelphia when the Eagles went on an eight-game losing streak. And when the Eagles made the postseason in 2013, he saw a boost in the entire city's morale. "It's a very unique city like that," Foles said. There was a real fascination with football in his native Texas that prepared him for the fanaticism. But the intensity of

Northeast fans was different, and the desperation in Philadelphia only exacerbated it. And so much of the fans' hope relied on his right arm.

"It's a great city to play in, it's a great city to be a quarterback," Foles said. "It's really what you make it. If you're out in the public a lot, if you're doing a lot of crazy stuff, it'll be one thing. But me, personally, I'm more of a simple guy. . . . I try to simplify things."

The 2014 season did not go as planned. The Eagles were winning, but Foles was not as efficient as he was in 2013. He threw more interceptions, with nine in the first seven games. Still, at the midway point the Eagles were in first place and Foles had started every game. He looked like he would bring the Eagles to the postseason for the second consecutive year, but in a Week 9 away game against the Houston Texans, Foles was sacked from behind by Texans linebacker Whitney Mercilus and sprawled out on the ground in pain. The diagnosis was a broken collarbone, and Foles did not play again for the remainder of the season. His standing in the organization seemed to fracture, too. He was no longer the quarterback for the "next thousand years." Kelly conceded the Eagles' quarterbacks committed too many turnovers that season and said the team would need to evaluate the position. In professional sports, being publicly noncommittal often reveals changes are afoot.

One month later, Foles attended the Super Bowl in Phoenix for promotional purposes. While he walked from one radio appearance to the next, a reporter asked him about a potential trade. It was an option he had never even considered. He blew it off as outside speculation unless and until he heard something from the Eagles.

That call came on March 10, 2015, when Chip Kelly blindsided Foles by telling him he had been traded to the St. Louis Rams in a quarterback swap for former No. 1 overall pick Sam Bradford, revealing that Foles's value was not all that high in Philly or across the NFL. Even though Bradford had missed the previous season with an injury and had never made the playoffs, the Eagles needed to include a valuable second-round draft pick as a sweetener to Foles.

The Rams handed Foles a two-year, $24.5 million contract extension and the starting job. His 2015 season opened with promise before he fell into the same inconsistencies that plagued his final year in Philadelphia. The Rams benched Foles after nine games for Case Keenum—the same Case Keenum that Foles would go on to beat in the 2018 NFC Championship game with the Eagles three years later, sending them to their elusive Super Bowl. He went 4–7 as a starter in St. Louis and threw more interceptions (ten) than touchdowns (seven). The Rams released Foles in July 2016.

Within sixteen months, after such a promising 2013 season, two teams had discarded Foles. Players learn early that the NFL is a business in which winning is the principal metric. It's seldom personal. That did not stop Foles, however, from growing disenchanted about the business and how unforgiving it had become.

Foles had lost his passion for the game. He wanted to retire. He went on a camping trip with his brother-in-law to do some fly-fishing and soul-searching. The expedition gave him a chance to gather his thoughts in solitude. Foles, who is deeply religious, used prayer for guidance. And it sounded like he prepared to say farewell to football. *Sports Illustrated* reported that Foles sent messages to those close to him confirming his decision.

"In my heart at that time, I was probably going to step away from the game," Foles said. "But I also knew I needed to take a few days to let the emotion settle."

He already devised a backup plan, taking steps to become a pastor and restaurateur. But there was a voice that tugged on Foles to return. It was Andy Reid's. After the Eagles fired Reid in 2012, he had gone on to become the Kansas City Chiefs head coach. And in August 2016, Reid offered Foles the backup quarterback job. It was a chance to reunite with the coach who first gave him a shot in the NFL.

"I knew he's a man that has always believed in me," Foles said. "I knew if I played [with] him, gave it one more shot, he'd find the joy. If I had joy in there, he'd bring it back out. And he did."

After one season in Kansas City, Foles again became a free agent. This time, there was one place he wanted to play: Philadelphia. The regime had changed. He shared positive relationships with Lurie, Roseman, and Pederson. And he missed playing quarterback for the Eagles. He knew that the NFL viewed him as a backup, and he was willing to be Carson Wentz's No. 2. The Eagles thought Foles's Rams experience was an outlier and were willing to make a notable investment, believing that Foles was better than the typical backup quarterback.

Because what happened if Wentz suffered an injury? The most quarterback-rich teams must think about this. Why buy an expensive car or a beachfront house without protecting it with the necessary insurance? Before the Eagles could sign Foles, they first needed to release 2016 backup quarterback Chase Daniel. That wasn't a simple transaction. The Eagles signed Daniel a year earlier to a three-year, $27 million contract—a questionable deal that included a $7 million hit against the salary cap even if they cut him in 2017. When Foles signed a two-year, $11 million contract with $7 million guaranteed in March, combined with the charge they incurred when they released Daniel, the Eagles guaranteed a payment of $14 million just to have Foles as Wentz's insurance policy instead of Daniel. At the time, it seemed like an outrageous luxury. But in retrospect, after Foles led the Eagles to the Super Bowl, it was worth every penny.

"We made such a concerted effort to make sure we could get Nick back on the team," Lurie said minutes after winning the NFC Championship and stamping their ticket to the Super Bowl. "Who knew it would come to this?"

A HOMETOWN DRAFT

The Eagles' Super Bowl parade ended on the steps of the Philadelphia Museum of Art on Benjamin Franklin Parkway, aka the "Rocky Steps," a reference to the 1976 film *Rocky*. But that was not the first football celebration that took place at the iconic museum. The NFL held its 2017 draft less than a year earlier on the same steps, with Philadelphia hosting the three-day event in April that drew 250,000 football fans to the tree-lined Parkway. When Philadelphia was awarded the draft on August 31, 2016, the Eagles did not own their 2017 first-round pick, having traded it to the Cleveland Browns in the deal that landed Wentz. They knew they needed to change that—not only to best fill their roster, but also to satisfy the hungry Philly crowd that would be in attendance.

At that point the draft was still nine months away, giving Howie Roseman plenty of time to make some sort of a move. Turns out, he needed just three days. On September 3, 2016, Roseman made one of his signature deals when he traded Sam Bradford to the Minnesota Vikings for the Vikings' 2017 first-round pick and 2018 fourth-round pick. The deal came together because the Vikings lost their starting quarterback, Teddy Bridgewater, to a major injury a week before the season opener. By trading Bradford, Roseman solved two problems. He cleared the way for Wentz to enter the starting lineup for Week 1 of his rookie season, and he secured the Eagles a first-round pick to elevate the excitement for Philadelphia's first NFL draft since the 1960 season. That, by the way, was the last season the Eagles won the NFL Championship, just six years before the inaugural Super Bowl.

It was also the Eagles' first draft with Joe Douglas in charge of ranking the draft prospects and overseeing the scouting process. Douglas, a seasoned scout, valued college production from draft prospects. And for each player, he seemed obsessed with finding the answer to the question, "How much does this guy love football?" Douglas mused that "when you get to this level, everybody's talented." So he wanted to know their intangibles, which could determine how much they can improve and handle the adjustment to the NFL.

The Eagles entered the draft with their biggest deficiencies at running back and cornerback, but since the organizational philosophy was to prioritize the offensive and defensive lines, they considered using their first-round pick on a pass rusher. Whoever they selected would still need to fit Douglas's criteria—proven playing chops and a passion for football.

"I think there's baseline levels of talent, height, weight, speed for every position," Douglas said. "I think the most important job our scouts have is to go deeper than that—get to know the player, the person, as best you can, the way he competes on a consistent basis. How he fits into the team, if he's a leader. All the things that you don't see on tape."

• • •

The first thirteen picks in the draft were made on the Art Museum steps on April 28, and there was excitement in the crowd for each one with fans from across the league in attendance. But it was nothing compared to what happened when the Eagles' ten-minute countdown clock started for the No. 14 pick. Music from *Rocky* played throughout the Parkway when Roger Goodell walked to the lectern. The *Rocky* connection can become a cliché when discussing Philadelphia sports, but the theme song has a way of energizing a Philadelphia crowd like nothing else. It's played before kickoff at every Eagles home game, too. Goodell welcomed members of Philadelphia's Martin Luther King High School football team to the stage as the crowd braced itself.

Then came the highlight of the weekend, as Goodell stepped to the microphone and announced: "With the 14th pick in the 2017 NFL draft, the Philadelphia Eagles select, Derek Barnett, defensive end, Tennessee."

Barnett, who was sitting in the green room behind the stage, was overcome with emotion when he heard his name, even though he knew the pick was coming. A few moments earlier, just miles away in South Philadelphia, Roseman had phoned Barnett.

"You want to stay in town, man?" Roseman asked Barnett, as captured by the team website. "You ready to roll? We're going to pick you here. We're excited to have you."

The throng of Eagles fans, who are known to boo at the slightest provocation, erupted in cheers. Barnett admitted he was nervous because he "didn't want to get boos." He appreciated the warm welcome. If you wanted to know if Barnett had the intangibles Douglas desired, his words minutes after the selection provided the answer.

"My first reaction, I'm glad I don't have to go too far so I can go straight to work," he said. "That's my mindset."

This mentality was bred into Barnett, who grew up in Nashville the son of a single mother who worked two or three jobs seven days a week to support three children. Barnett attended the University of Tennessee and became a day-one starter. Barnett's physical measurements didn't distinguish him in the draft class, but his college playing production did. That's what Douglas valued the most. Barnett set Tennessee's career sack record with thirty-three in three years. The record he broke had been set by NFL Hall of Famer Reggie White, one of the best players in Eagles history. Barnett was a first-team All-American during his junior season and was only twenty years old. So why was he even available at the No. 14 pick? Some of it had to do with his athletic testing. Barnett, who is 6-foot-3 and 259 pounds, ran a 4.88-second 40-yard dash at the scouting combine—a substandard time for an elite pass rusher. Barnett said he's "a great football player . . . not a track star." Roseman pointed out that Barnett was sick the day of testing and still elected to work out in front of scouts—a characteristic that endeared Barnett to the Eagles more than what his test results would have suggested.

"It was an important job interview and if I didn't run it, a lot of people would have questioned my toughness," Barnett said. "I'm not going to run from anything. I'm a very competitive person."

Barnett's standard of excellence was best understood by the shadow under which he stood. At Tennessee, Barnett played at Neyland Stadium, which bears the image of Reggie White on its scoreboard. In Philadelphia, he arrived for his opening news conference at the auditorium inside the team's practice facility, which features a giant mural of White. Barnett was linked to White before he came to Philadelphia, and he didn't run from the White connection upon joining the Eagles. Barnett often watched film of White's college games because he wanted to adopt some of White's pass-rushing moves. After Barnett eclipsed White's record at Tennessee, White's widow, Sara White, called Barnett to congratulate him.

"Even though I broke the record, I told her Reggie is still Reggie," Barnett said. "I don't think I'm better than Reggie. I told her thanks a lot, and I really appreciate it."

Leading up to the draft, Barnett wrote a "cover letter" to NFL general managers and coaches on the *Players' Tribune*. He said that he knows he'll be identified as the player who broke White's sack record. He'd prefer to be known as someone who wins Super Bowls.

In Barnett's rookie season, he already won one.

• • •

The Eagles added cornerbacks in the second and third rounds of the draft, although only one was expected to play for much of the season. The Eagles gambled in the second round by selecting Sidney Jones, a highly touted prospect from the University of Washington who tore his Achilles tendon the month before the draft. Jones started the pre-draft process among the draft's top prospects, but the injury put his 2017 season in peril and plunged his draft stock. So with the No. 43 overall pick—after their top targeted running backs were already taken—the Eagles decided to make an investment in the future and pick Jones. It was a double risk because there was no certainty that Jones would recover and because the Eagles had passed on a chance to take an immediate contributor at a position of need. It signaled that the Eagles were thinking about the long term as much as the short term.

"That was an upside decision, obviously, with the organization," Jeffrey Lurie said. "It hurt the short term, but . . . we don't expect to be drafting in the top ten for a while, hopefully for a decade or more. And it's hard to get cornerbacks that you rate in the top one or two in the draft."

Roseman indicated that before Jones's injury, the Eagles considered taking him with the No. 14 pick. So by taking Barnett and Jones, in their estimation they secured two of the top fourteen players on their board. Jones "had a feeling" the Eagles would take him because he received a handwritten note from Anthony Patch, the Eagles' senior director of college scouting, after the injury. Jones said other teams sent text messages. No other team wrote a letter.

In the third round, the Eagles drafted cornerback Rasul Douglas. A raw prospect from West Virginia University, Douglas led college football in interceptions in 2016. The Eagles drafted two players in the fourth round (wide receiver Mack Hollins and running back Donnel Pumphrey), two in the fifth round (wide receiver Shelton Gibson and linebacker Nate Gerry), and one in the sixth round (defensive tackle Elijah Qualls) to complete their draft. Even though their later-round picks had little-to-mediocre production as rookies later that year, they were all part of the organization through the Super Bowl and were part of the parade. Their rookie seasons ended the same place their names were called: the Rocky Steps at the Art Museum.

COMPLETING THE PUZZLE

After the start of free agency and the NFL Draft came and went, many teams knew what their roster would look like come the regular season. But not the Eagles. Their front office never intended to limit team-building to those two events. They still had a lot of work to do, and they would add to their roster throughout the spring and summer, not to mention key acquisitions made after the season started.

The running back slot in particular remained a weakness after the draft, so the Eagles added veteran free agent running back LeGarrette Blount on May 17. Blount, who won two Super Bowls in New England, led the NFL with eighteen rushing touchdowns in 2016. He was expected to find a role as the Eagles' bruising running back, but he turned into much more.

At the start of training camp, the Eagles' decision-makers decided to make a change at left guard. Veteran Allen Barbre, a two-year starter for the Eagles, was traded on July 26 to the Denver Broncos to open the spot for second-year offensive lineman Isaac Seumalo. The Eagles didn't open up the job to competition, even though veterans such as Stefen Wisniewski and Chance Warmack offered more experience. Seumalo, the second player selected by the Eagles in the 2016 draft after Wentz, appeared to be a key part of the Eagles' future. The only way to realize his potential would be to play him.

Always seeking to add depth and experienced players, on August 3, during the second week of camp, the Eagles dipped back into the free agent market to sign veteran safety Corey Graham as a reserve. This was another example of the organizational emphasis on deepening the bench in case injuries beset the team. Graham was yet another pickup who already sported a Super Bowl ring, fitting the type of player that Joe Douglas wanted on the roster.

"I think sometimes the sum is greater than the whole of its parts," Roseman said. "You're going to have injuries over the course of the year. . . . If one injury derails your ability to compete, we didn't want that to happen. We wanted to build up as much depth as possible. I think you've seen in the past, we would maybe go for younger players. But here we brought in some veteran guys to fill in those roles. We wanted to be able to have this 'next-man-up' mentality."

The Eagles were fortunate to escape the preseason without major injuries (those would come during the regular season), although there were two lingering setbacks that could have derailed their goals. At the end of the first week of training camp, Alshon Jeffery fell hard on his right shoulder and drew the attention of trainers. He practiced the next day before missing almost a full week. It was initially described as a strained shoulder before Pederson said the Eagles were simply resting Jeffery. While it was not the smoothest introduction to his new team, Jeffery recovered and proved to be a key player during the season and even more so throughout the playoffs. In fact, his playoff heroics turned out to be even more impressive when it was learned that Jeffery needed surgery following the Super Bowl to repair a torn rotator cuff. He played with the injury throughout the entire season, passing on surgery during the preseason and instead relying on rehab and grit.

The other lingering injury throughout the summer could have doomed the Super Bowl run. Nick Foles did not play any of the preseason games because of elbow soreness that forced him to miss most of training camp. Foles said there were days when the elbow felt "OK" and days when it felt "horrible," with inflammation often a problem. Foles started wearing a tight sleeve around his elbow to keep his elbow warm (he also wore one during the Super Bowl), and added an elaborate pre-practice warm-up routine that focused on loosening his arm and massaging the muscles around the elbow to ensure blood flow. Foles returned by the start of the season, though, and the elbow was not a problem during the playoffs.

The most notable summer transaction came the morning after the first exhibition game when Roseman traded wide receiver Jordan Matthews and a 2018 third-round draft pick to the Buffalo Bills for cornerback Ronald Darby. On the surface, the deal made sense. The Eagles badly needed cornerback help—that was obvious early in training camp—and Darby was a young, promising player who could immediately step into the starting lineup, allowing

Patrick Robinson to move inside to the slot cornerback position. Matthews, who led the Eagles in receiving yards in 2015 and 2016, was entering the last year of his contract and was expendable after the team's recent overhaul at wide receiver, where they were deeper than they had been in years.

However, the decision was more nuanced. Matthews had developed into one of the team's leaders on and off the field, and was one of Wentz's closest friends. They traveled together on a Christian service trip to Haiti during the summer and developed a connection away from football. On the night of the trade, Wentz and three other teammates took Matthews out to dinner and drove him to the airport for an emotional farewell.

"It's tough," Wentz said of the trade. "It's one of those things where there's the personal side to things and the football side to things. The football side of things, you just got to trust what they're doing upstairs. Ultimately, they're the ones that make those decisions. And what they think is best for the team, I'm going to be in support of one hundred percent. They haven't let me down or haven't let this team down yet."

Wentz added that it would not be easy to replace someone like Matthews in the locker room, and Matthews was not the last popular locker room figure sent packing before the season started.

During the final week of the preseason, Roseman dealt long snapper Jon Dorenbos to the New Orleans Saints for a late round draft pick. Ordinarily, trading a long snapper would not move the meter. But Dorenbos was different. The longest-tenured player on the Eagles, Dorenbos joined the team in 2006 and his 162 consecutive games played tied a franchise record. His fame transcended football when he appeared on *America's Got Talent* in 2016. He revealed to a TV audience what the locker room saw every day: that Dorenbos could amaze with magic tricks and corresponding theatrics. Dorenbos's overwhelming positivity came after a turbulent childhood. His father killed his mother during a dispute in their home and was convicted of second-degree murder. Dorenbos was sent to foster care, and he turned to magic as an escape. He reached the NFL as a long snapper and connected with Eagles fans, often signing autographs during practices open to the public when he was not needed on the field. Lurie called

Dorenbos "one of the most inspiring people I have ever known."

As it turned out, the trade saved Dorenbos's life. During his physical examination in New Orleans, a Saints doctor discovered an aortic aneurysm. Dorenbos required emergency open-heart surgery. His career was finished, but his life was saved. The Eagles welcomed Dorenbos back to games as an honorary Eagle. He attended the Super Bowl, partied in the postgame locker room, rode in the parade with his former teammates, and was even given a Super Bowl ring.

A WINNING CULTURE

More than anything, the off-season program was a chance to establish the team's culture. Pederson emphasized competition in his second season with the Eagles and wanted that to permeate everything the players did. Instead of simply lifting weights because it was mandated, players were awarded points for their performance in the weight room, and the winners received preferred parking spots. Pederson instituted tug-of-war challenges and tag-team races. Competition was encouraged during the 11-on-11 work in practices—it wasn't just about installing the offense and defense, but beating the other side of the ball.

"Iron sharpens iron, and [when] your senses are on high alert, the juices are flowing, it makes you better as a football team," Pederson said.

Pederson installed a Pop-A-Shot basketball net in the locker room, offering another place for the players to compete. One day, he even cancelled practice and took the team on a paintball excursion. Players referenced that day later in the season when the team was lauded for its chemistry. This was not by accident. Listen to Pederson enough and you'll be reminded that he played in the NFL. He believes his experience in the trenches created "an understanding of the dynamic of what a team needs." Pederson's ability to read his team and nudge morale in the right direction when necessary remained a strength throughout the season, whether it was introducing big personalities into the locker room or knowing when to push and back off during practices. He said it's part of "that emotional intelligence" Jeffrey Lurie had famously mentioned, and he certainly saw the return on investment in 2017.

"You have to be honest. You have to be transparent. You have to be upfront. There has to be tough love with the players. They have to see that you care," Pederson said. "You can't be a phony standing up in front of the room. I'll shoot them straight. That's just the way you get through that stuff. They have to see that, as a head coach, you go through those tough moments, but on Monday or Tuesday when you stand in front of that team, it's chest up, shoulders back, and let's go to work this week."

AN EMERGING LEADER

One big difference with the 2017 off-season was Wentz's growing role in the locker room. As a rookie, even though he was the future franchise quarterback, Wentz spent the summer as the third quarterback on the depth chart. He didn't know many of his teammates and he tried to blend in, which went against Wentz's nature as a born leader. He admitted to biting his tongue more than usual.

"It was a challenge," Wentz said about the previous summer. "I do like to take charge to some extent. . . . Now if I was a sixth-round pick and I knew my role from the jump, I would have owned that role, made the most of it. But I knew it was just a matter of time. So it was, 'How do I assert myself now when I'm the three?' And it was some interesting waters to some extent. But I tried to not be too vocal and let my work and my play speak for itself with how I interacted with guys and treated guys, without overexerting myself."

In 2017, he did not need to worry about a back seat. By his own admission, he felt more comfortable around the facility and in the locker room. One year earlier, Wentz was still trying to learn all of his teammates' names. Now, his actions set the temperature in the building. And he made sure he took care of those who took care of him.

In April, when the team began the off-season program, Wentz hosted his offensive linemen at his property in South Jersey for a social gathering. Wentz grilled steaks for his teammates and took them to fire guns—specifically, the Silver Pigeon Berettas he gifted his linemen the previous Christmas. It was a way for the players to bond away from the facility, and to let them know they mattered to their quarterback.

"It was good to get those guys out, hang out, do things," Wentz said. "We went down the road and shot some shotguns, just hung out and bonded. Some of the guys love shooting guns and did it a lot; some guys, it was very new. And [it was great to] also cook up steaks and eat and just enjoy time with each other."

In July, during the team's extended break between the off-season workouts and training camp, Wentz hosted many of his wide receivers and tight ends in Fargo for throwing sessions and group activities. They spent three days passing and catching, eating bison burgers, golfing, and paddle boarding.

The football workouts were successful. The golf outings . . . not so much. Wentz laughed at the memory of his teammates swinging a golf club, calling it a "disaster." It took eight men more than four-and-a-half hours to finish a best-ball scramble. Wentz said the players were fish out of water on the golf course, but they were also fish out of water in Fargo. They had never been to North Dakota. The trip gave teammates a chance to learn about Wentz.

"We're out here in North Dakota, man," Jordan Matthews said on a Periscope video posted by Alshon Jeffery. "Ain't no rap stations on the radio or nothing, baby. It's straight bison burgers, country music, and redheads—shout-out to Carson Wentz."

Wentz has said he planned on hosting a similar gathering every summer. Pederson said the initiative "shows the leadership that Carson has."

UNDERDOGS FROM THE START

If a gambler visited Las Vegas the week before the 2017 season and placed a $100 futures bet on the Eagles winning the Super Bowl, he or she would have won $4,000 when they did. The Eagles' odds to win the Super Bowl were measured at 40:1. Eagles fans have been teased in past years by much greater Super Bowl aspirations that went bust. In 2017, while there was excitement about their chance to improve, it was tempered by the understanding that they still had a young quarterback and an unproven coach who were both entering their second season on the job. Even the rhetoric from the front office suggested the Eagles were still building toward becoming a legitimate contender, and that they didn't necessarily think this was "the year."

Inside the locker room, there was optimism. Don't dare tell the veterans this year was part of a rebuilding process. They saw an improved roster with a real chance to win.

"You start to look at each position group-by-group, they're either going into another year at their position, a little more experienced, or we have another guy there that's showing a lot of potential on paper," captain Malcolm Jenkins said before the season. "When you can go down our roster on a list, we feel really good about where we are."

However, Jenkins said the leaders on the team needed to make sure they tempered expectations. It was Jenkins's fourth season in Philadelphia, and he experienced the same emotional pendulum that Eagles fans live on. Win a few games, and fans might check February flight prices from Philadelphia to Minneapolis. "If we get this thing rolling and we start looking good on paper, we'll be hearing praises," Jenkins said. He wanted the team to stay focused each week, knowing that a trip to the playoffs comes after "sixteen steps." Nobody clinches the playoffs in September.

Pederson even assigned full-season team captains, a departure from his 2016 approach of changing the captains each week. Jenkins, Wentz, Jason Peters, Brandon Graham, and Chris Maragos were elected by their teammates as the five representatives—two from offense, two from defense, one from special teams. There would be a sixth captain rotated on a weekly basis, too. Pederson wanted the players to take ownership of the season, and he thought that having them choose captains would "put the onus back on the players." The captains did not replace the nine-man leadership council Pederson installed in 2016, a group that met with the coach weekly to express and discuss the concerns of the players. This was the sort of quality Las Vegas oddsmakers couldn't account for when evaluating the 2017 Eagles' prospects—the behind-the-scenes chemistry Pederson was creating and nurturing.

PEDERSON 2.0

Nobody changed their reputation more in 2017 than Doug Pederson. He wasn't the fans' first-choice hire one year earlier and, depending upon who you ask, might not have been the team's top choice, either. His only prior head-coaching experience was at the high school level in Shreveport, Louisiana. And he spent only two seasons as an NFL offensive coordinator, but didn't even call the plays.

"There was doubt, there was some skepticism, there was, call it whatever it is," Pederson said. "First-time head coach. What did he know about running a team? And hopefully I've proven people wrong."

The results were mixed during Pederson's first season. He oversaw key changes to the team's culture and schemes, and he demonstrated the aggressiveness and ingenuity that proved to be his hallmarks during the Super Bowl campaign. But he also fumbled the ball a few times in his own public speaking. He navigated several players' off-field issues involving a legal problem, an anxiety condition, and a crisis of confidence. There was a midseason stretch when the Eagles lost seven of eight games. And while the team's 7–9 finish was not a disaster, nobody lined up to name Doug Pederson Coach of the Year. Entering his second season, Pederson realized how much more confident he was in articulating his message to the public, and in his standing as a head coach.

"Going into the second year, going into situations [like meeting with reporters], are not as intimidating as they were a year ago, quite honestly," Pederson said in June.

He also knew that the days of a coach arriving to a new city with a five-year plan were finished. The life cycle of a coach had condensed. More immediate results were expected, even with a young team. The Eagles didn't make the investments in improving the roster during the previous few months to stagnate as a mediocre team. Pederson needed to produce results in his second season.

"Sometimes when you're building a [Super Bowl] roster . . . it takes three years, four years, five years in, and if you constantly change, I don't see how you can get there," Pederson said in June. "With that being said, there has to be consistency and there has to be improvement this year. I get that. I'm not naïve to that or anything."

Pederson's job status—and his fitness for the role—became a hot-button topic when former NFL executive Mike Lombardi said on *The Ringer* podcast that Pederson "might be less qualified to coach a team than anyone I've ever seen in my thirty-plus years in the NFL," and wondered when the Eagles "would admit their mistake." A *Philadelphia Inquirer* column even wondered whether Jim Schwartz, the Eagles' respected defensive coordinator, was angling for Pederson's job. (Schwartz, who admitted to having a "brash," "in-your-face" demeanor, insisted that Pederson felt comfortable with their relationship.)

Pederson said he wasn't aware of Lombardi's comments, so he didn't have a response. But he did note that Jeffrey Lurie and Howie Roseman thought he was qualified enough for the job. Lurie held an impromptu news conference three days before the season to publicly defend his coach and to rebuke Lombardi's comments.

"Those comments, you guys call it 'click bait' or 'hot takes,'" Lurie said. Lurie acknowledged there were "growing pains" in Pederson's first season, which Lurie insisted was not something exclusive to Pederson. Andy Reid had them. Chip Kelly had them. Lurie suggested that Pederson would "keep improving," touted the relationship Pederson built with the players, and made it known that the "future is in front of him . . . for the taking."

Lurie would not put the expectation of a specific win total on Pederson's second season—only saying that he expected improvement from 2016. He thought the Eagles could "compete strongly" with a year under Wentz's belt, yet his comments mostly focused on sticking to the blueprint of continuing to build around their young quarterback. When asked specifically if anything other than the playoffs would be a disappointment to him, Lurie countered that "thirty-one teams are going to be disappointed," meaning a Super Bowl win was the end goal for all teams. It was a stock answer, but Lurie didn't want to make a playoff-or-else public decree. A Super Bowl win would have been a difficult standard to set for Pederson, although Pederson himself saw seeds of a Super Bowl team.

"I look back on my time in Green Bay as a player when we were making those playoff runs, those Super Bowl runs there. And do we have as much talent on this team [as] we did then? We probably have more talent," Pederson said. "But we also had a lot of talent in 2010, here, and where did that get us?"

Pederson's point was that so much needed to work—whether it was luck with injuries, cohesion in the locker room, development on the roster, and the performance of the coaching staff. Yet the tone from Pederson before the season wasn't that the Eagles were in the second year of a rebuilding job. He was ready to win—and win big.

"If we go 8–8, is that a successful year?" Pederson said. "I don't coach to be average—I'll tell you that."

PART 2

THE RACE FOR FIRST PLACE

The Regular Season

WEEK 1

A SPLASHY OPENING WIN

GAME DAY: WASHINGTON REDSKINS :: W 30–17

Doug Pederson's season started the way it finished—with a Gatorade shower.

Wet and sticky, Pederson could not stop smiling. It was seconds after the Eagles' 30–17 season-opening win over the Washington Redskins in the nation's capital, and his players decided to drench him with celebratory electrolytes. After a Super Bowl or a championship game win, that's customary. After a Week 1 win? Not so much.

But this was more than a typical Week 1 game for the Eagles. The constant criticism of Pederson created an undercurrent through the week, and recent history didn't bode well for Philly. The Eagles had lost five in a row to the Redskins, and they'd dropped their last seven road games of the 2016 season. His players wanted badly to win it for him. Pederson, meanwhile, wanted to set a winning tone for the season.

"We haven't played well, and especially here," Pederson said. "Five times against these guys; we got the monkey off our back."

Signs that the 2017 season could be special were evident from the offense's opening drive. Backed up on a third-and-twelve, Carson Wentz spun away from pressure, eluded an oncoming defender, broke away from a sack, and hurled a deep pass to Nelson Agholor downfield. Immediately distancing himself from an awful 2016 season in which many called the rookie receiver a bust, Agholor pulled in Wentz's pass and broke free for a 58-yard touchdown.

"Now y'all know! Never quit!" Wentz shouted to his teammates on the sideline, as captured by NFL Films.

The Eagles led for all but 4:39 of the game. In the final two minutes, they clung to a five-point lead as Washington tried for the go-ahead score.

The Eagles' 2017 defense was built around their D-line with the intention to dominate the line of scrimmage. That's exactly what happened on the game-clinching play, when Brandon Graham stripped the ball from Redskins quarterback Kirk Cousins and Fletcher Cox scooped it up and rumbled for a touchdown. He celebrated by channeling his inner Michael Jackson and performing the "Thriller" dance, showing impressive nimbleness for a 310-pound man.

With the win sealed, reserve linebacker Kamu Grugier-Hill and defensive end Steven Means chased down Pederson to bathe him in Gatorade. As much as Pederson tries to insulate his players from distracting commentary, they were all aware of the outside discussion questioning the Eagles and their head coach entering the season.

"That's Philly. Second-year head coach—pressure's on him, pressure's on us," left tackle Jason Peters told the *Philadelphia Inquirer* after the game. "Doug is kind of like an Andy Reid guy. He mentored under Andy Reid, and he's more of a players' coach, and when you have a players' coach, you tend to play harder for that guy. He knows how it feels to get tired, so he'll take something off a little bit. You tend to lay it all on the line for a players' coach like that."

THE LIFE OF THE FRANCHISE QUARTERBACK

Carson Wentz has survived Philadelphia's fishbowl by sticking to his routine and keeping up the lifestyle that fits his personality. He arrives at the Eagles' training facility every morning at 6 a.m. after a thirty-minute drive from his rural New Jersey home. He listens to worship music or to podcasts of sermons during the ride because "it kind of just gets my mind right." He also adds audio books into the rotation, such as *Forgotten God* by Francis Chan.

From 6 a.m. to 8 a.m., Wentz watches film. It's part of a routine brought to Philadelphia by former quarterback Chase Daniel, who learned it from New Orleans Saints quarterback Drew Brees. Those two hours each morning gives Wentz a chance to do his own work before team requirements. The meetings begin during the 8 a.m. hour and are followed by the team's daily routine: installation of that week's game plan, position meetings, on-field practice, game simulation walk-through, lunch, and then more individual meetings.

Wentz eats on the go with little time to waste in his day. He's not one to lounge around the locker room, even after practice. Wentz showers and changes quickly at his corner locker that was once occupied by Donovan McNabb and Michael Vick, then he's off to another obligation. Even team chef Tim Lopez knows Wentz seldom has time to sit and eat, so he always has the quarterback's standard sandwich ready to grab and go. It's become known in the Eagles facility as "the Wentz"—smoked turkey, ham, crispy bacon, melted provolone cheese, seared tomato, and mayonnaise on whole grain toast, as described by Lopez in a team podcast. In addition to his eponymous sandwich, he'll snack on a protein shake and fruit during the day to stay fueled, only reluctantly eating vegetables. His guilty pleasure at the team facility is biscuits and gravy for breakfast. He once suggested that Lopez use multigrain flour for the biscuits, but the chef countered that the defensive linemen would protest.

Wentz usually leaves the team facility around 6:30 p.m. after putting in a twelve-hour day. Most nights he brings dinner home from the team's cafeteria, and about twice a week he has dinner with his brother Zach and sister-in-law Andrea, who moved to the area with Carson and live just ten minutes away. A few times a month he goes out to dinner with the offensive linemen.

He enjoys spending time with his dogs, Henley and Jersey, romping around his expansive property and playing fetch. Sometimes he'll drive around at night on his electric bicycle with the dogs in chase.

"I'm free out there to some extent, gives me a little peace of mind," Wentz said.

Wentz tries to read every night. He watches *Monday Night Football* and the Thursday night game, although when the television is on in his home, it's usually programmed to the Outdoor Channel. Carson and Zach started a YouTube channel called "Wentz Bros Outdoors" to document their hunting trips. He's always looking for new ideas to expand the channel.

Wentz also uses this time to make phone calls to family, friends, and agents. Just don't ask him about football. That goes for everyone—his mother included.

"There's times where I'll be talking to my mom and she'll be asking me football questions and I'll be like, 'Mom, I'm going to hang up,'" Wentz said. "Like, 'I'll call you to see how you're doing, but I don't want to talk about football.'" Even Wentz's brother Zach, his best friend, knows not to bring up football in conversation. Any such discussion will begin and end with "good game."

If there's some public debate going on about him or his performance, Wentz finds out from the team's media relations staff or can infer it from the lines of questioning in his weekly press conference. He doesn't like to directly consume whatever the issues are on a given day, and "sometimes, having to talk about it, to call a spade a spade, can be really annoying at times."

But he knew what comes with the territory of being the franchise quarterback. Wentz was ready for it from the day he arrived, even though it was quite an adjustment from North Dakota.

• • •

Wentz often frequented the enormous Scheels department store in Fargo while in college, mostly perusing their hunting section. After he was drafted, they displayed two mannequins in the middle of the sporting goods department with Wentz's North Dakota State jersey and an Eagles jersey. The store had never carried Eagles merchandise in the past, but Wentz made it Eagles territory. One week after the draft, kids posed for selfies in front of the mannequins, including one eight-year-old boy who said he has signed posters of Wentz at home. Many shoppers have had their own Wentz encounters.

"It's Wentz-a-palooza around here," said the boy's father. "We're a small state. When somebody does good, everybody jumps on."

About a quarter of the 760,000 North Dakota residents live in either Wentz's hometown of Bismarck or in Fargo, where he spent five years in college. During a reporter's visit to North Dakota in May 2016, it seemed impossible to walk around without encountering someone who knew Wentz. The woman at the front desk of a Bismarck hotel went to high school with him. Inside the office of then-gubernatorial candidate Doug Burgum (now the North Dakota governor), Wentz's stepbrother worked the desk and answered phones. At the university's student union and the coffee shops, a random encounter often yielded a Wentz story, or someone had bought insurance from his father, or another lived in the same neighborhood as his mother, and yet another had a class with his older brother. At a Bismarck barbershop, where Wentz was often a popular topic of conversation during haircuts, the 6 p.m. appointments on the night of the 2016 draft were canceled so customers could watch Wentz cross the stage as the No. 2 overall pick. North Dakotans see a piece of themselves in Wentz.

"As you get to know Carson, and people get to know Carson, that's the best image of North Dakota you can get," said Easton Stick, Wentz's backup quarterback at North Dakota State.

Margie Trickle worked the front desk of North Dakota State's football offices for more than thirty years. For five seasons, every time Wentz walked into the office where she sat, he greeted her by name.

Such descriptions of Wentz reached mythical proportions. North Dakotans take pride in their friendliness, and even have a name for it: "North Dakota Nice." Along the nearly two-hundred mile, three-hour stretch of interstate between Bismarck and Fargo that passes a forty-six-foot, sixty-ton statue in Jamestown billed as the "world's largest buffalo," there are white signs that instruct drivers to "Be Nice" and "Be Polite." And they say Wentz fits the bill perfectly, with one teacher explaining how all Wentz's success was so meaningful because "you want it to be a deserving person."

Part of Wentz's appeal was that he was not prepackaged to be the franchise quarterback. He stood just 5-foot-8 as a high school freshman before going through a growth spurt and reaching 6-foot-5 by graduation. His high school photos show him as a tall, lanky redhead. He added thirty pounds while in college to fill out his body. That was due in part to the strength training of

Jim Kramer, North Dakota State's director of athletic performance, but also to Wentz's huge appetite. During a spring cookout before his final year of college, he ate thirty-six ounces of steak—more than some of his blockers.

Many people claimed Wentz had never received a B or lower in his school career—a fact confirmed by his teachers. In a freshman psychology class, he came close to falling below 90 percent because of missed time during football season, but then recovered and earned an A.

When Wentz played basketball at Century High School, he sat next to his coach on the bus rides home so he could complete his homework. Wentz's high school football coach, Ron Wingenbach, also taught him in pre-calculus. If Wentz missed a question, he would study the wrong answer until he understood the concept and got it right.

Wentz majored in health and physical education at North Dakota State. During one class, students were tasked to teach something unusual that they didn't know. Wentz's professor, Jenny Linker, assigned him break dancing.

"Really?" Wentz said.

"Let's see what you've got," Linker replied.

Wentz learned everything he could about break dancing. He showed up for his demonstration with a bucket hat and Hawaiian shirt, ready and fully able to "do the six step."

"And he went out to a middle school with his teaching partner, and they taught it with the middle school kids," Linker said. "He's something special."

But he was also insulated in North Dakota. There was a small-town aura to Wentz, a charming naivety that could change when moving to a big city. This could also create an unfair caricature. Hal Rosenbluth is a former travel executive who splits his time between Philadelphia and his ranch about sixty miles south of Bismarck. He still owns Eagles season tickets and flies in for games, although he's fallen for the North Dakota culture. He drives from his ranch to Bismarck in the same amount of time it takes him to drive from a suburb on the Philadelphia city line to Center City at rush hour, and he can wave to any car he passes along the way in North Dakota. Rosenbluth has seen both lifestyles, and before Wentz came to the East Coast, he warned Philadelphians not to think Wentz couldn't handle the culture shock.

"You can't equate nice with not being tough," Rosenbluth said. "Nice and tough are the same thing out here. . . . Most people out here are tough to begin with, or you probably wouldn't be in North Dakota. You'd choose to leave."

Wentz's toughness became one of his defining qualities. He looks forward each year to the inclement weather in Philadelphia. He practices in short sleeves even when others shiver. He invites contact when he runs—sometimes to his detriment. And he manages the increased fan and media attention the same way he did Linker's break-dancing assignment.

"We have a saying around here: 'You can't fake farming,'" Rosenbluth said. "Something either grows or it doesn't grow. So there's no need to try to create a false image of yourself."

• • •

The attention he got in North Dakota prepared Wentz for Philadelphia. He couldn't blend in much in his new environment, either—there were just more people to notice him.

In the spring after his first season with the Eagles, Wentz went shopping one day at the Deptford Mall in southern New Jersey, right outside Philadelphia. A fan approached him, and Wentz entertained him for twenty minutes before realizing there was a line of shoppers twenty deep who wanted his time, too.

"Guys, I literally have to go," Wentz said. "This isn't going to work."

Wentz learned that that level of attention just comes with the territory of playing for the Eagles and its rabid fan base. On another occasion that spring, he went out to eat in Center City with his brother and sister-in-law when a fan walked by and screamed, "You're the f—ing man!" He then broke into the team's main cheer, "E-A-G-L-E-S, Eagles!" with passersby on the street joining in. What started as an evening out in the spring, suddenly felt like an autumn Sunday at the stadium.

"That's Philly right there," Wentz said.

The recognition even extends to his brother, who bears a slight resemblance.

Zach went to an Italian restaurant in Philadelphia during the preseason and received a free dinner when the servers mistook him for Carson. When Zach told them they had the wrong Wentz, they still picked up the tab. It pays to be a tall redhead in Philadelphia in 2017.

When Wentz stops at the local Target to pick up household items, he'll keep his head down and the phone pressed to his ear. He purposefully chose to live outside the hustle of the city, and after two years in South Jersey, he's finally found places near home where his presence has become normal and the commotion has subsided. Wentz could have been drafted by the Los Angeles Rams and carved his life out amid the sunshine and the glitz of Southern California. But he is happy he came to Philadelphia, where the team facility is a short drive from rural areas that offer space to hunt and play with his dogs outdoors, bringing his North Dakota life with him to the East.

"To some extent," Wentz said. "It's just the things I like about North Dakota, that's who I am. I'm not going to let the culture I live in and where I live kind of change me. I'm just going to keep being me. If other people embrace it, that's cool. If they don't, I'm OK with it because I'm comfortable with who I am. Like the hunting and all that stuff, I'm fortunate enough that I can do that out in New Jersey. I can kind of get that peace of mind to get away from the game."

Although Wentz says he likes his privacy, he's not reclusive. He's active on social media, outspoken about his faith, and comfortable with himself. When he accidentally locked himself in a gas station bathroom when he first arrived in Philadelphia, he gladly shared the story on Twitter and had a laugh at his own expense. And when he proposed to his girlfriend the week after the Super Bowl, he shared photos on Instagram.

Wentz often arrives on game day wearing a suit outfitted by teammate Malcolm Jenkins's Philadelphia clothing store, Damari Savile. Yet teammate Lane Johnson described Wentz's everyday appearance in a *Players' Tribune* article as "North Dakotan as hell," which meant he's "looking like he's ready to scale Kilimanjaro—camo hat, boots, backpack with a bunch of hooks on it." He will often wear Birkenstocks during the summer, and often lets his auburn stubble grow out.

At midweek news conferences during the season, Wentz throws a hat on his head sporting the logo "AO1" which represents the Audience of One Foundation he founded in 2017 to support underprivileged youth, the physically disabled, and American veterans. He even has the logo tattooed on his right wrist. His brother handles the foundation and much of Wentz's nonfootball responsibilities, allowing Wentz to focus on his day job. He signs autographs whenever children ask, although he's also become aware of collectors, and tries to avoid giving them a payday.

"If I have time, I want to help," Wentz said. "The fans are great. I was that fan once. I used to be a kid and wanted autographs. Now there are also other adults that I'm [like], 'Do you really need me to sign that?' . . . If we have time, I'm going to do my best to help interact with them because they love the Birds and I'm going to show them love right back as best as I can."

That comes with being the "face of the franchise." Wentz never uses that term to describe himself because he doesn't want it to affect his relationship with his teammates. But they all know his standing in the organization and the city, and he's aware of the responsibilities that come with it.

"During the season I like to be focused on football and then go home and be insulated," Wentz said. "So it's kind of pick and choose and knowing when you're comfortable with those things. . . . I'm learning every time I go do something, the reaction and everything."

WEEK 2

STUCK ON THE GROUND

GAME DAY: **KANSAS CITY CHIEFS :: L 20–27**

One of the most popular laments during Andy Reid's fourteen seasons in Philadelphia was his proclivity for passing the ball and his seeming aversion to running it. Perhaps Pederson channeled his inner-Reid in the visit to Kansas City, because the Eagles called only thirteen running plays in a 27–20 loss to the Chiefs.

In the Arrowhead Stadium press box, there's a graphic display of famed Chiefs coach Hank Stram with a big quote that read, "You cannot win if you cannot run." Pederson called runs on only 19 percent of the plays against the Chiefs, a drop from 30 percent in Week 1 and 40 percent from the entire 2016 season. That alarming ratio in Week 2 happened despite the fact that Pederson spent the days leading up to the game touting the necessity to run.

"We've just got to get it fixed," Pederson said afterward of the Birds' running game. "No ifs, ands, or buts."

One idea expressed by many was that they should have handed the ball to LeGarrette Blount. The veteran free-agent off-season addition did not log a single carry against the Chiefs, an eye-popping anomaly in a season he later finished as the Eagles' leading rusher. It was the first time Blount went without a carry in a game since November 2014 while playing for the Pittsburgh Steelers. In that instance, he stormed off the field before the game ended and the Steelers released him less than twenty-four hours later.

Fortunately, that was not the Blount the Eagles experienced. Wearing sunglasses while surrounded by television cameras, he passed on a ripe chance to pout and calmly deferred the question about his usage (or lack thereof) to Pederson. No running back is happy after they don't carry the ball in a game, especially a loss, but the Eagles could have experienced worse from Blount that afternoon. It proved to be a sign of the locker room's strength.

The Eagles also needed to evaluate their offensive line after taking the loss. They so badly wanted Isaac Seumalo to establish himself as a starter, yet the second-year lineman appeared overmatched while allowing three sacks against the Chiefs.

Still, despite the loss, the Eagles looked strong against the team that defeated the defending Super Bowl champions ten days earlier. Wentz continued his excellence, including throwing his first touchdown pass to Alshon Jeffery. He even led the team in rushing with four carries for fifty-five yards—a statistic that spoke to both Wentz's athletic ability and the Eagles' rushing issues that day. The one blemish on Wentz's performance was a fourth-quarter interception that led to Kansas City's go-ahead touchdown.

"The takeaway is you're right there," Pederson said. "A team that lit the scoreboard up in Week 1 in New England, to keep them tied, keep them held down for three quarters, the takeaway is, offensively, we have to address our own needs and how we're playing."

In the locker room after the game, the players felt like they were every bit the caliber of team as the Chiefs, the defending AFC West champions. Malcolm Jenkins said the Eagles "had control" of the game for more than three quarters. They lamented plays that slipped away, but there was confidence on the flight home to Philadelphia that they were a good team—and they were determined to show it in their home opener against the New York Giants the following week.

THE TEACHER VS. PROTÉGÉ

Entering Week 2 versus the Kansas City Chiefs, the biggest storyline was the head-coaching matchup of Doug Pederson vs. Andy Reid. For fourteen seasons, Reid roamed the Eagles sideline and was one of the polarizing figures in Philadelphia sports. He won more games than any coach in franchise history and had more playoff success than any of them, too (until Pederson won the Super Bowl, that is). The one stain on Reid's résumé was that he left without bringing home the ultimate prize.

During Reid's first season in Philadelphia, in 1999, he signed a veteran quarterback to start the season as a bridge to eventual franchise quarterback Donovan McNabb. That veteran was Pederson, whom Reid had coached the prior three seasons in Green Bay. The two remained close when Pederson left Philadelphia after just one season. Ten years later, Reid jump-started Pederson's NFL coaching career by hiring him as an assistant for the Eagles in 2009, promoting him from quality control coach to quarterbacks coach, and later bringing him to Kansas City as offensive coordinator in January 2013.

Reid's tenure with the Chiefs shared similarities to his time in Philadelphia—considerable success, but no championship. The Chiefs looked like a Super Bowl contender in their first game of the 2017 season when they dominated the New England Patriots, the defending Super Bowl champions, and offered a significant early-season challenge for the 1–0 Eagles. It didn't help the Eagles that Reid had always feasted on his former assistants when they battled as opposing coaches—the Chiefs had won eight of the previous eleven such matchups entering Week 2 of the 2017 season.

"I think sometimes, in my position, I don't want to put any added stress or pressure on myself to go perform," Pederson said before the game. "It's that chess match, and moving our pieces against their pieces. And for me, I just can't get caught up in that record. I can't get caught up on who's on the other sideline."

Although Pederson played for other respected coaches such as Don Shula and Mike Holmgren, Reid was his biggest influence. When the Eagles first hired Pederson as head coach, he insisted that he would bring his own personality to the team. Early in his tenure, though, much of what his Eagles did resembled a Reid-coached team, starting with his daily schedule during his first off-season. But Pederson added his own mark as he gained experience, and by his second season, he was truly beginning to forge his own path.

He changed the players' off day from Tuesday to Monday in an effort to maximize their recovery periods. He added more competitive elements to practices, including times when the deep reserves practiced against each other on a separate field to get more work instead of watching the starters. When calling plays, he eliminated the offensive coordinator as the middleman and sent the calls directly to the quarterback—a break from the way it was done under Reid. Pederson made a personal pledge to be aggressive on fourth downs. He adapted to suggestions his assistant coaches made—even those who were holdovers from Chip Kelly's tenure. And most of all, he welcomed and tried to implement his players' input.

"I find myself, as I go every day and . . . month to month, finding new ways to do something," Pederson said. "I'm a big believer that you don't change just to change. It's got to benefit the team and it's got to help you win games. . . . It's a little bit more my personality, and also, I want to hear from the players, too. You keep your eyes and ears open, you listen to the guys, you listen to what other teams might be doing from around the league."

Reid noticed how Pederson could connect to players as a former player. That perspective proved valuable in earning trust from the locker room. Reid said Pederson was attuned to "when to crank on the guys" and "when to pull off." But that should not be confused with being soft. In fact, when Pederson took over as head coach, the holdovers from the Andy Reid era warned their teammates that training camp practices would be more intense than they were under Chip Kelly. They would be longer. There would be tackling.

"If it's anything like Andy's training camp," Fletcher Cox told teammates, "it's going to be a grind."

Only eight of the fifty-three players on the Eagles roster for that 2017 Chiefs game had played for Reid in Philadelphia—Cox, Peters, Graham, Foles, Jason Kelce, Brent Celek, Vinny Curry, and Mychal Kendricks. They maintained a sense of loyalty to Reid, who was always more popular inside his locker room than he was outside of it.

"There's something about him, anyone who plays for him would tell you," Foles said. "You want to play for him. He has something special with all his players."

Some of their best Reid memories did not involve anything that happened on the field. Pederson remembered late nights in Kansas City in the office putting a game plan together with the Zac Brown Band playing in the background, the two coaches cracking each other up with old stories. Jeffrey Lurie has not forgotten the second dinner out with the rotund Reid, when Reid ordered three steaks.

"Three!" Lurie said. "And it was like normal. It was sort of like, 'OK!'"

Regardless of how his tenure in Philadelphia ended, Reid emphasized his fondness for the team and the city. He remains in regular contact with Pederson, Lurie, Roseman, and others in the building. He lived in the area for longer than any other city in his professional life. He'll one day join the team's Hall of Fame.

"You don't stay some place for fourteen years and not have a fondness for a place," Reid said. "And I always wish them the best, except when we play them."

Reid experienced—and bore the brunt of—the desperation and criticism of the fan base. A few weeks after the 2017 Super Bowl, reporters asked Reid if he thought the Eagles head coaching job was different now that the region's hunger for a title has been satisfied. Maybe there would be less venom from the fans and less criticism from the media? Maybe a coach would receive the benefit of the doubt more often? Reid laughed, reminding the reporter of former Phillies manager Charlie Manuel and his fate after the Phillies won the 2008 World Series.

"He came out the first game [the next season], the ring ceremony, and they're losing and they boo him," Reid said. "Hey, that's a badge of honor in Philly!"

WEEK 3

A SEASON-CHANGING KICK

GAME DAY: NEW YORK GIANTS :: W 27–24

Points were precious early in the Eagles' Week 3 win over the New York Giants. It was only 7–0 at halftime, and the Eagles fell short of adding to that lead when rookie kicker Jake Elliott missed a 52-yard field goal in the third quarter.

Elliott had joined the team in Week 2 after the Eagles lost Caleb Sturgis, a veteran who set the franchise record for field goals one year earlier, to a hip injury in the season opener. The Eagles picked up Elliott from the Cincinnati Bengals practice squad, and he promptly missed two of his first four field goals with the Eagles. After his third-quarter miss against the Giants, future Hall-of-Fame left tackle Jason Peters found Elliott on the sideline.

"Hey, Elliott, c'mon baby," Peters said, as captured by NFL Films. "We're going to need you, man. No more misses. No more misses, bro."

Peters wasn't just trying to encourage Elliott; he was trying to intimidate him. Don't miss again! Peters is a tone-setter for the Eagles, a venerable fourteen-year veteran whose words carried weight. His body also carried weight, as the 6-foot-4, 328-pound Peters cast an intimidating shadow over the 5-foot-9, 167-pound Elliott.

Meanwhile, Doug Pederson was rethinking his running-game strategy. After calling for just thirty-three rushes during the first two weeks, the Eagles rushed thirty-nine times against the Giants alone, although one of those rushes would prove costly when the team's most versatile offensive weapon, Darren Sproles, left the game with an injury.

The ground attack helped the Eagles build a 14–0 lead that they carried into the fourth quarter, but the Giants tied the score with two TDs within two minutes, then took the lead with a 77-yard touchdown pass.

The teams then traded scores, and with fifty-six seconds on the clock, Elliott faced a pressure-packed 46-yard field-goal attempt to tie the game and redeem himself. Peters's words hung over the young kicker, as did his future employment prospects. He nailed the kick with room to spare—the ball looked like it could have made it from 60 yards—and it appeared the teams would head to overtime.

But on the Giants' ensuing possession, two penalties stopped the clock and forced them to punt from their own 34-yard line with nineteen seconds left. The punt shanked out of bounds after 28 yards, giving the Eagles the ball at their 38-yard line with just thirteen seconds remaining.

After an incomplete pass took six seconds off the clock, the Eagles needed a 27-yard completion to reach Elliott's field-goal range of 52 yards. That's difficult to do in seven seconds. Pederson called a sideline pass that, if executed perfectly, would get Elliott in range and take five to six seconds off the clock. The Eagles practiced this play during their walkthrough twenty-four hours before the game, just in case they were in this type of situation.

"It's a little bit like a Hail Mary," Pederson said. "It's kind of a desperation attempt, but it's something we execute every week."

Wentz heard the play call and thought "seven seconds was definitely pushing it with the route," which was designed to go about 15 yards. He needed to be as precise as he's ever been. And even if there was tight coverage, he needed to trust Alshon Jeffery and throw the ball anyway. This was why they signed the free-agent receiver.

"Sometimes, with a guy like Alshon," Wentz said, "you just have to give him a chance."

Jeffery lined up on the same side with two other wide receivers. The Giants did not pressure the receivers at the line of scrimmage. That allowed Jeffery a free release, giving him a chance to run his route on time. Wentz took three steps out of the shotgun, glanced to a short pass to draw a defender toward

Nelson Agholor, then fired a fastball to Jeffery with two defenders converging. Jeffery caught the pass between the defenders and then searched immediately for the sideline. He found the chalk at the Giants' 43-yard line with just one second remaining on the clock.

"Get out of bounds and we'll take our chances with a Hail Mary or a kick," Jeffery thought to himself. "If there was more time left, I think I would have kept going."

The Eagles had gained 19 yards—but that didn't seem like enough. Elliott ran toward Pederson and special teams coordinator Dave Fipp and pleaded for a chance to kick the field goal. It was 9 yards longer than the range the coaches planned for Elliott that day. But Pederson reasoned that a perfect kick would offer a better chance of points than a 38-yard heave from Wentz. Jeffery came to the sideline and asked Fipp about Elliott's leg.

"He can make it from sixty-one yards," Fipp said.

Elliott had never made a kick longer than 57 yards in a game. But at an especially windy practice, he once put a kick through the uprights from 75 yards away. Pederson watched confidently from the sideline. He also thought Elliott could hit the field goal.

"The guy's a superhero if he makes this," Wentz said on the sideline, as captured by NFL Films. "I'll friggin' give him my paycheck. I'll give him my game check if he makes it."

Then, all the sudden, boom!

"Sounded like a cannon off his foot," Pederson said.

Elliott's low-flying kick just cleared the crossbar as time expired. It was the longest kick in franchise history. Pandemonium overtook the stadium.

"Ahhh! Ahhh! You son of a gun!" screamed Wentz, who later pledged to donate part of his $31,764.71 game check to a charity of Elliott's choice.

The Eagles came out of the game with a crucial early-season W, and they did it in a more dramatic fashion than any other moment until the Super Bowl. Even when it looked improbable, it foretold what would happen over the next five months.

"That's why we never die," Wentz said as he walked off the field. "Never quit."

NO LONGER STICKING TO SPORTS

On September 22, two days before the Eagles' home opener against the New York Giants, President Donald Trump attended a campaign rally in Huntsville, Alabama, for U.S. Senate candidate Luther Strange. During his speech, with the American flag hanging behind him, Trump decided the venue would be the forum to attack the NFL.

"Wouldn't you love to see one of these NFL owners, when somebody disrespects our flag, to say, 'Get that son of a b— off the field right now. Out. He's fired. He's fired!'" Trump said. "You know, some owner is going to do that. He's going to say, 'That guy that disrespects our flag, he's fired.' And that owner, they don't know it. They don't know it. They'll be the most popular person, for a week. They'll be the most popular person in this country."

Since former San Francisco 49ers quarterback Colin Kaepernick started kneeling during the national anthem during the 2016 preseason, dozens of players throughout the NFL protested for social-justice reform during the anthem. Eagles safety Malcolm Jenkins, one of the NFL's most outspoken players on social issues, decided in Week 2 of that season to raise his fist in the air during the anthem—similar to Tommie Smith and John Carlos at the 1968 Olympics—instead of kneeling, and continued to do so throughout the 2016 season and into 2017.

The protests had been a hot-button issue for thirteen months, especially with Kaepernick unsigned for the 2017 season. The debate reached its crescendo with Trump's comments. The NFL was a topic of conversation on more than the sports networks that Sunday morning.

Jeffrey Lurie, among other owners, released statements following Trump's remarks. Lurie supported his players "as they take their courage, character, and commitment into our communities to make them better or to call attention to injustice." He added that his players respect the national anthem "and all it represents" and that the Eagles "firmly believe that in this difficult time of division and conflict, it is more important than ever for football to be a great unifier."

There was widespread curiosity about how players across the league would react to Trump's comments. As it turned out, according to ESPN's website, Week 3 saw by far the most activity with more than 150 individuals protesting on their own and nearly twenty teams doing so together. By contrast, in each of the first two weeks, there were zero team demonstrations and fewer than thirty individual participants league-wide. Around the same time that Jenkins tweeted his request to Eagles fans to lock arms during the anthem, the first NFL game of the day kicked off in London with a preview of what would follow across the league. Several players on the Baltimore Ravens and Jacksonville Jaguars knelt during the anthem, while the entire Jacksonville team, along with some executives, locked arms. No player from either team had demonstrated in the first two weeks of the season.

At Lincoln Financial Field, Lurie remained on the field during the national anthem along with team president Don Smolenski and Howie Roseman. They locked arms with players and coaches and police officers and military members. (The only player who did not lock arms was linebacker Mychal Kendricks, although that was only because he came to the field late and did not realize what was happening.) Retired U.S. Navy Petty Officer Generald Wilson sang the national anthem in front of a flag stretching the length of the field. Jenkins held his right fist in the air. Chris Long, who is white, placed one arm on Jenkins's shoulder and his other hand on his heart, as he had done for weeks.

"We just talked about how we were going to do something as a team to show solidarity," Long said. "Because it kind of gets distorted, you know there are things that guys are protesting about, but then when the president calls us out, we're kind of also now protesting the right to protest. Which you wouldn't think you'd have to do in this country. This is a wonderful, wonderful country with things that we can improve, and that's all those guys are trying to do is improve some things."

Jenkins was suddenly thrust into the national spotlight. He had spent more than a year trying to promote social change, achieving remarkable success but little fanfare. The president's criticism of NFL players brought more eyeballs to the issues and triggered more players' involvement. But Jenkins had discussed the issues and taken significant action in the community long before Trump was elected, and he continued even when Trump's scandal du jour transferred from the NFL to the FBI. It didn't even faze Jenkins to hear the president of the United States call one his fellow players a "son of a b——."

"I've gotten a lot worse on Twitter," Jenkins said. "When you're in the limelight, and especially with what we've been doing over the past year, you hear a lot. So it's nothing out of the ordinary. It's another internet troll."

• • •

With Jenkins taking on a larger profile in social advocacy, he developed a leadership role in the Players Coalition, including attending meetings with NFL owners and officials. In Week 13, after spending one-and-a-half seasons raising his fist during the national anthem, Jenkins decided to stop. It came after the league pledged $89 million to social justice causes.

"I felt like when I started demonstrating, my whole motivation was to draw awareness to disenfranchised people, communities of color, injustices around the country, our criminal justice system," Jenkins said. "And obviously through this year and talking with the league and what they've kind of proposed, I feel like has presented a bigger and better platform to continue to raise that awareness and continue to fluctuate positive change. Not only with the money that they've put up, because I think that's probably the least important part of the deal, but with the resources and platform that they proposed to build."

Jenkins rejected the criticism that the league threw money at the problem to prompt him to stop. He said he "wouldn't just accept a check and move on"—the motivation was more about the platform that the league provided to fight causes and the commitment they made to address issues in "our communities, communities of color, criminal justice system, education system, and really tell those stories." That was the reason Jenkins started raising his fist in the first place. The decision was not popular with everyone who demonstrated, creating a rift in the coalition. But what's always been clear is that Jenkins backs up his talk with action. Just look at his off-season calendar, and you'll see how committed he is to different causes and ventures.

From the end of the 2016 season to the beginning of the 2017 training camp, Jenkins had more than 70 engagements around the country. Those included speaking with U.S. Senator Cory Booker to discuss how to collaborate for criminal justice reform; a keynote address at a University of Pennsylvania Law School symposium exploring hate speech and the First Amendment; a visit with inmates at Graterford Prison in Schwenksville, Pennsylvania; meeting with legislators in Washington; sitting on an Ohio State panel about the role athletes play in social change; a public-service announcement on behalf of the ACLU to encourage voting; and a free football camp in Piscataway. On his final Friday before training camp started, Jenkins hosted and funded a camp for West Philadelphia middle school students to learn how the Eagles use science and technology.

"At the end of the day, when I'm done playing, I don't want my entire life's work to be what I've done on the field," Jenkins said. "Because there's always going to be somebody that's going to be more after me, and then you're forgotten. So I want to build a legacy that will last, and I want to see the fruits of the labor."

"The NFL's Wokest Team"

On the morning after the Eagles played a *Monday Night Football* game in October, Jenkins, Smith, and Long boarded an Amtrak train for a two-hour ride to the Pennsylvania State Capitol in Harrisburg. Football players often have trouble getting out of bed the morning after a game, with lingering soreness comparable to waking up the day after a car accident. But Jenkins, Smith, and Long surrendered their off day to lobby lawmakers for criminal justice reform.

This type of civic engagement was not an outlier in the Eagles season. During the Super Bowl Week, the Eagles were described by Bleacher Report as "the NFL's wokest team." Whenever there was a microphone around—whether it was a nondescript Friday during the season or after the president called out football players—Jenkins used it as a forum to deliver his message.

"I think telling our story and opening up will change a lot of people's perspective," Jenkins said. "When you can show them systematic oppression, systematic problems that we have, and how they disproportionally affect a different group of people—one, I think they can better digest it and understand it, and two, they can actually see something they can help. . . . One thing you can change is our laws, our justice system, our schooling, our housing. All of that can be changed. And that comes from understanding that comes from voting, that comes from the people. We have that unique opportunity to bring people to the table and point to those issues, give people solutions, and educate people. Hopefully, we'll continue to push that and not get into fights about what's right, what's wrong, and really focus on what needs to happen."

Jenkins was far from the only one who fits into this category. Some players realized the value of their platform and refused to be silent. There's a common criticism that athletes—and the reporters who cover them—should "stick to sports." FOX News host Laura Ingraham responded to political commentary from NBA star LeBron James by suggesting that James should "shut up and dribble." This was not the modus operandi of some in the Eagles locker room. Long, who is from Charlottesville, Virginia, and attended the University of Virginia, was so disheartened by the August 2017 riots in his hometown following a white nationalist rally that he felt an obligation both as an NFL player and a Charlottesville native to speak about it.

"Some people are tired of hearing me tweet because they want me to 'stick to football,'" Long said. "But I like to use social media like I was a regular guy, because I think I am. I don't tell people to stick to their job when they want to talk politics. And this isn't political. That's the thing—everybody wants to turn this political. This isn't a political issue. This is right and wrong. I believe you're on one side or the other. For me, being from Charlottesville, nobody wants to sit idly by and not say anything. And I wish there was more categorical denials from some very important people in this country who have had the opportunity to strike it down but didn't."

Long put his money where his mouth was, donating his entire base salary to charity—half went to fund scholarships at his prep school in Charlottesville, and the other half went to organizations supporting educational equity in the three cities where Long played during his distinguished NFL career. And while he himself did not take a knee in protest during the national anthem, he showed support for those who did by putting his arm around Jenkins's shoulder while his teammate held his fist in the air.

At the Super Bowl, Roseman was asked how the Eagles were able to win in 2017 despite players such as Jenkins and Long having agendas outside of football. Roseman disagreed with the premise of the question. He explained how well those players functioned with the team, and noted that Lurie wants his players to be well-rounded. Before the season, Lurie emphasized how significant a problem social injustice is around the globe. He was in favor of any proactive activity from his players, as long as it was "respectful" toward the military and emergency responders. Lurie did not believe "protesting the national anthem, in and of itself, is very respectful." He wanted to know the reason for it and understand the "proactive nature" behind it. Lurie and Jenkins have had discussions about Jenkins's activity, and Jenkins had Lurie's full support. Lurie wants the Eagles to be viewed as a civic-minded organization, and it's not just lip service. In an *ESPN The Magazine* article about a league meeting among the thirty-two owners discussing the national anthem protest, Lurie was cast as one of the league's "thoughtful leaders" who spoke up during the meeting to support players' right to kneel. It was not the popular opinion in the room.

"I would be disappointed if every year we weren't a very good community-dedicated team," Lurie said. "To me, owning a sports team, you've got to be a great partner with your city, fan base, and region. If you don't do everything you can within your community, it'll be disappointing. They're not mutually exclusive. They actually go very well together."

• • •

For Pederson, what mattered most about the Eagles locking arms during the Giants game was that the team did it together. He considered it a sign of unity, part of the fabric of what made the 2017 team successful. An NFL locker room is filled with fifty-three players of different ages and backgrounds. A few Eagles were noticeably outspoken throughout the season—and especially after the Giants game because of the president's remarks that day—but that should not suggest everyone in the locker room was thrilled to be answering questions about the president or the national anthem.

"It's just really a distraction," said Lane Johnson, a veteran offensive lineman whose charity helps support Philadelphia public schools. "I don't like to get involved in politics and I don't think politicians should get involved in sports. It just creates a lot of noise and a lot of distraction that takes away from your main goal of winning games."

But on that particular Sunday, there was no avoiding it. Trump's comments brought it to the forefront, and it was more than just football fans who paid attention to how the league and its players reacted. Of course, once Wilson finished singing the line "and the home of the brave" and the applause subsided, the story was football again.

"It's not like guys are out there and protesting during the game," Long said. "I keep hearing 'keep politics out of sports' and I think some of the things that the guys are fighting for are more equality type of things, and I don't think that's political. Once the game starts, fans don't have to look at that stuff. Don't turn on the national anthem if you don't like it. We're still going to play hard."

An Invitation Rescinded

When a team wins the Super Bowl, they're typically honored by the president at the White House. It was a loaded invitation for the Eagles, though. A few players—notably Jenkins, Long, and Smith—made clear they would not visit if the team was invited. Jenkins was not interested in a photo opportunity. He wanted to discuss real issues. Add in President Trump sparring with the NFL, and the White House visit was a complicated topic for the Eagles. Nearly two months after the Super Bowl, Lurie wouldn't answer whether the Eagles would visit. And even after the White House eventually extended the invitation in April and the Eagles accepted, the team remained ambiguous about the visit, with a few players wishing to take Trump on the invitation and others vehemently opposed to going. Around the same time, the NFL established a national anthem policy that required everyone on the field to stand for the anthem. Players were given the option to remain in the locker room if they did not wish to stand for the anthem, but they were no longer permitted to be on the field and choose to kneel. The new policy was praised by the Trump administration.

A June 5 date had been set for the Eagles to visit. The Eagles had settled on only sending a small delegation, and President Trump rescinded the invitation. The team remained silent while the White House accused the Eagles of a "political stunt" and said the "vast majority of the Eagles team decided to abandon their fans." President Trump turned it into an anthem issue, suggesting that the players disagreed with Trump's stance on the anthem. Even if the anthem was not the reason some players objected to visiting, the Eagles were caught in a political hailstorm. It was another example of how the Eagles could not—and would not—stick to sports.

WEEK 4

‖‖‖

RUNNING BACK ON TRACK

GAME DAY: LOS ANGELES CHARGERS :: W 26–24

Jake Elliott carried the momentum from his game-winning field goal against the Giants into the Eagles' 26–24 Week 4 win over the Chargers, connecting on four field goals from 40 yards or more.

But the difference this day was the running game. After looking like they would be stymied all season, the Eagles suddenly had an effective ground attack—even without Darren Sproles.

"It's sort of the direction that I think our offense needs to go in," Doug Pederson said the day after the game.

The key was LeGarrette Blount. His zero-carry outing against Kansas City was long forgotten on the West Coast as he rushed for a season-high 136 yards, a performance that would make any linebacker wish he'd have called in sick.

"That man's angry," quarterback Carson Wentz joked, referring to Blount's punishing running style.

His best run came in the fourth quarter after the Chargers cut the Eagles' lead to 19–17. Wentz handed the ball to the 250-pound Blount, who ran 68 bruising yards through the Chargers defense, breaking four tackles along the way and demoralizing the defense with a physicality that few in the NFL could match. Wentz called it one of the most impressive runs he had ever seen. Considering that Blount led the NFL in rushing touchdowns one year earlier, it's hard to imagine that he had to wait through two months of free agency before signing a relatively paltry one-year contract with a base salary of just

$1.25 million (with incentives that could bring it up to $2.8 million). Blount took it in stride.

"I don't have any grudges against anybody," said Blount, wearing a T-shirt that read "Passion and Purpose." "I'm one of the better backs in this league as far as running the football."

He would continue to prove that statement throughout the 2017 season. It didn't hurt that he ran behind one of the NFL's best offensive lines. The Eagles benched Isaac Seumalo after Week 2 due to lackluster performance, calling up veterans Stefen Wisniewski and Chance Warmack to play left guard. Wisniewski eventually won the full-time job, solidifying the line for the road to the Super Bowl.

In Los Angeles, the line helped spark the running game and wear down the Chargers in the fourth quarter. In fact, after getting the ball with 6:44 to play after the Chargers had cut the lead to two points, the Eagles never gave it back. They rushed eight times for four first downs, moving the chains and winding down the clock until Wentz could finally take a knee and take the clock to zero. The final first down was gained by Blount.

"We were hoping we were going to end in the victory formation or end in the end zone," Wentz said.

The Eagles moved to 3–1 on the season, with back-to-back wins by tiny margins (three and two points, respectively). One year earlier, those close games usually ended with a loss. In Pederson's first season, the Eagles went 1–6 in games decided by seven points or fewer. Winning close games was an off-season talking point; during the season, it became part of the team's identity. Pederson credited veteran leadership that "really bought into . . . whatever I'm speaking about or selling." Center Jason Kelce pointed out that in 2016, the Eagles outscored their opponents overall and failed to make the postseason. The biggest reason for that failure their inability to finish games the way they did against the Chargers.

"That shows maturity, overcoming adversity," Kelce said. "And that's, really, in this league, what comes down to the difference of [making the] playoffs or not."

Pederson asked his players for a favor after the game. They were about to head to the airport to board a long flight home before facing two games over the next eleven days. Pederson asked his players to invest in those eleven days before they could catch their breath during an extended break. It was an easier ask for the veterans who bought into Pederson's message and witnessed the benefits in the standings, but newcomers took it to heart as well.

"You're starting to feel a little bit of this family environment," Pederson told his players in his postgame speech, as captured by the team website. "And it's contagious. Winning is a contagious."

EAGLES NATION

Wendell Smallwood started warming up on the turf of the StubHub Center in Carson, California, before the Eagles' game against the Chargers. He heard boos and figured Carson Wentz had come running onto the field—the opposing quarterback is usually serenaded with boos when taking the field on the road. When Smallwood looked up, he noticed that the boos were actually coming from Eagles fans who were heckling Chargers players.

"Man, this is crazy," Smallwood thought. "This is a home game for us."

Eagles fans are already known to travel in unusually large numbers to opposing stadiums, but the Chargers game brought it to a different level. There were a few factors at play. It was the Chargers' first season in the Los Angeles area, so they were still developing their fan base. They played in a 27,000-seat stadium—the smallest in the NFL by far—so Eagles fans made up a bigger chunk of the crowd than at any other away game. And when the scoreboard message incited the home crowd to cheer for the Chargers, the Eagles fans took it as their cue and drowned them out. After many big plays by the Birds, their fans' familiar "E-A-G-L-E-S, Eagles!" cheer echoed throughout the stadium. They even started chanting "Cowboys suck!"—a sentiment that would seem odd at a game that didn't involve Dallas if it wasn't coming from fans in midnight green. Even NFL fans used to seeing Eagles fans travel never saw them overtake a stadium like they did in Carson.

"I can't recall a time [like that]," Doug Pederson said. "It was great to see Eagle Nation out there, the fans to come support the guys. It's a long trip for us, obviously. . . . It was a fun atmosphere."

Chargers quarterback Philip Rivers admitted to the *San Diego Union-Tribune* that "it's just not a home game." Malcolm Jenkins said the defensive players were waving toward the stands to summon crowd noise as if they were playing at Lincoln Financial Field. He also had never experienced something that drastic on the road. It was a credit to Eagles fans who were starting to see the seeds of a special team.

"I'm kind of starting to not be stunned by our fans," Wentz said. "It's unbelievable."

A LITTLE MAN, A BIG LOSS

Inside the Eagles' locker room, few players command more respect than Darren Sproles. At age 34, the running back and kick returner was still one of the team's most dynamic players. That's why the joy of the Eagles' dramatic victory over the Giants was diminished one day later when they learned that Sproles had torn the anterior cruciate ligament in his left knee and broken his right forearm. The injuries, which occurred on the same rushing play, ended Sproles's season.

Sproles was the first of several high-profile players the Eagles lost to injury in 2017, and they would be forced to make adjustments after losing of one of the most versatile veterans in the NFL. Sproles had previously hinted that 2017 would be his final season, and these devastating injuries added to that speculation.

"For guys around here who see how hard he works and how much effort and preparation he puts into what he does on Sundays, it's tough," Malcolm Jenkins said. "I think everyone anticipated this being his last season. . . . You just feel for him more so as a friend. He's definitely a huge weapon we kind of hung our hat on all year. To lose that is big. You can't really replace a Darren Sproles."

In a sport that focuses on position prototypes, Sproles is unique. At 5-foot-6 and 190 pounds, Sproles is one of the NFL's smallest players. His size was what allowed the San Diego Chargers to draft him in the fourth round in 2005 despite prolific college production at Kansas State. Sproles was told that if he was 5-foot-10, he would have been a first-round pick. He's outlasted twelve of the thirteen running backs that were drafted ahead of him, and from the time he entered the league, no player in the NFL amassed more all-purpose yards. He helped his teams on the ground, through the air, and on punt returns, affecting the outcome of games more than most nonquarterbacks on the roster.

Yet Sproles didn't make the Pro Bowl until his ninth NFL season. During his first of three Pro Bowls, higher-profile players lit up when discussing Sproles, indicating their respect and admiration for him. Drew Brees, a future Hall of Fame quarterback who played with Sproles in San Diego and New Orleans, wanted the NFL to add an "all-purpose" category to the Pro Bowl so a player as versatile as Sproles could receive recognition. Hall of Fame running back LaDainian Tomlinson, who played with Sproles in San Diego, said "someone like Darren, you can't put a value on what they bring to the team."

With such a great reputation, it came as no surprise when Chip Kelly acquired Sproles in 2014. When the Eagles were preparing for the Saints playoff game the previous season, former Eagles defensive coordinator Bill Davis had walked into Kelly's office specifically to discuss how to defend against Sproles. And when Sproles arrived in Philadelphia—the Eagles picked him up from the Saints in 2014 in exchange for a 5th-round draft pick—Kelly quickly learned that Sundays might have been the least impressive part of Sproles's week, stating that Sproles was the "best practice player" he'd coached. There was no half-speed with Sproles. Teammates marveled at the strength he packed into his frame. Sproles's father, Larry, who is 5-foot-5, told his son at a young age that he would be short, but he could be strong. The two went to the gym together every day when Sproles was a kid in Olathe, Kansas.

"I mean this in the most complimentary way possible: He's a freak," Frank Reich said. "He is a genetic and physical specimen. We all know the size thing, but he's probably the strongest guy pound-for-pound on the team. There's something to be said for that."

Reich coached in San Diego from 2013 to 2015, and while Sproles had not played for the Chargers since 2010, players and employees still gushed about him. Reich once called him "legendary" in the weight room.

"Sproles is one of my favorite people—one of my favorite teammates I've ever had," Brees said. "His work ethic is second to none. His focus, his intensity. He's the epitome of what you would want in a teammate."

It's often easier for others to speak to Sproles's talent than it is for him to toot his own horn. He has a speech impediment, a stutter, which kept him away from the television cameras through the early part of his career. Friends noted that his stutter was more pronounced when he was most nervous, which included public speaking, and that his communication skills were underrated because of it. So throughout his NFL career, Sproles worked on becoming more comfortable with public speaking and eventually became a spokesman for the National Stuttering Foundation.

While Sproles was more comfortable on the field than in the spotlight, at age thirty-four his opportunity to play football was dwindling. He gave up precious time with his wife and children at home in Southern California to attend off-season workouts in Philadelphia. Knowing his years in the NFL were winding down, he made sure to savor every moment. When asked if this would be his last season in the NFL, Sproles told the reporter to check with him after the playoffs. It was a good response in June. But it was a cruel irony that Sproles reached his first Super Bowl on the injury list.

"You don't want to be forced out," Sproles said. "You want to leave on your own terms."

Sure enough, Sproles decided to return after the Super Bowl. An injury was not the right way to go out.

WEEK 5

A BIG-PLAY OFFENSE

GAME DAY: **ARIZONA CARDINALS** :: **W 34–7**

After winning two close games in a row, the Eagles sealed their 34–7 Week 5 win over the Arizona Cardinals by the end of the first quarter. Carson Wentz threw touchdowns on the Eagles' first three drives to build a 21–0 lead.

They looked like a juggernaut throughout the afternoon, using a big-play offense that had been missing one year earlier and delivering a third-down efficiency rating of sixty-four percent that's seldom seen in the NFL. On third down alone, Wentz went 11 of 12 for 225 yards and threw three of his four touchdown passes on third down. Making plays on third down is one big way quarterbacks distinguish themselves in the NFL.

Wentz and center Jason Kelce spend considerable time together in the days before each game to discuss offensive line protections. They spend considerable time on third-down protection in particular, as defenses often put their best pass rushers in the game on third downs. It's up to the center and the quarterback to see where the pressure is coming and adjust pre-snap. After his rookie season, Wentz often discussed "situational football"—third downs and red zone—as an area he could improve. And that's exactly what he did, finishing the season with the second-best percentage on third-down conversions of any starting quarterback.

"That's what separates good teams," Wentz said. "To be effective on third down and staying on the field, that helps time of possession and that helps the defense. It's a big part of the game. [We] call it the 'money down.'"

At one point, watching a long third down from the sideline during the Cardinals game, Malcolm Jenkins joked that he didn't even need to pick up his helmet. He figured Wentz would convert. Wentz did.

The "big plays" were also an area of improvement from 2016 to 2017. Wentz threw touchdowns of 72 yards and 59 yards against the Cardinals—two of the four longest touchdown passes of his career. During his rookie season Wentz threw for just four touchdowns of 20 yards or more; he had 10 TDs of that length in his second season.

Wentz likes the big play. Former Eagles wide receiver Jordan Matthews recalled becoming sold on Wentz as a big-time player in the quarterback's very first practice with the Eagles. They were running a play known as a "Y-stick concept," which calls for two slot receivers, the primary targets, to run "out" patterns while a wide receiver runs a "go" route—straight and deep—as a decoy to clear space for them.

"Nobody's ever thrown [the go route] since the history of football," Matthews said, yet Wentz threw the go route the first time they ran the play.

Matthews was in disbelief. "This dude's first day on the job?" he thought. He realized then that Wentz was unafraid to compete. Wentz didn't have a deep-threat receiver during his rookie season to allow him to stretch the field, and the Eagles wanted it to be a bigger part of the offense in 2017 and beyond. So in addition to Alshon Jeffery, they added Torrey Smith to provide a vertical element, drafted two of the top big-play receivers (Mack Hollins and Shelton Gibson) coming out of college, and replaced Jordan Matthews with Nelson Agholor in the slot to have a more dynamic presence. The results were evident all season—Wentz tied for second in the NFL in 2017 in "air yards" on completions, a statistic that tracks how many yards a ball traveled in the air. In 2016, Wentz ranked near the bottom of the NFL in that category. His completions traveled an average of nearly 2 more yards in the air than they did in 2016.

"Carson is known to chuck it," said Nelson Agholor, who caught the 72-yarder against the Cardinals. "He's going to chuck it and you have to get under it. We have fun with it. The deep ball is a great way to keep defenses honest and to help guys all around the football field."

Pederson said after the twenty-seven-point victory that the "sky's the limit" for the Eagles. And if there was any skepticism about the Eagles' 4–1 record, they had a chance to answer it four days later on the road against the impressive Carolina Panthers.

BROOKS: BLOCKING OUT ANXIETY

With Brandon Brooks playing all sixteen games in 2017, the Eagles' offensive line excelled. This was no coincidence. The combination of Lane Johnson at right tackle and Brooks at right guard provided the Eagles the best right side of an offensive line in the NFL. Both players had missed time in 2016—Johnson because of PED suspension, and Brooks because of a game-day illness related to an anxiety condition.

Throughout Brooks's career, he would wake up on the morning of games and vomit. While it is not unheard of for athletes to feel anxiety before games, Brooks's condition worsened to the point that he required hospitalization and intravenous fluids just to be able to stand upright. He first thought the vomiting was due to a stomach condition and underwent endoscopies and other medical tests, but his doctors couldn't pinpoint the problem. Not until he missed two games within three weeks late in the 2016 season did Brooks learn it wasn't his stomach; it was his mind. He suffered from an anxiety condition.

"What I mean by anxiety condition is not nervousness or fear of the game," Brooks said in 2016. "I have an obsession with the game. It's an unhealthy obsession right now."

Brooks went on medication and started seeing a therapist. His aim was to determine "why I'm constantly searching to be perfect"—and how his body was affected when he thought he fell short. He wanted to learn to turn his brain off—to "chill," as he explained it.

In 2017, Brooks found the peace of mind he desired. He still wakes up on the day of games and vomits in the hotel room bathroom. But now he laughs about it and sends a text message to Lane Johnson. He realized it was his body's way of priming for the game. He controlled the anxiety. He did not allow it to control him.

"I'm always going to be anxious," Brooks said. "But I realize it's OK to be anxious. Really, how I look at it, it's your body knowing you're about to go out there and play. . . . It's how my body handles it. But it's OK. It's not something I need to panic about."

Brooks, who is 6-foot-5 and 335 pounds, signed a five-year, $40-million contract with the Eagles in March 2016. He has the size and the skills of few people in the world. But when he made a mistake on the field, Brooks wondered what others would think of him. He considered the fans. He considered the commentators. But in time, he realized that all eyes are not locked on the right guard on every play. In fact, most casual observers wouldn't know if Brooks executed his block as required.

"It's like, 'Oh s—, that block wasn't perfect. Who saw that?'" Brooks said. "I was making a bigger deal about it than it was."

Brooks accepted that mistakes will be made, but he just needed to win more blocks than he lost. And while he realized each play was not "life and death," it didn't mean he took the game less seriously. He just stopped paralyzing himself with his thoughts, and stopped focusing on the complexity of football.

"People say this is just a game, but it's not at all," Brooks said. "If it was just a game, people wouldn't be able to make careers off it. Not just players but reporters, coaches, et cetera. . . . You almost get locked in a mindset of you can't make a mistake, or if you make a mistake, it's the end of the world. That's not the case. Everybody [makes mistakes], top down. If I make a mistake, I laugh about that s—. There's more plays to play. Life goes on."

His pregame routine has changed, too. Brooks used to arrive at the stadium wearing headphones, distancing himself from everyone around him while envisioning how he needed "to go out there and be perfect." In 2017, Brooks stopped bringing headphones to the stadium. He spent pregames joking with his teammates, finding a sense of calmness that he missed in past years.

"Last year, I was like f—ing about to go to war," Brooks said. "That's probably the thing. [This year] on game day, man, I'm just thinking I put all the time into prepare. I know what I'm doing. . . . And my last thought is to go out there and have fun."

Brooks's personal goal going into the season was not to make the Pro Bowl or to hit certain stats, but to simply play sixteen games. He wanted to prove to himself that he could overcome the anxiety. And that's exactly what he did. Not only did he play every game, but he played so well that he also made his first Pro Bowl.

Brooks met with a therapist after every game, usually on Tuesdays. Those sessions were just as important to him as working with the team's athletic trainer to prepare himself physically. It just wasn't viewed the same way amid the machismo of sports.

"I guess the mental awareness tip was just like, if you pull a hamstring and you need ice to [stimulate] your rehab, it's the same thing mentally," Brooks said. "Sometimes you need someone to talk to. Sometimes things are deeper than what you think, or you have something from your past that's affecting you, and you don't even know. But it's nice to be able to talk to somebody on a confidential level and get PhD advice."

Brooks went public about his anxiety condition in December of 2016, and he now views that day as one of the highlights of his time in Philadelphia. Before doing so, he met with the team's media relations department to determine the public message. Until then, the team had been cryptic about Brooks's absences. But Brooks decided to be honest. He answered every question from reporters, exhibiting a vulnerability that's rare for a professional athlete. Brooks is now unafraid to speak about his condition, and he won't turn away interviews when anxiety is discussed.

Brooks's candor in discussing the stigmatized topic proved inspirational for others. It also prompted greater support from the Philadelphia fan base. One of his neighbors slid a message under the door in his Philadelphia condominium that read: "Don't worry about being perfect. Our imperfections are what make us who we are."

Being so vocal about his mental health struggles made him even more relatable than he already was. Brooks had long transcended football with interests outside the sport. He worked toward his MBA while playing in Houston. After his first season with the Eagles, he interned in the Philadelphia revenue department and also with a private equity firm. He can discuss Philadelphia's tax structure and the way city tax affects businesses. Brooks is also an avid reader whose favorite books are *Zero to One* by Peter Thiel, *Outliers* by Malcolm Gladwell, and *The Road to Character* by David Brooks. He was always more than a football player, and his anxiety condition earned the empathy of those who don't need to worry about blocking a defensive tackle on national television.

"I heard about the fans before I came here, how passionate they were," Brooks said. "And I'm a regular dude, man. I live downtown. I walk around all the time. I'm grabbing food, just walking around. It's not something like where I'm too big-time."

There was little reason for disappointment in 2017. By his own admission, football was fun again. He established himself as one of the best players on the Eagles and in the NFL. And he conquered what had once almost conquered him.

"You can overcome it," Brooks said. "Although there are times when there's darkness, there will be brighter days coming."

WEEK 6

LEGITIMATE CONTENDERS

GAME DAY: **CAROLINA PANTHERS :: W 28–23**

The Eagles were 4–1 through their first five games, but skepticism remained about whether they were for real. Their four wins came against opponents that were a combined 5–14 at that point in the season. A signature win would change the reputation of the Eagles.

That came in Week 6 against the Carolina Panthers, who also entered the nationally televised Thursday night contest with a 4–1 record. The Panthers were the home team on a short week—often considered an advantage—and the Eagles were notably undermanned because of injuries. Sproles was out for the season. Cornerback Ronald Darby remained sidelined with a dislocated ankle suffered in Week 1. Right tackle Lane Johnson missed the game with a concussion sustained against Arizona. Linebacker Jordan Hicks left the game early with an ankle injury. Chris Maragos, the Eagles' best special teams player, suffered a season-ending knee injury that night.

Given all of this, an Eagles loss would have been understandable. But the team was not deterred. When cornerback Jalen Mills secured a fourth-quarter interception to help clinch the 28–23 road victory, it was a pivotal point in the season. The Eagles were contenders, and everyone around the league knew it. There was no rationalizing or scrutinizing necessary.

"I told them tonight after the game," Pederson said, "that I haven't been a part of a team that has battled through so much injury and adversity through the first month of the season, to stay together."

Carson Wentz, who threw three touchdowns in the game, believed the victory was the result of the "different character makeup in the locker room." He said the 2017 group was "built differently" after injuries crippled their 2016 campaign, and he would not tolerate excuses from his teammates. Halapoulivaati Vaitai stepped in at right tackle for the injured Johnson, and after allowing an early sack, he settled down and had a solid game the rest of the way. He looked like a different player than the rookie who struggled one year earlier during Johnson's ten-game suspension.

"We just have a bunch of guys that believe no matter the situation, we can win the ball game," Wentz said.

The defense bullied quarterback Cam Newton throughout the night, forcing three interceptions by the former MVP. When the Eagles trailed by a touchdown in the second quarter, Fletcher Cox crushed Newton in midpass allowing rookie cornerback Rasul Douglas to intercept the fluttering ball and set up Wentz's game-tying touchdown pass to tight end Zach Ertz. Two of the Eagles' three interceptions led to touchdowns, and the other ended the game. Coming into the game the Panthers were viewed as one of the top teams in the NFC, and the Eagles outplayed them in their own stadium.

"We just put the league on notice," safety Rodney McLeod said afterward.

Standing tall with a 5–1 record—tops in the NFC—Ertz admitted that he did not expect that type of start to the season given the injuries the Eagles had already accumulated. (Of course, more devastating blows would follow.) But the resilience that would become the hallmark of their Super Bowl run was evident early on. Before the Eagles boarded a flight back to Philadelphia for extended rest and a three-game home stand, Pederson, as seen on the team's website, succinctly explained to his players that there would be no slowing down.

"Sky is the freaking limit for this football team, you got me?" Pederson said.

GET TO KNOW NIGEL

Late in the win over Carolina, after one of linebacker Nigel Bradham's ten tackles, an offensive player on the Panthers approached him to say that he didn't know Bradham before the game, but that Bradham was a "beast."

"You don't know who I am?" Bradham responded, according to NBC Sports Philadelphia. "You must not know football. But you know me today."

As the 2017 season progressed, Bradham started receiving more attention for his standout performances. He wondered what took so long. It wasn't as if Bradham was an out-of-nowhere rookie—he was in his sixth season in the NFL and second starting for the Eagles. Bradham long thought he was one of the NFL's best linebackers. It just took longer for others to take notice.

"I played like that last year," Bradham said. "That's what's funny to me."

Malcolm Jenkins called Bradham the Eagles' "enforcer," roaming the field looking for big hits and talking trash to opponents thereafter. If there's ever a skirmish after a play, Bradham never plays the bystander. Jenkins said Bradham "brings a little juice" to the group.

But he's not all brawn, either. One week after the Panthers game, the Eagles would lose standout linebacker and defensive signal-caller Jordan Hicks for the season with a torn Achilles tendon. Bradham picked up Hicks's signal-calling responsibilities—receiving play calls from the sideline and aligning the defense accordingly—and did so seamlessly. Defensive Coordinator Jim Schwartz thought Bradham's adjustment was "one of the unsung stories" to the Eagles' success.

"Nigel has always been a fiery guy," Schwartz said. "Sometimes I think he runs about five extra miles trying to get to the pile to make sure he's delivering whatever message he's going to deliver, and it brings us a lot of energy, it really does."

Bradham and Schwartz share a close bond. Bradham played his best football in Buffalo when Schwartz was his defensive coordinator there. As a free agent in 2016, Bradham signed a two-year, $7-million contract with the Eagles so he could reunite with Schwartz. He would immediately join the starting lineup, but not before dealing with a couple of controversial off-the-field incidents.

Before Bradham even played a game in an Eagles uniform, he was charged with aggravated assault for striking a hotel worker in Miami. (He accepted a deferred prosecution program and the case has since closed.) A few weeks later, Bradham was charged with a misdemeanor for bringing a weapon to the Miami airport. For a guy joining a new team, it was a bad first impression . . . and second impression. The disappointment for Schwartz, who vouched for Bradham, was that the transgressions overshadowed all the positive qualities Schwartz saw in him—how trustworthy Bradham is as a player, how devoted he is as a teammate, and how ardent he is as a worker.

"But hey, facts are facts," Schwartz said. "You do dumbass things, pretty soon you're going to be labeled a dumbass."

Since Schwartz made that statement in October 2016, there have been no public incidents involving Bradham. He continued thriving in the defense, where his aggression is invited. When Bradham's performance helped carry the defense against the Panthers in front of a national audience, Schwartz was unsurprised.

"He plays tough, he plays mean," Schwartz said. "He plays with a lot of spirit. Players feed off of him. He feeds off of the guys. He's sort of stuck with it through some tough times. But we never really lost our belief in him."

One month after the Super Bowl, Bradham signed a five-year, $40-million contract to continue playing in Philadelphia. He had traveled a long way from a modest Crawfordville, Florida, childhood in a wooden trailer eluding rats and cockroaches, and it wasn't just for the paycheck. Bradham also sought recognition, and he intended to make sure there was no longer any surprise when he's swarming the field in a 10-tackle performance.

"Respect. That's what we're playing for. That's all I want," Bradham said. "At the end of the day, I want my peers to see me on film and say, 'I want to play with that guy' or 'I respect that guy.'"

WEEK 7

"I DON'T KNOW HOW YOU STOP THAT"

GAME DAY: **WASHINGTON REDSKINS :: W 34–24**

Carson Wentz delivered a standout performance in the Eagles' 34–24 win over Washington in Week 7, completing 17 of 25 passes for 268 yards and four touchdowns while also leading the team with 63 rushing yards. But two plays in particular will surely make his career highlight reel.

With the Eagles holding a seven-point lead in the fourth quarter and facing a third-and-8 from their own 27-yard line, Wentz took the shotgun snap and immediately felt the pocket collapse against the Redskins blitz. He appeared to be all but buried between four defenders and four blockers, but somehow Wentz squirmed away like a worm, found a sliver of space, and accelerated for a 17-yard gain and a first down.

"How in the world did that happen?" ESPN announcer Sean McDonough asked in disbelief on the telecast.

"Was he down?" analyst Jon Gruden asked. "Where did he go? Amazing! He came out of a pile of bodies."

"That was ridiculous," tight end Zach Ertz said after the game. "I don't know how you stop that as a defense."

While that play will likely go down as the game's signature highlight, it might not have been Wentz's most impressive moment.

In the third quarter, on a third-and-goal from the 9-yard line, Redskins defenders collapsed the line of scrimmage and quickly surrounded Wentz in the backfield. He somehow remained upright in a mass of linemen, stepped forward into space, and then hurled a pass to the side of the end zone as two pass rushers converged upon him. The pass found Corey Clement—Wentz's last read in his progression—along the sideline in the end zone for the touchdown.

"How does he get away from all these free rushers and make throws like that?" Gruden asked on the telecast.

"I thought maybe that time it was going to be a sack," Pederson said after the game. "One of the best plays I've seen in a long, long time."

The play design was inspired by a play Wentz ran at North Dakota State called "Bison." Offensive coordinator Frank Reich, an ex-quarterback himself, explained that some plays just have a "good mojo" for a particular quarterback, and that it would be foolish for a coaching staff not to add such plays to the inventory. It took only a few weeks from the time Wentz introduced the play to the time it was installed in the game plan.

"I had to call NDSU [and] get the old film out so I could show them what's going on, and then run it in practice and just kind of convince them on it," Wentz said. "It's cool to have that relationship, that dynamic with Coach Reich, with Coach Pederson, [and] that they respect my opinion when I bring them things like that."

Wentz and Pederson met every Thursday night through most of the season. Sometimes, they talked about hunting or told old Brett Favre stories. (Pederson and Favre were close friends in Green Bay. Favre was Wentz's favorite player as a kid.) Other times, they discussed Xs and Os so Pederson—the play-caller—was on the same page as Wentz.

That bond was clear throughout the win over Washington that advanced the Eagles to 6–1 and continued to elevate Wentz's confidence. He connected with Mack Hollins on a 64-yard touchdown. He hit Zach Ertz on all five intended targets, including a 4-yard score. A quarterback who didn't throw more than two touchdowns in a game as a rookie now had two four-touchdown games in three weeks. It was the team's best start to a season since they reached the Super Bowl thirteen years earlier, and they were doing it behind a player who was quickly becoming an MVP candidate. In fact, the fans chanted "M-V-P!" after some of Wentz's most spectacular plays. But it was another chant that would add bitterness to a night that was otherwise so sweet.

WENTZ: BECOMING A STAR

If you had to identify the point in the season when Carson Wentz ascended to stardom—when it started to become obvious that the great performances throughout the first few weeks of the season weren't dumb luck—you would say it happened in the Week 7 *Monday Night Football* showdown against the division rival Washington Redskins.

Entering the game, Redskins coach Jay Gruden said that Wentz had "progressed at a rate as fast as anybody I've seen" and that, only twenty-two games into his career, "he's already proven . . . he's one of the top quarterbacks in the league." This wasn't just lip service. Wentz was already on pace to set the Eagles' franchise record for yards and touchdowns, and one Las Vegas sportsbook ranked Wentz the favorite to win the MVP before the game.

"I know that he's probably going to be in those conversations," Doug Pederson said, "probably for the rest of his career."

To add to Wentz's growing mystique, ESPN ran a story that week about his relationship with Wilmington, Delaware, native Lukas Kusters, who died of stomach cancer at age ten. Nicknamed the "Dutch Destroyer" for his own football prowess, Kusters watched Wentz's rookie season while undergoing treatment in 2016. Kusters's family adorned his hospital room with Eagles regalia, including Wentz's No. 11 jersey. Wentz sent a personal video to lift the boy's spirits after the team learned of Kusters's story.

When they boy's cancer spread and became terminal, his request to the Make a Wish Foundation was simple—he just wanted a chance to thank Wentz for the video. The Eagles granted the wish in style, sending a limo to pick up Kusters and his family and deliver them to the Eagles' facility to meet with Wentz and linebacker Jordan Hicks. They gave Kusters a tour of the facility, and the boy gave Wentz a green bracelet inscribed with his nickname, "Dutch Destroyer."

Two weeks after meeting Wentz, Kusters succumbed to cancer. He was buried in Wentz's Eagles jersey. Meanwhile, Wentz never took off the bracelet. The Eagles invited the Kusters family to the *Monday Night Football* game against Washington, where Wentz met with them before the game and later gave them the ball from one of his touchdown passes. (Wentz later sent them to the Super Bowl, too.)

"I feel Lukas all the time," Wentz said. "It's always nice just to have him on my wrist. It's a constant reminder that it's so much bigger than football. And I have just been praying for that family, praying for them for a long time. It's a very moving story, obviously. It's pretty cool to be able to be in this position and make that impact."

It was all part of a groundswell of positive publicity leading up to Wentz's second consecutive nationally televised game. By the end of that game, Wentz had become a bona fide star.

A BITTERSWEET VICTORY

Almost every player on the Eagles sideline ran onto the field less than a minute into the third quarter as future Hall-of-Fame lineman Jason Peters sat on the turf clutching his right knee. The injury looked bad, and in moments a motorized cart was speeding onto the field toward Peters. Teammates shook his hand and offered encouraging words as he was taken off the field. Even players from the Redskins came over to pay their respects. If that wasn't enough, the 69,596 fans at Lincoln Financial Field started to chant together, *"Ja-son-Pe-ters! . . . Ja-son-Pe-ters!"*

As he was carted off the field, Peters, always a leader, barked instructions and inspiration to second-year tackle Halapoulivaati Vaitai, who would step in for him at left tackle.

When Peters arrived in the trainer's room, linebacker Jordan Hicks was already sitting on a table. Two quarters earlier, Hicks had left the field with an apparent leg injury. Peters encouraged both men to stay positive, but the team's worst fears were confirmed the next day. Peters had suffered a torn anterior cruciate ligament and torn medial collateral ligament, and Hicks ruptured the Achilles tendon in his right leg. Both were lost for the rest of the season.

If you compiled a list naming the best players and best leaders on the Eagles, Peters and Hicks would be near the top of both. And in one game, they were both gone.

Leader in the Clubhouse

When Jordan Hicks came to Philadelphia as a third-round pick under Chip Kelly in 2015, it looked like he would be buried on the depth chart behind established inside linebackers DeMeco Ryans, Mychal Kendricks, and Kiko Alonso. Ryans, a wily veteran, had earned the nickname "Mufasa" in a reference to *The Lion King*. In practice, Hicks quickly established himself as a younger version of Ryans, but with a maturity beyond his years, and was given the nickname "Simba" from the same movie. On game days, Hicks proved to be the most productive of all of the inside linebackers that season—until his rookie year was cut short by a torn pectoral muscle.

There has been little question about Hicks's contributions during his Eagles career, but there have many questions about his health. When he played all sixteen games in 2016, there was optimism that he would take the next step and become a Pro Bowl–caliber player in 2017. Jim Schwartz puts great responsibility on his middle linebacker, including relaying the play call and setting up the defense. He quickly realized "there's nothing that we've thrown at him that he has not been able to handle." "It's awesome not coming off injury," Hicks said during the spring of 2017. "It's awesome not having to learn a new defense. You're comfortable. You don't have to waste time learning. You already know. Now it's just taking the next step mentally because you know you're there physically."

Hicks's personal life was also taking shape in the 2017 off-season. He got married and went on his honeymoon in Greece before training camp opened in late July. Everything was moving in the right direction for the budding star until he slipped on a pool deck at a Mykonos resort and braced for the fall with his right hand, feeling immediate pain. Seeking an X-ray, Hicks took the ferry to Santorini to meet with a doctor, who puffed on a cigarette while examining Hicks's hand. The X-ray revealed a broken bone in his pinkie finger; it didn't require a cast, but he would need surgery. Hicks finished the final days of his honeymoon before returning to the States, where a pin was inserted into his pinkie to stabilize the bone.

Hicks was familiar with sustaining injuries on the football field. But a honeymoon injury added a new layer to the dreaded "injury-prone" label that all players fear.

"I had done this stuff on the field," Hicks told reporters at the start of training camp. "I've done my share. But off the field, I've really never had anything like that, so the fact that it happened and I was so far away . . . adds a bit more stress, a bit more pressure."

That injury would not cause him to miss the start of the season, although it was an ominous start. When a groin injury slowed him during training camp, Schwartz decided to experiment with other linebacker combinations just in case Hicks went down during the season, planting the seeds of the eventual Nigel Bradham–Mychal Kendricks partnership that the Eagles relied on after Hicks was injured.

Sure enough, the injury bug began to bite once the season started. Hicks suffered a minor ankle injury in Week 3 against the Giants that caused him to leave the game, but he returned the following week. He played two games without incident, then left the Carolina game with another ankle tweak. When he returned, he began using his right leg more to compensate for his ailing left ankle, leaving him vulnerable. When he collapsed to the ground against Washington with a ruptured Achilles tendon, Hicks didn't even need to wait for the diagnosis.

"I knew exactly what happened," Hicks said.

The Eagles lost one of their best players and leaders. A season that offered such promise for Hicks ended as too many did before: on the injury list. He wondered what would have happened had he let his ankle heal more thoroughly. Hicks realized too late that missing a few weeks is better than missing a few months.

"I think a part of it is knowing when to cut back," Hicks said. "But I'm a professional athlete. You put me in a position to go play, and I'm going to compete as hard as I can."

Next Man Up

The Eagles traded a first-round pick for Jason Peters in 2009, paying the Buffalo Bills' high asking price because, as then-coach Andy Reid said, "Jason Peters is the best left tackle in football." Since coming to the Eagles, he's made seven Pro Bowls and solidified himself as a bona fide Hall of Fame candidate. Nicknamed "the Bodyguard," Peters will be remembered as the best offensive tackle in Eagles history.

The Eagles have already given him three contract extensions, the latest coming in June 2017 before the Super Bowl season began. The three-year, $32.5-million deal seemed steep for a thirty-five-year-old player—until you listen to his explanation.

"Do you want to win a Super Bowl or do you want to save money?" Peters said. "It's their decision. I give us a good chance on a line to help all the other guys and get where we want to go."

Peters said when he signed the last contract that he was "year-to-year," admitting he was chasing a ring. That's what kept him playing. He had not won a playoff game since coming to Philadelphia, and that was his singular goal.

"The fans deserve a Super Bowl," Peters said. "Get in the playoffs, make the Linc rock, get home field, and go from there. The city of Philly deserves it."

In addition to being a fan favorite, Peters is revered in the locker room. His booming voice carries even more weight than his 340-pound frame. He is also a personal favorite of owner Jeffrey Lurie, with Peters calling the two "best friends."

"I love Jason," Lurie said. "Jason is just very special."

Peters is one of the NFL's great success stories. He was signed by the Buffalo Bills as an undrafted tight end, started his career on the practice squad, joined the active roster as a special teams player, and started to learn the position of offensive tackle because it appeared to be his only opportunity to get onto the field. An intelligent and diligent worker, Peters has since mastered the craft. Before Eagles offensive line coach Jeff Stoutland came to Philadelphia in 2013, he was a position coach at Alabama. During his time there, Stoutland often showed his college players film of the Eagles' Peters as an example of how to best play the position. Peters's athleticism and strength are unique, but his technique is world-class.

He is a natural leader who takes it upon himself to help younger players whenever he can. After a long training-camp practice in July, the thirty-five-year-old Peters stayed on the field to help twenty-one-year-old Derek Barnett add a new pass-rush move to his repertoire. After his injury, Peters continued to mentor his replacement Vaitai throughout the season, even passing along instructions to the younger player during games.

It was a tough responsibility for Vaitai to replace Peters, someone he admired even before they were teammates. Vaitai was a junior at Texas Christian University in 2015 when he walked through a Dallas-area shopping mall and spotted Peters. He approached his future teammate to introduce himself and ask for advice.

"Work your butt off," Peters said, "and you'll be up here."

The Eagles drafted Vaitai one year later. Vaitai shared the story upon his arrival and quickly received a phone call from Peters.

"Remember me?" Peters asked.

"I didn't know it was going to be literally *here*," Vaitai said with a smile, remembering the story.

Vaitai insisted that nobody could replace Peters. He wanted to play his best for Peters, and was eager to embrace his tutelage. Following his injury, Peters phoned Vaitai with a simple message: "Work your ass off." It was now Vaitai's job, and everyone was counting on him, especially the franchise quarterback.

For the first time in Wentz's career, he wouldn't have the Bodyguard protecting his blindside. "I guess it's something I've never really had to think of," Wentz said. "JP's been dynamite back there. But I have a ton of confidence in whoever's over there."

WEEK 8

||||||||||||||||||||||||||||||||||||||||||||||||||||||||||||||||||||||||||||||||||||||||||||||||||||||||||||||||||||||||||||||||||||||||||

MORE OF THE SAME,
TIME FOR A CHANGE

GAME DAY: SAN FRANCISCO 49ERS :: W 33–10

With two major injuries to deal with, it sure helped that the Eagles' Week 8 opponent was the San Francisco 49ers.

No matter how the Eagles tried to spin it, the winless 49ers were far from an intimidating foe at that point in the season. But there was still concern among fans that it could be a "trap game"—one that proves more difficult than it should, due to timing and other circumstances. With the Eagles coming off two straight emotional victories, there was a chance for a letdown. Instead, they delivered another dominant performance to move to a league-best 7–1 record.

"We're halfway through the season, we're right where we want to be," veteran defensive end Brandon Graham said. "But things can go downhill real easily if you start [acting impressed with] yourself. So we need to make sure . . . we don't worry about 7–1 until we get done [the season] and they say, 'Hey, we're going to the playoffs.' That's when we can have a different mindset. But right now, we haven't done anything."

The Eagles entered the game as thirteen-point favorites, and they easily covered that point spread in a 33–10 victory. The win was mostly attributed to the Eagles defense, which hit 49ers rookie quarterback C. J. Beathard twelve times, caused four sacks, and made two interceptions.

Without Jordan Hicks, the Eagles turned to Mychal Kendricks to play a bigger role. Kendricks had been a starting linebacker since joining the Eagles as a second-round pick in 2012, but he took on a diminished role in recent years when the rest of the linebackers were healthy. Because the NFL has shifted to a passing league, defenses usually play a nickel package that has five defensive backs and only two linebackers on the field. When Bradham and Hicks were in the lineup, Kendricks was the odd man out because the Eagles did not need three linebackers. With Hicks injured, Kendricks ascended to a top-two linebacker for the Eagles.

"When you're not in there and not playing, you don't have anything to lose when you get your chance," Kendricks said. "You play free, and it's a good feeling."

Unlike past weeks, Carson Wentz did not have a MVP performance. He was sacked three times, threw one interception, and had his second-worst passer rating of the season. Yet the Eagles still scored thirty-three points, including three offensive touchdowns. It wasn't exactly a bad day at the office.

There was nothing to fix with Wentz and his receiving crew. However, the Eagles thought they needed to improve on the ground after averaging fewer than 4 yards per carry for the fourth consecutive game. Pederson was committed to calling running plays, but they needed to have more success when he did. Fortunately, the deficiency didn't matter much against the 49ers. But there was going to be a time when the Eagles would need more production on the ground, and Howie Roseman was already considering how they might achieve that.

MILLS: A CONFIDENT CORNERBACK

Jalen Mills took a moment to think about his answer. The question was whether he had ever in his life lacked the bravado that is just as big a part of his finger-wagging, green-hair-wearing reputation as all the big plays he's made on the field.

Finally, Mills said he remembered a moment in grade school, more than fifteen years prior. (Never mind that he was merely a seventh-round draft pick who needed to first earn a roster spot, and then a starting spot, on the Eagles.) As a seven-year-old growing up in the Dallas area, many of Mills's classmates wore new sneakers. But Mills came from a single-mother home where money was tight and they watched every dollar. There would be no new shoes for Mills, but there would be a lesson. Don't compare yourself to others, his mother and grandmother told him. Be confident in who you are and be happy with what you have.

Since then, Mills has used their advice as a marching order. He has almost incomparable bravado in a locker room full of alpha males.

On the first day of training camp as a rookie, Mills defied the norm and avoided anonymity. It's said that rookies are sometimes better seen than heard, but most would agree that dyeing your hair a bright shade of Kelly green doesn't exactly fall under that adage. Mills wasn't looking to lay low; he wanted to be noticed. "Nobody had to coach him . . . on confidence," safety Malcolm Jenkins said.

"If you're going to be wearing that green hair," Jim Schwartz told Mills, "you better be out here making plays."

That's exactly what Mills did. The Eagles reconfigured the depth chart in 2016 because of the way Mills played as a rookie. He looked like a steal in the seventh round out of LSU, although his draft stock was affected by a broken ankle and a legal issue (a charge of battery) that was later dropped. He waited 232 picks before the Eagles selected him. Upon arriving in Philadelphia, Mills asked to wear No. 31 as a reminder of all the other teams that passed on drafting him.

"I love the hell out of that kid," Schwartz said. "I really do. He is a competitor. People talk about speed, people talk about ability to play the ball. To me, the number one criteria for playing corner is you have to be a competitor, and he is."

Mills's mother, Kisa Jackson, said the confidence was "embedded in him" from a young age. She told her two children that they must always stand up for themselves. "As a little kid, he was always just the man," said Jackson. Although Mills needed prodding in high school to improve his grades and avoid bad influences in order to make it to college, he thrived once he got to LSU. Despite playing on a team with several future NFL stars, Mills didn't take a back seat to anyone, starting all four years.

"It's one thing to be confident, but it's another thing to be able to back it up," said New York Giants star receiver Odell Beckham Jr., a college teammate. "And that's what he does."

Whenever a pass targeted for a wide receiver falls incomplete, Mills wags his finger. It doesn't matter if the receiver caught the previous pass. Bravado doesn't take breaks.

"It shows he's confident," Jackson said. "It shows, 'Not on me, you're not doing it.'"

Going into the 2017 season, cornerback was considered a weakness for the Eagles, but Mills refused to hear it. When the Eagles traded for Ronald Darby, it appeared Darby would become the No. 1 cornerback. But a Week 1 injury sidelined Darby, putting even more pressure on Mills. But he believed he carried the burden all along.

Mills recorded three interceptions in 2017, including one that he ran back for a touchdown. That touchdown came in the Week 8 win against San Francisco, and it showed that Mills was far more than flash. He had clearly improved the mental side of his game, and he credits the growth in part to observing the preparation of players such as Jenkins and Rodney McLeod who showed him how to "really *study* study."

Mills studied 49ers rookie quarterback C. J. Beathard in the week leading up to the game to spot Beathard's tendencies. On the interception, he identified the play and knew Beathard was going to throw it toward Pierre Garçon. Mills jumped in front of the veteran receiver, picked off the ball, and navigated through traffic for a 37-yard touchdown. The interception wasn't just a key play in the game; it was a sign of Mills's growth and a validation of his confidence.

"It's hard to cover on the outside part of the field if you don't have confidence," Schwartz said. "Jalen has never lacked for confidence, but his preparation is a big part of that."

WEEK 9

TRADER HOWIE

Back on that couch in college, Howie Roseman pledged to his roommate that if he got the chance, he would make more trades than had ever been seen in the NFL. He wasn't exaggerating.

For many years, trades were relatively uncommon in the NFL, especially those involving players as opposed to draft picks. Roseman was part of a new wave of executives who were more active in making trades. He completed sixty-two trades from the time he was named general manager in 2010 through the 2017 season, including forty-two involving players. His forty-second trade came at the trade deadline on October 31, just before the Eagles' game against the Denver Broncos in Week 9.

With the Eagles at 7–1 and considered to be legitimate postseason contenders, Roseman acquired Pro Bowl running back Jay Ajayi from the Miami Dolphins in exchange for a 2018 fourth-round draft pick. Ajayi starred for the Dolphins in 2016 when he rushed for 1,272 yards and 8 touchdowns, although his production—and reputation—took a dive to begin the 2017 season.

After the trade, the *Miami Herald* reported that the Dolphins had concerns about team chemistry and how Ajayi fit within their locker-room culture. The report indicated that he complained about not carrying the ball enough and had stormed out of the locker room after victories if he felt he didn't get enough touches. They also had concerns about the long-term health of Ajayi's knees.

Before the trade deadline, Doug Pederson seemed cautious about making any moves. He emphasized that the Eagles could not do a deal that would disrupt the locker room, stressing the value of the chemistry that had been built. Roseman insisted he would not add anyone that would affect that, and after pulling the trigger on the Ajayi deal, explained that the Eagles felt "very confident and comfortable" about Ajayi. Roseman and Pederson both declared that LeGarrette Blount would remain the starting running back, deferring to Blount's past reputation and current performance as an Eagle. Also, they didn't want to necessarily rebuild their highly effective ground attack, which was ranked No. 5 in the NFL at the time, but rather to enhance it. Roseman even notified Blount of the deal before it was consummated.

"I trust the guys on this team to handle the players. Everybody's got a past," Pederson said. "I was in a situation where we brought in a player and there were reports of character issues and all kinds of things. You know what? The guys rallied around him and there was not one issue whatsoever. And we went on to win the Super Bowl."

Pederson's reference was to the Green Bay Packers' late-season addition of notorious receiver Andre Rison in 1996, when Pederson was a backup quarterback there. This was another example of Pederson's playing experience proving beneficial to his coaching. He met with Ajayi to better understand the running back, and Ajayi said he viewed the trade as a fresh start. The organization was also confident that running backs coach and former Eagles back Duce Staley, whom Pederson called "the equalizer," could manage the personalities in his group. Staley had worked with Pro Bowlers LeSean McCoy and DeMarco Murray in the past, so adding another high-profile player should not be a problem.

Most importantly, the Eagles thought Ajayi could help the offense based on his production for the Dolphins and on first-hand experience. Before the season started, the Dolphins had practiced with the Eagles in joint sessions in Philadelphia. The Eagles coaches and scouting staff were all on the field and saw Ajayi up close. They didn't know then that they might trade for him, but they were impressed with his skill set.

"He's one of the guys that when we came back after those practices, we said, 'That's our kind of guy,'" Roseman said. "He's got the mentality that we're looking for. He brings the kind of presence and he plays the kind of way that we want to play and that we want to represent our football team and our fans with."

When Ajayi arrived in Philadelphia, the Eagles showed him his spot in the middle of the locker room. It was the same stall that once belonged to McCoy, the franchise's all-time leading rusher. The team issued Ajayi No. 36, which was worn by former Pro Bowl running back Brian Westbrook. This was the company Ajayi joined as an Eagles running back.

Ajayi is a London native who stands 6 feet tall and 223 pounds with blond highlights mixed into his dreadlocks. He's mild-mannered off the field, often wearing a beanie on his head and speaking with a quiet British accent. But when Ajayi is on the field, he says he's something different. He wears a gold locomotive-shaped medallion around his neck in reference to his nickname, the "Jay Train," and the metaphor matches his on-field persona.

Ajayi got the nickname while playing at Boise State University in 2013. He wanted to create an alter-ego for himself, and was somewhat jealous of a defensive teammate whose postsack dance became popular among fans. When a fan on social media Photoshopped a picture of Ajayi on a train, Ajayi thought it was clever and adopted the "Jay Train" nickname from it. He even came up with a touchdown celebration in which he'd simulate a train conductor pulling a whistle. He wanted the Eagles to sound a train horn after he scored. (Ajayi made the comment during the playoffs and did not score after he said it.)

"When I'm on the field, I can turn into the Jay Train, become kind of violent, physical," Ajayi said. "It's almost like you can be violent on the field and it's legal a little bit because it's football. That's kind of where I can go with that persona and use it to be physical, to be a dog on the field. Use all those emotions to run and make plays for the team."

Even with his deserved reputation as perhaps the most aggressive executive in the NFL, Roseman seldom sought a major upgrade via an in-season trade. It's hard for a player to adjust from one scheme to another in the NFL, and besides, most teams just don't trade players in-season. In a 2012 *New York Times* interview, Roseman explained how football trades were different than baseball trades. A third baseman can play third base whether it's for the Philadelphia Phillies or New York Yankees. It's a matter of changing colors of the pinstripes. In football, a player must learn new plays, and the role of a player from one team to another could be completely different depending on the scheme. That's why it's easier to make trades during the off-season, when there is ample practice time to get a player acclimated.

But opportunity is not a lengthy visitor. And Roseman was not going to pass on a chance to pick up a player like Ajayi.

"It's certainly different when you are 7–1 than if you're having a losing season," Roseman said. "If there are opportunities to improve our team, and improve where we're at, we have a responsibility to the people on the field, to the people off the field, and to our fans to evaluate everything."

GAME DAY: DENVER BRONCOS :: W 51–23

It did not take long for the Philadelphia crowd to realize the quality of player that Howie Roseman acquired. Doug Pederson planned to limit Jay Ajayi to ten-to-fifteen plays in his first game, a 51–23 Week 9 victory over the Denver Broncos, and Ajayi made the most of them. Late in the second quarter he took a handoff at the Broncos' 46-yard line and ran through a hole big enough to provide an unimpeded view of the Philadelphia skyline in the distance. An adoring crowd erupted while Ajayi sprinted for the long touchdown.

"I don't think it could have been written any better than that," Ajayi said.

That touchdown gave the Eagles a 31–9 halftime lead, an accurate reflection of their domination. There was little for talk-radio callers to gripe about the day after this victory. The Eagles topped fifty points for the first time since 2013, even though the Broncos entered the game with the NFL's top-ranked defense.

"They keep hearing all week how good [Denver's] defense is," Pederson said. "Our guys have a lot of pride, too."

Right tackle Lane Johnson stonewalled Broncos' pass rusher Von Miller, one of the NFL's elite players. Alshon Jeffery beat five-time Pro Bowler Aqib

Talib for a touchdown—"I'm a Pro Bowl wide receiver, too," Jeffery scoffed. Rookie running back Corey Clement rushed for two touchdowns and caught another, becoming the first rookie with those statistics in an Eagles uniform in nearly sixty-four years. And Carson Wentz had *another* four-touchdown performance.

The Broncos offense was also outmatched by the Eagles defense, which forced two turnovers. It was the most complete game the Eagles had played, and by then, it was not a surprise to anyone. They had turned into a juggernaut. The players paraded into the locker room hooting and hollering, proud owners of the best record in the NFL. The crowd chanted, "We want Dallas! We want Dallas!" The city's most hated rival was next up after the Eagles' much needed bye week.

In his postgame speech seen on the team's website, Pederson told his players that it was "a kickass performance like I've ever seen." He recited the stats to show just how lopsided the game had been, with the players cheering along.

"We said we'd be what?" Pederson asked his players.

"Eight and one!" they shouted back.

"However," the coach continued, "if you realize where you're sitting right now, you don't want to jeopardize that, right? We've got a lot of unfinished business to do, right? You started something special, let's finish something special the remainder of this season, OK? You take this time, yes, you reflect on the first half of the season, these first nine weeks. But then, you know what? We make an even stronger push when we come back."

At that point, everyone knew what was coming next. The team's bye week had just begun, and the players hoped to get a little time off before resuming practice. But just in case, they started to egg on their coach with catcalls and friendly shoves. After a dramatic pause, Pederson cracked a smile and let the cat out of the bag.

"Hey! We'll see you guys in a week!" Pederson yelled to a roar of cheers.

CLEMENT: CROSSING THE RIVER TO STARDOM

It was great to have Ajayi on board to bolster the running game. But it was the team's least-heralded running back who stood out most against Denver. Five years before Corey Clement scored three touchdowns against the Broncos at Lincoln Financial Field, he celebrated his eighteenth birthday a mere twenty-minute drive away at Glassboro High School in New Jersey. Clement, who set a South Jersey high school record with 6,245 career rushing yards, decided that day that he would play college football at the University of Wisconsin.

However, Clement became an afterthought in the touted running back draft class of 2017. He was not particularly fast, he was not notably big, and he didn't catch or block often at Wisconsin. Plus, he had served a suspension in college for a fight at an apartment complex that he initially lied about to his coaches, prompting off-field concerns.

"You either learn from it or you don't," Clement said. "I took the learning path."

The Eagles were not so worried about the off-field issues, as they had good intelligence on Clement. Dom DiSandro, the head of team security who's responsible for doing research into player backgrounds, had known Clement well since Clement was a child in Glassboro. Running backs coach Duce Staley was also familiar with Clement from his playing days when DiSandro brought Clement around the Eagles' facility. Clement has said DiSandro played a "magnificent" role in his life, including advocating for him within the Eagles organization. And when Clement went undrafted, the Eagles made it a priority to sign him.

Still, Clement had a long way to go to make the roster. He arrived at training camp sixth on the Eagles' running back depth chart behind Darren Sproles, LeGarrette Blount, Wendell Smallwood, Byron

Marshall, and 2017 fourth-round draft pick Donnel Pumphrey. A team usually keeps four running backs on their roster during the season, and Clement appeared far more likely to get cut than to play on Sundays.

That didn't stop him. He focused less on the depth chart and more on fulfilling what the coaches asked of him. He dropped twelve pounds because he thought he could be quicker if he was leaner. He impressed during practice and was the best running back during preseason games. If the coaches disregarded draft status and just looked at the way the running backs played, it would have been hard to leave him off the team. But it rarely works that way.

"I've been fighting all camp from the bottom, trying to work my way to the top," Clement said during the summer. "If anybody understands the amount of sacrificing I had to do to keep going up the depth chart, it's a lot."

Clement worked on his blocking and showed the coaches he can catch. This was not the Clement from the college film; this was an NFL player. Carson Wentz noticed him as a player "that wanted to work and wanted to learn." Most important, Clement embraced his responsibilities on special teams. The bottom-of-the-roster players have their best chance of making the roster by impressing in this less-heralded phase of the game where coaches don't like to expose their starting players to injury. Clement wasn't trying to win a starting job in August. He was trying to prove he was one of the fifty-three best players on the squad so he could stick around.

"I'd rather them say 'he can block' first before 'he can run,'" Clement said. "I try to show that every down I was out there to protect the quarterbacks, not to let [up] sacks. I hold that as a chip on my shoulder to know I can stay in on third downs. . . . Then I can run, I can catch the ball out of the backfield. And to be the total package . . . getting on [special teams coordinator Dave] Fipp's [radar]."

On cut-down day, the Eagles decided to keep Clement. He was too valuable. They went with five running backs to make sure they could also carry Pumphrey, whose status as a draft pick all but ensured him a spot, but by then Clement was ahead of Pumphrey on the depth chart. In the season opener against Washington, Clement lined up on the coverage unit for the opening kickoff and made the Eagles' first tackle of the season.

With Clement proving himself on special teams, the coaching staff slowly began to give him opportunities on offense. He got just nine offensive plays in the first three games, but his playing time got a bump in October. He then jumped over Smallwood on the depth chart, joining a three-man running back committee with Blount and Jay Ajayi. The three-touchdown game against the Broncos only raised his profile.

"Hey, I can only imagine what you're going to be like now!" veteran defensive end Chris Long joked with Clement after the third touchdown, as seen on the Eagles website. "I thought you changed ever since you caught that touchdown on Monday night [against Washington]. What was it, a hat trick today? Congrats!"

By the postseason, Clement had become the Eagles' third-down running back—responsible mostly for blocking and catching. That responsibility is rare for a rookie, especially an undrafted one. In the Super Bowl, it was Clement—not Alshon Jeffery, not Zach Ertz, not Nelson Agholor—who led the Eagles in receiving yards. He caught a pivotal touchdown, took the snap on the famous "Philly Special" play, and earned his place in Eagles history.

On a team that took pride in being underdogs, Clement fit the bill as much as anyone. Here was a local kid who went undrafted, worked his way up from the bottom of the depth chart, secured his position as a regular-season contributor, and delivered one of the best performances in the biggest game in franchise history.

"It's all a blessing," Clement said after the Super Bowl. "Going back to when the season started, and then to this moment, it is awesome . . . . Going back to New Jersey, small high school, I've achieved my dreams, man."

WEEK 11

BACK FROM THE BYE

GAME DAY: DALLAS COWBOYS :: W 37-9

The Eagles' bye week seemed to last thirty minutes longer than planned. The team appeared listless in the first half of their Week 11 Sunday night game against the Dallas Cowboys, entering halftime trailing 9–7. To make matters worse, kicker Jake Elliott sustained a concussion making a touchdown-saving tackle on the opening kickoff and missed the rest of the game.

"The [halftime] message was that we were OK, we were fine," Pederson said. "Let's just get back to basics. No one panic."

In the second half, the Eagles got back to normal, scoring thirty unanswered points en route to a 37–9 rout. The defense forced four turnovers and pummeled Cowboys quarterback Dak Prescott throughout the game. Derek Barnett, the first-round pick who was quiet early in the season, finished with two sacks and a forced fumble. Cornerback Ronald Darby returned from an ankle injury that had sidelined him for ten weeks and showed the Eagles what they missed with an interception. Jim Schwartz's unit had a number of dominant performances throughout the 2017 season, but their effort against the Cowboys kept the Eagles in the game early. The Cowboys never reached the end zone and only twice brought the ball inside the Eagles' red zone. Schwartz values "points allowed" more than any other defensive metric.

"However you do that—takeaways, third-down stops, fourth-down stops . . . forcing punts—keeping points off the board is the name of the game, and I think they did a good job of doing that," Schwartz said.

The offense rebounded in the second half by turning to the running game. Remember when Pederson abandoned the run early in the season? That was long forgotten by November, especially with Ajayi in the mix. The Eagles took the lead in the third quarter on an eight-play, 75-yard drive that included five running plays, with their offensive line overpowering the Cowboys' defensive front. By the end of the game, the Eagles rushed for a season-best 215 yards and 6.5 yards per carry. Ajayi's 71-yard rush in the third quarter was the Eagles' longest of the season, and it came behind left tackle Halapoulivaati Vaitai who by now was comfortable as Jason Peters's replacement.

"We just wanted to commit to the run," Pederson said. "We didn't really change anything at halftime. We just committed to the same runs we had."

The team's resiliency was exhibited all season, but it was personified against the Cowboys by reserve linebacker Kamu Grugier-Hill, who was pressed into service as the emergency kicker. All NFL teams carry only one kicker, so when Elliott left the game in the first half, there was no plan B. The coaching staff had to scramble to determine who would handle kickoffs, and the job fell to the Hawaii native who was in his second season with the Eagles. Typically his main duty was making tackles on kickoffs and punts, but on this night, he found himself on the other side of the ball. He had kicked off just once in his life—in practice a few weeks earlier—but had been a punter in high school and played soccer as a child. This, of course, was different.

Before Grugier-Hill took his first practice kick into a net on the sideline, punter Donnie Jones asked if he wanted the net moved closer. Grugier-Hill declined, thinking he could kick the ball straight. He missed the net on his first kick, sending the ball into the stands.

"This is going to be a little rough," Grugier-Hill said.

That was his worst kick of the night. His kicking proved passable, and he even sailed one of his four kickoffs into the end zone for a touchback. The Eagles survived. Elliott was back the next week. They had a "next man up" mentality all season, and this was but another example. In Pederson's postgame speech, he singled out Grugier-Hill, whose teammates swarmed him with hugs.

The Eagles had reached 9–1.

"Coaches and players, you're the best team in football right now," Pederson said, as seen on the Eagles website. "But we still have a long way to go."

STAYING IN THE LANE

Lane Johnson was still angry. He had returned to Oklahoma, where he went to college, during the 2016 season and watched the Eagles falter without him while he served a ten-game suspension for violating the league's performance-enhancing drug (PED) policy. It was the second such suspension in Johnson's career. He said he took a supplement in which all the ingredients were approved, but there were apparently unapproved ingredients that weren't listed. He appealed the suspension to the league and even fought the NFL Players' Association to back him, but to no avail. Johnson had developed into a foundational piece for the Eagles, inking a lucrative six-year contract with a maximum value of $63 million in January 2016. It looked like 2016 would be the first year he became a Pro Bowl player, until the suspension was levied. The Eagles were 3–1 to start the 2016 season, but then Johnson left and they went 2–8 in his absence.

"I failed the team," Johnson said. He was labeled a cheater, no matter his story. Two suspensions don't give a player the benefit of the doubt. He returned in 2017 an irritated player on a mission—or as he described it, "pissed off."

"All last year, ever since I left the building, I had a long time to think," Johnson said. "When I got back on the field, I was going to make it count. I was going to make my opponents remember who I am. So whenever you game-plan the Eagles, you better know who I am. That's been my whole mentality."

He heard taunts early in the season about the drug issue. Before the Chargers game, a former teammate, in a seemingly joking manner, called him "'roid boy." Johnson didn't find it funny. He took it out on the field in dominating fashion.

It was a marvel that Johnson ever became a 325-pound offensive lineman. He grew up a quarterback in Groveton, Texas, a logging town of eleven-hundred people. His mother worked at the local prison as a social worker, his father worked for the highway department, and his stepfather coached high school football.

"You either work for the state, a teacher, you work for the government, or you're a ranger," said James Evans, Johnson's stepfather. "And that's all there is there."

Johnson was the starting quarterback for his Texas high school team, but it was different than *Friday Night Lights*. There were only thirty-three students in his graduating class, hardly enough to fill a stadium. In fact, Groveton High School was in the lowest division in the state. College coaches didn't come by recruiting him, even though he was 6-foot-6 and 202 pounds and played basketball and baseball, ran track, and threw the shotput.

With no college scholarships in the offing, Johnson chose to attend Kilgore College, a junior college where he thought he could play quarterback. He was the backup until the eighth game when the starter was suspended for fighting. Johnson finally got his chance, but it didn't last long. He was relieved of QB duties after just three quarters, and never played the position again. "It was a really tough year for me," he said.

But with his athletic ability and a desire to continue playing football, Johnson shifted to tight end. Bigger colleges started to notice. He added fifty pounds and ran the 40-yard dash in 4.5 seconds. It's rare to find a 255-pounder who could do that. After one year in junior college, he transferred to the big time to play for the University of Oklahoma. Once there, he continued adding muscle and was moved to defensive end, that is, until the team needed an extra offensive lineman. Bob Stoops, the famed Oklahoma head coach, asked a strength and conditioning coach what it would take for Johnson to reach 300 pounds. "A cheeseburger and a week," Stoops was told.

Within the first few practices, Stoops realized Johnson could become an NFL first-round pick. During sprints, Johnson finished 10 to 15 yards ahead of the other offensive and defensive linemen. He played offensive tackle at Oklahoma for two years, and even though he was raw and unpolished at the outset, in time his NFL potential seemed limitless.

"Nobody ever considers going from a skill position to playing tackle," Johnson said. "After going to tackle, I just grew into it, and now I feel natural."

At the scouting combine, Johnson put on a show. His 4.72-second 40-yard dash and 34-inch vertical leap were almost unheard of for a 303-pound player. They were the second-best totals recorded by an offensive lineman since 2000. He was an athletic marvel. The Eagles invested the No. 4 overall pick in the 2013 draft on Johnson. It was their highest draft pick since Donovan McNabb in 1999. Two offensive linemen were drafted ahead of Johnson that year, but he has developed into the best one.

With Pro Bowler Jason Peters at left tackle, the Eagles put Johnson on the right side. He played his first three seasons at around 317 pounds, and the only games he missed were because of suspensions. Regardless of Johnson's explanation regarding the PED suspensions, they cast a shadow of doubt upon whether his muscle gain from quarterback to offensive tackle was natural. When he arrived at training camp in 2017 weighing 325 pounds—the heaviest he had been since joining the Eagles—Johnson said his new body was the result of an old-fashioned regimen of food and fitness.

"Everybody expects me to be like the Steve Latimer from *The Program* and come back and weigh one-eighty and all my skills and talents were going to leave me," Johnson said, referring to a character in the 1993 film. "That's what people think. But, hey, look where I am now."

After the suspensions, with no margin for error and encountering a healthy dose of skepticism, Johnson vowed to adhere to clean eating with zero supplements. He cut out sweets and fried foods because they caused inflammation. He stuck to chicken, beef, fish, potatoes, and vegetables such as kale and spinach, with the occasional indulgence of a cheeseburger. Even if the training staff approved a supplement, Johnson would not take the risk. And on the field, he was better than he had ever been.

Traditionally in the NFL, the left tackle is considered the superior offensive lineman, as he is responsible for protecting against rushers attacking the blind side of a right-handed quarterback. But the NFL has evolved, and the list of pass rushers the Eagles saw from Johnson's side could also wreck game plans. So when Jason Peters suffered a season-ending injury in Week 7, the Eagles did not feel compelled to move Johnson to left tackle. And each week, Johnson answered the bell and contained his counterpart—whether it was Denver's Von Miller, Oakland's Khalil Mack, Dallas's DeMarcus Lawrence, Washington's Ryan Kerrigan, the Los Angeles Chargers' Joey Bosa—and established himself beyond any doubt as an elite offensive lineman. Miller even told the *Denver Post* that Johnson was the "premier right tackle" in the NFL.

"I think I'm probably the best version of myself in terms of strength," Johnson said. "I'm bigger than I have been, I think I use my hands more effectively. And as far as my temperament, I try to play angry. I know what the stigma [about the suspensions] is about my name and my story. I know the idea that runs through people's heads when they think of me. I just hope they do some re-evaluating over the next part of my career."

Despite his angry on-field persona, guys in the locker room consider him one of the funniest players on the team. He's certainly one of the most outspoken. It was Johnson who spearheaded the idea that the Eagles would wear dog masks when they were underdogs in the 2017 playoffs. Before the Super Bowl, Johnson didn't hesitate to call Tom Brady a "pretty boy." His production backed up his words through every game of the season.

Back in training camp, Johnson confessed that he owed much to the city of Philadelphia. If the Eagles ever won a Super Bowl, he said, beers were on him. When Bud Light representatives heard this, they sent a message on social media that they would supply the beer on Johnson's behalf if the Birds won it all. And when they did, Johnson made sure the beer company remembered this promise, coordinating with them to have free Bud Light available for fans attending the celebratory parade up Broad Street. Fans returned the favor by tossing beers to Johnson as he rode by on the parade bus. In the end, all was forgiven.

WEEK 12

||||||||||||||||||||||||||||||||||||||||||||||||||||||||||||||||||||||||||||||||||||||||||||||||||||||||||||||||||||||||||||||||||||||||||||||

REASON TO CELEBRATE

GAME DAY: **CHICAGO BEARS :: W 31–3**

The Eagles hosted the Chicago Bears for a football game, not a wedding reception. But late in the fourth quarter of a 31–3 Week 12 win, it was hard to tell the difference when a dozen Eagles gathered after an interception and performed the Electric Slide in unison.

And that wasn't the only choreographed celebration that day. There was one in which ten players set up as bowling pins, and Alshon Jeffery bowled a strike and they all fell down. And another one where they pretended that they were posing for a family photo. These were part of a hilarious repertoire of celebrations the team performed throughout the season—from starting a fire to robbing a bank to charging a pitcher's mound. Fans looked forward to what they created each week. And there were plenty of opportunities to celebrate.

"I think guys are enjoying the process every week and so when we're here on Sundays and it's game time, we cut loose," safety Malcolm Jenkins said. "We work hard so we feel like the least we can do is have fun out there. It gets the crowd involved and excited. That permeates throughout the whole team."

These elaborate celebrations—and, in fact, any sort of celebration—were against the rules until May of 2017 when the league announced that such displays would no longer be penalized or fined. Just a year before, dozens of players were hit with hundreds of thousands of dollars in fines for celebrating, prompting fans to refer to the NFL as the "No Fun League." Fortunately, the league relaxed their policy, and every team took full advantage of it to the fans' great pleasure.

Against the Bears, the Eagles' opportunities to celebrate included three passing touchdowns by Carson Wentz plus two interceptions and two sacks by the defense, which limited the Bears to just 140 total yards. The Bears came into the game as one of the NFL's worst scoring offenses, and they were completely outmatched by Jim Schwartz's scorching unit. The Eagles' game plan was to stop the run and make the Bears offense one-dimensional. Despite their scoring woes, Chicago entered the game ranked fifth in the NFL with 131.8 rushing yards per game. Against the Eagles, their running backs combined to rush for minus-6 yards. It was the best performance of the season by the Eagles unit that ended the year as the NFL's top-ranked run defense.

"They are one of the best defenses that I have ever played against," said Bears offensive lineman Kyle Long, the brother of Eagles defensive end Chris Long.

The win over the Bears was the Eagles' ninth consecutive victory and their fourth consecutive by twenty-plus points. They had not done that since their 2004 Super Bowl season. They had never won three games in the same season by twenty-eight points or more until 2017, though. It was a sign they were a special squad. With five games remaining on the schedule, they needed just one more win to clinch the NFC East crown and the prospect of home-field advantage throughout the playoffs was also within reach.

The Eagles had become so dominant that Lincoln Financial Field staff ran out of fireworks against the Bears after so many celebrations. And the players seemed to have a dance or skit prepared for each one. Jeffery was one of the organizers for the offense, and Jenkins approved of the Electric Slide for the defense, noting that he's twenty-nine and he needed a dance that he would know. Only in football is twenty-nine considered old.

"You can see everyone jumping in them and joining, and that's just the brotherhood that we have right now. It's a blast," Wentz said.

Pederson, who takes pride in his player-friendly ways, was fine with the players having fun as long as they kept it among themselves and did not incur a penalty for a delay of game.

"I think it's great that they can show the excitement, the enthusiasm, and

[that] they are doing it with their teammates," Pederson said. "It's not about one guy, [and] this team has really embraced that."

Come Monday, though, Pederson needed to make sure his players were focused. They would spend the next five days practicing in Philadelphia before departing on a nine-day, two-game trip to the West Coast that could change their entire season.

JEFFERY: NEW KID IN TOWN

At the end of the Chicago Bears' 3-13 season in 2016, during which their top receiver Alshon Jeffery scored just two touchdowns (a career-low), the soft-spoken wide receiver made a bold proclamation to reporters.

"I guarantee you we're winning the Super Bowl next season," he said.

Three months later, Jeffery signed with the Eagles. When the Eagles prepared to play the Chicago Bears in November, the Eagles entered the game 9-1 and the Bears entered the game 3-7.

When asked about the guarantee he made, Jeffery said with a smile, "I never said a team."

It was a shrewd response from a player who majors in cool. Jeffery became the Eagles' highest-profile free-agent wide receiver since Terrell Owens in 2004.

One week earlier, in the Eagles' nationally televised win over the Dallas Cowboys, Jeffery sought out an NBC camera and started screaming to the audience at home. Viewers could see his lips move, but couldn't hear what he said. So Jeffery filled them in during a locker-room interview after the game.

"I was saying, 'They ain't f—ing with us. Nobody's f—ing with us,'"

Jeffery said. "In this locker room, that's how we feel. We're the best."

Jeffery flew back to Philadelphia wearing a T-shirt featuring a Brian Dawkins caricature. It read: "BLEED GREEN." Hours after Jeffery arrived back at the Linc, he drove across the street to catch the 76ers–Utah Jazz basketball game at the Wells Fargo Center. He took to Philadelphia, living in the heart of the city and soaking in the experience. When he signed a one-year deal, he could have been a hired mercenary and looked for a bigger payday elsewhere next year. He wasn't interested in just dating Philadelphia, though. He wanted a commitment. He wanted to stay.

"Man, I love it here in Philly," Jeffery said. "Philly is a great city, great town. Everyone has welcomed me with open arms."

One week after making those comments, Jeffery proved he meant them by signing a four-year, $52-million contract extension. For their part, the Eagles were adamant that they wouldn't have signed Jeffery to a one-year contract if they had no interest in extending the relationship. That was not lip service, either. The Eagles viewed Jeffery as a key part of Wentz's development, especially after seeing the special connection the two were forming on the field. In addition to his production, Jeffery brought stability, as Pederson didn't want Wentz to have a revolving door at No. 1 receiver. From his perspective, Jeffery said Wentz was a big reason he came to Philadelphia in the first place. He had watched Wentz from afar the year before and thought the young quarterback only needed a few pieces to become an MVP candidate. Just like his Super Bowl prediction, Jeffery was prescient on this one, too.

"We're both pretty stoked about what the future holds," Wentz said. "At the same time, we're really focused on this year, too. But I'm really thrilled that he's going to be here for a couple of years."

The Eagles also liked the way Jeffery bought into the team-first ethos that Pederson insisted upon, especially on offense where players often count the number of touches they get per game. Jeffery's numbers were not nearly as prolific as anticipated, partly because he played with a torn rotator cuff, but also because Wentz liked to spread the ball around. Under different circumstances, Jeffery could have been a diva and complained, but this circumstance was special. Jeffery said on his first day in the locker room that he knew he wanted to play for the Eagles for "a long time." He noted that his teammates were the reason.

"I'll treat those guys to dinner," Jeffery said. "The whole locker room."

Even though the Eagles spread the ball around to all their skill players, make no mistake about it: Jeffery was the alpha dog of the unit. He might not have been a diva, but he carried himself like a superstar. And when the Eagles needed a spectacular play, Jeffery often delivered. Jeffery likes to say that a "50-50 ball"—a pass that's up for grabs between the receiver and defender—does not apply to him. Like a great rebounder in basketball, he's positive that he's the one who will come down with it. This attitude has defined Jeffery's football career, and considering that his first love was basketball, it makes sense. Even in the Eagles locker room he's more apt to engage in conversation about the NBA rather than the NFL.

Jeffery grew up in St. Mathews, South Carolina, a town of two-thousand residents described in a *Philadelphia Inquirer* story in September 2017 as having "two traffic lights, one Hardee's, and an overwhelming sociocultural sense . . . that, over time, little in life changes much." Jeffery was part of the Calhoun County High School basketball team that won four state championships. He later joined the school's football team and quickly became a standout wide receiver in his two seasons of play. While his 6-foot-3 body didn't set him apart on the basketball court, it proved to be a big advantage on the football field. Coaches from the top college football programs came to St. Mathews to see Jeffery. A USC recruiter watched him make a catch and gasped, "Wow. That guy is a freak. This guy will be playing on Sunday."

Despite making a verbal commitment to USC, Jeffery ended up attending South Carolina and helped lead the Gamecocks to their first-ever SEC Championship appearance. By his junior year, ESPN called him the best player in the conference. The Chicago Bears picked him in the second round of the 2012 draft, and after a modest rookie season he made the Pro Bowl his second year. By the time he signed with the Eagles, Jeffery had established himself as one of the top receivers in the NFL, although he had never played in a playoff game. From his perspective, going to Philly was not about the money.

It was about "winning championships," Jeffery said. "A lot of players make a lot of money, but some of them never make the playoffs, never get to experience a lot of things."

By the end of the season, Jeffery had secured both the money and the championship.

WEEK 13

A LOSS AND A WARNING

GAME DAY: SEATTLE SEAHAWKS :: L 10–24

This is what losing felt like. The Eagles had not experienced a losing locker room since Week 2. Their nine-game winning streak was halted by the Seattle Seahawks in a 10–24 road loss that brought the team down to Earth. So many of the elements that worked through the first three months of the season seemed to malfunction in Seattle.

The pivotal moment came in the third quarter when the Eagles drove to the Seahawks' 6-yard line with a chance to tie the game. On second-and-goal, Carson Wentz faked a handoff, tucked the ball away, sprinted through the middle of the line, and dove toward the end zone. Just inches from the goal line, two Seattle defenders converged on Wentz and knocked the ball loose. It bounced a few times and landed in the white paint outside the back of the end zone, resulting in a touchback and a Seahawks possession. The Eagles had no points to show for the drive.

"I saw the goal line, so I thought it was going to be close," Wentz said. "Made that extra lunge and it cost me."

There were questionable decisions by Doug Pederson in the game, too, from unsuccessful fourth-down calls to failing to challenge a likely fumble. But Wentz's fumble was the most costly mistake. For the first time all season, Wentz was not the best quarterback on the field. He was outplayed by Seattle's Russell Wilson, who threw for three touchdowns and did not commit a turnover. Wentz threw for one touchdown with an interception and the fumble.

"That's the story of the game, really," Wentz said. "We turned the ball over and they didn't. On the road in this atmosphere against a great team like they are, it's tough to win when you do that."

After the game, Pederson told his players, "You can't just show up and expect to win against good football teams." Throughout the locker room, there was a sense that the loss was a wake-up call. They were not making excuses, but rather acknowledging that come playoff time, turnovers and penalties could haunt them like they did that day. They were determined to learn from their mistakes.

Football players don't tend to brush off defeat. There are so few games, and they put their bodies through so much trauma, that a loss stings the players more than it does the fans. However, this loss was not a matter of the Eagles being big-headed or unprepared. They lost to a good team with a hot quarterback in a tough atmosphere.

If anything required scrutinizing, it was Wentz's fumble. Pederson applauded Wentz going for the touchdown, but said Wentz needed to know he would encounter traffic and keep two hands on the ball. But the fact that Wentz fumbled wasn't as much of a problem as his decision to jump forward and expose himself to that type of contact. Part of Wentz's appeal is his creativity and toughness, two factors that suggest a play is seldom dead no matter how bleak the situation appears to be. He has the inclination and the ability to capture extra yards for his teammates in almost any situation. But at what price?

"You've got to be careful of taking the aggression away from your quarterback . . . because I don't ever want to do that," Pederson said. "At the same time, we've got to continue to educate and talk to him about sliding and protecting himself, getting down, all of that—the longevity of the season and his well-being. It's a fine line, but we'll just continue to talk to him about those issues."

The upside was gaining points needed to win the game. The downside was a fumble. And the worst-case scenario would be an injury. It was a point of discussion for the next few days, and it would prove to be an ominous line of questioning. One week later, on a similar play, Wentz wouldn't be so lucky.

THE EMERGENCE OF NELSON AGHOLOR

Before the 2017 season, Nelson Agholor appeared on the verge of earning the dreaded "bust" label that goes to a first-round pick who fails to fulfill expectations. By the end of the season, when Agholor finished a breakout season and led the Eagles in receptions in the Super Bowl, Agholor took a moment with confetti raining on his shoulders to appreciate what had happened.

Whenever a team selects a player in the first round, they typically hold a news conference one day later during which the player holds his new jersey in a photo opportunity. Agholor's photo was different than any of the other top picks that year—or any in Eagles history. That was because Chip Kelly, who was then the coach, asked Troy Robinson, the popular janitor at the NovaCare Complex, to pose in the photo. Kelly did not publicize why he asked Robinson to join the photo. It seemed an odd inclusion. But there was a reason: Agholor's father, Felix, was a janitor at the University of South Florida. The photo was a quiet tribute to Agholor's upbringing.

A Nigerian immigrant whose family moved to the United States when he was five, Agholor watched his mother work at a nursing home and his father ride his bike to multiple jobs before he could afford a car. That was how they raised four children in a three-bedroom apartment.

"I think I understand the way life works," Agholor said. "I don't feel like I'm entitled to anything. . . . Work like a peasant. That's the mindset."

As a rookie, Agholor wanted his work ethic to become a distinguishing characteristic. During his first spring with the Eagles, Agholor set his alarm for 5:30 a.m. and scheduled a 6 a.m. taxi from his Philadelphia hotel. He arrived at the team facility by 6:15

a.m.—an hour before the rookie shuttle was to leave for the NovaCare Complex.

"That's where I get time to do most of my extra stuff," Agholor said. "It's not to do anything separate. It's my comfort level. It's not trying to separate [from other rookies]. But I feel comfortable preparing. It's something I can control."

That ethos did not translate into results during Agholor's rookie season. He finished with only 23 catches for 283 yards and one touchdown, failing to fulfill the expectations carried by a first-round pick. His statistics marginally improved during his second season, but his reputation took a major hit with an unfortunate off-the-field incident. On the afternoon of June 9, the final day of the 2016 off-season activity, Agholor and a couple of teammates visited a Philadelphia strip club where an exotic dancer accused Agholor of sexual assault. The accusation was made public the next day, and an investigation ensued. It took more than a month for officials to announce that no charges would be filed, noting that security video and witness interviews proved the allegations false. There was no change to Agholor's status on the team throughout the process, but the lingering accusation nonetheless caused a stain on his reputation.

Agholor was "in shock" when he first heard about the allegation. His parents were disappointed in him. It was an uncharacteristic scenario for a player hailed for his character and maturity upon joining the team. He knew the public had a reason to wonder what he did wrong, and he vowed to rebuild his image.

"I put myself in a poor situation, and the most important thing for me was to realize that no matter what's going on, if I make the right decision, I won't be there," Agholor said. "To be honest with you, there were points I thought an opportunity that was given to me to play for this organization, and to have the life I have, could have been taken from me. So it allows you to be more grateful and to have a good perspective on life."

Carson Wentz's emergence into an MVP candidate made the Eagles a contender in 2017. His progress in his second year was evident from the Eagles' season-opening victory against Washington (above), although a December knee injury halted his season before the Super Bowl

alcolm Jenkins's leadership was pivotal in the Eagles' Super Bowl campaign. Jenkins rallied
s teammates before games and gave postgame locker room speeches. He'd end his pregame
beeches with the cheer, "We all we got . . . we all we need!"

One of the most memorable moments of the Eagles' regular season came in Week 3 when rookie kicker Jake Elliott set a franchise record with a 61-yard, game-winning field goal as time expired against the rival New York Giants.

Chris Long (above) and Lane Johnson came up with the idea of wearing dog masks after the Eagles won their opening playoff game as underdogs. The Eagles were underdogs throughout the playoffs, and the dog masks became popular among fans.

The Eagles' only sack of the Super Bowl came when Brandon Graham (center) sacked Tom Brady and forced a fumble late in the fourth quarter to help clinch the victory. Brady had been known for leading comebacks in the postseason.

The most memorable play of the Super Bowl came at the end of the first half when Nick Foles caught a touchdown on a play called "Philly Special." The trick play, which came on a fourth down, showed coach Doug Pederson's aggressiveness and creativity as a play-caller.

Fans flooded Philadelphia's streets to celebrate the first Super Bowl victory in Eagles history. Police officers greased light poles to make them too slippery to climb, although some fans still tried. It was the franchise's first championship since 1960, before the creation of the Super Bowl.

Owner Jeffrey Lurie, top executive Howie Roseman, and coach Doug Pederson put the plan in place to bring a Super Bowl to Philadelphia. Carson Wentz and Nick Foles, also pictured, demonstrated the team's commitment to finding a franchise quarterback and quarterback depth.

The Eagles celebrated their Super Bowl with a parade in Philadelphia on February 8, 2018. The parade started outside the stadium complex in South Philadelphia, went up Broad Street and the Benjamin Franklin Parkway, and finished on the Rocky Steps at the Museum of Art

The most memorable moment of the parade was center Jason Kelce's epic speech, when Kelce explained the underdog mentality of the team and galvanized the fan base with a rant entrenched in Philadelphia lore.

Agholor fulfilled his pledge to be better off the field. His on-the-field performance, however, was a different story. Following a strong start to the 2016 season, including a touchdown in the season opener, Agholor's production cratered. He dropped passes he should have caught and he wasn't scoring points. But his biggest issues seemed to be mental. During a November 20 loss to the Seattle Seahawks, Agholor failed to line up correctly on a play that resulted in a 57-yard touchdown. Agholor's mistake drew a penalty and negated the play—a score the Eagles badly needed. On the next drive, Agholor dropped a wide-open pass. He grabbed his helmet in clear anger with himself, his frustration evident for all to see. Agholor had suffered a crisis of confidence.

"I've got to get out of my own head," Agholor said after the game. "Pressing so much and worried about so many things."

When the team returned to Philadelphia, Doug Pederson met with Agholor. Pederson believed that for a struggling player like Agholor, "sometimes you have to take a step back in order to go forward." He understood the pressure that was on Agholor and decided to bench him for the next game. Pederson didn't make this move to penalize the young receiver, but rather to give him the chance to clear his head and unburden himself from the attention surrounding his struggles.

"I don't want to expose him to anything that will hurt him there as an individual, as a human being, because I just know that this is also about life, and it's about him as a person, and it's not so much about football anymore," Pederson said. "So if it means lessening the load, then I'll lessen the load and try to take a little bit off of his plate."

Agholor returned to the field for the final month of the season. His production was modest, but his perspective had clearly changed after working with a sports psychologist. After the season, Agholor admitted he needed to learn to relax his mind and "come to peace with myself, with my life."

"I think too many times in the season, when I was in those moments,

I was trying to be the controller of things," Agholor said after the 2016 season. "And I'm not. . . . I'm just a player, and this is a reaction game. When I go on the field, my only objective is to react. I know I have talent, but I just react. I can't control what comes my way. I can't control everything. Thinking too much almost takes away those natural abilities of reaction and instinct. Now that I'm away from it, I'm like, 'Man, you know what you can do. Train, and let what you train [for] show itself on a Sunday.'"

The Eagles added wide receivers Alshon Jeffery and Torrey Smith at the beginning of the 2017 off-season, pushing Agholor down the depth chart. Agholor didn't need a demotion to inspire him, though. His newfound perspective bolstered an already-promising skill set. Agholor keeps a whiteboard in his locker stall, and during the spring of 2017, he created two separate sections—on one part he tracked his drops during practice, and on the other he wrote a quote for motivation: *When change is necessary, not to change is destructive.*

That quote was his takeaway from an encounter with Hall of Fame running back Curtis Martin at a wedding. Agholor took Martin's advice to heart. He needed to be honest with himself. He realized that "things aren't going well for a reason," so he needed to "find change."

That change included rediscovering his confidence. In the off-season, he returned to his hometown of Tampa and worked with Yo Murphy, a former NFL receiver who became Agholor's trainer. Agholor wanted to slow his brain and just rely on his athletic ability, noting that "every time something special happens, I play fast." He realized that in the November 2016 Seahawks game, he "showed a sign of defeat I didn't need to." He wanted to become mentally tougher and to develop the "ability to shake things off." Of course, that's not a skill featured on a scouting report.

"It could have gone one of two ways: He could have gone in the dumps and you never would have heard from him again . . . or he did what he does, which is work his butt off and try to excel and do everything right," said tight end Zach Ertz, who has witnessed Agholor's whole career in Philadelphia.

That's what happened throughout off-season workouts in 2017, when Agholor appeared to be a different player. In fact, he was clearly one of the best players on the field. Safety Malcolm Jenkins noticed it immediately and identified "confidence" as the biggest difference. Agholor also benefited from the arrival of veteran wide receivers coach Mike Groh, a change that others on the Eagles cited as beneficial for Agholor. Since Groh didn't work with Agholor in 2015 and 2016, he would judge Agholor by what came thereafter. It was just the fresh start Agholor needed, and he welcomed the tough coaching Groh provided. In their first meeting, Agholor asked what must improve and Groh singled in on his stance. Together they focused on the proper foot alignment and crouch on the line so that Agholor could be more explosive when the ball was snapped.

"Nelson is mentally tough," Groh said. "He's certainly very skillful. And he set out with a plan and he's executed his plan each and every day, whether it be Monday or Friday or Sunday. He has a routine he goes through and he doesn't deviate from it."

Agholor's progress continued early in training camp. NFL Network analyst Daniel Jeremiah, a former scout for the Eagles, visited Philadelphia to watch practice early in training camp. One of his takeaways was that Agholor would be the Eagles' slot receiver in 2017, and he didn't know where that left Jordan Matthews. The comment raised eyebrows considering Matthews was the Eagles' leading receiver the previous two seasons, but the team didn't necessarily try to quiet the speculation. In fact, offensive coordinator Frank Reich admitted that the slot receiver spot would "be a little bit different than last year." He did not temper praise for Agholor, suggesting that Agholor has "gotten over the hump."

The burning question of who would be the slot receiver was answered during the preseason when the Eagles traded Matthews and a third-round pick to the Buffalo Bills for cornerback Ronald Darby. From that point forward, it was clear that the Eagles would rely on Agholor in the slot, despite the fact that he had played mostly as an outside receiver during his first two seasons in Philadelphia. The only question now was whether Agholor could handle the position change. The slot receiver, who stands between the offensive line and the wide receiver nearest to the sideline, must navigate through more traffic because his routes are in the middle of the field. And Agholor, at 6 feet tall and 198 pounds, is shorter and wirier than the muscular Matthews. But he's also quicker with more agility and impressive acceleration.

Once Agholor took his new position, Malcolm Jenkins wanted to challenge him. A fierce competitor, Jenkins often uses practice to try to push his teammates. After Agholor caught a pass over him in practice, Jenkins shoved him hard and the two started chirping at each other. When they next faced off, Jenkins jammed Agholor at the line of scrimmage, playing more physical than one might expect in an August practice. But there was a method to Jenkins's approach.

"I saw an opportunity for him," Jenkins said. "You brought in Alshon, Torrey, now you lose Jordan, and that slot position was wide open. Even though he's a first-round pick, I felt like this year, at the beginning of the year, he was in competition to make the team. So I saw an opportunity for him to get better and take hold of that spot. But since he's gotten here, I feel he's been our most talented receiver, when you talk about flat talent. He just hasn't performed up to par. In order for us to win games, I knew we'd have to get the best out of him."

That's exactly what happened. Starting in Week 1, Agholor emerged as one of the team's biggest threats. By Week 6 against Arizona, when Agholor caught a 72-yard touchdown pass, it was clear that his presence would be one of the biggest differences for the Eagles in 2017. His best game of the season came in Seattle—the site of his huge faux pas one year earlier—when he made seven catches for a career-high

141 yards. In the Super Bowl, Agholor led the Eagles with nine catches. A player who once appeared on the verge of being a "bust" had turned into one of the Eagles' most clutch players in their biggest game.

"It all changed," Agholor said, "when I told myself I'm not going to be denied."

Agholor was yet another Eagle who had been close to being written off, only to redeem himself in 2017.

WEEK 14

THE PLAY THAT CHANGED EVERYTHING

GAME DAY: LOS ANGELES RAMS :: W 43–35

There was considerable hype for the Eagles-Rams game in Week 14. Both were upstart teams bound for the playoffs. Both had thriving second-year quarterbacks in Jared Goff and Carson Wentz, the top two picks in the 2016 draft, who would be linked throughout their careers. The two developed a fast friendship in the pre-draft process while working out together in Irvine, California, after signing with the same agency.

When the schedule came out in April, an NFL executive called Rams officials to run down each game. The 12th game was on December 10, Eagles vs. Rams in Los Angeles.

"The Goff vs. Wentz Bowl," Rams general manager Les Snead said, as captured by the Rams website.

Snead had considered drafting Wentz when the Rams traded up to the No. 1 pick. Wentz even visited the Rams' facility, just as Goff visited Philadelphia. Ultimately, the Rams chose Goff and the Eagles got the guy they most wanted in Wentz. Wentz said both players ended up in the right place—Wentz's hardnosed style fit the Philadelphia market while Goff, a Ryan Gosling lookalike, appealed to the Southern California crowd. Wentz had far more success as a rookie, but Goff took a big jump in his second season.

The Eagles-Rams game was television gold. FOX moved its live studio show to a remote location at the stadium to further pump up the game. The

Eagles were 10–2 and the Rams were 9–3, so both teams were an attraction. But the quarterbacks made it a marquee matchup.

"I think it's exciting any time two young quarterbacks like us face off," Wentz said. "I think it's definitely exciting for the league, and Jared and I are both excited about it."

After throwing an interception on the opening drive, Wentz quickly settled down and played like the MVP candidate he had become. He threw touchdown passes on his next three drives and entered halftime with 236 passing yards. It looked like he was on his way to a record-setting game.

After the Rams took a 28–24 lead in the third quarter, Wentz led the Eagles on a potential go-ahead drive the length of the field, converting three third downs along the way. With the Eagles at the 2-yard line, Wentz took the shotgun snap, found no open receivers, rolled to his right and lunged forward toward the end zone in a play eerily similar to the one in Seattle a week earlier. One Rams defender tried tackling him low as another tried tackling him high. They sandwiched him with great force, but the 237-pound Wentz bullied through for a touchdown.

"He got hit hard," Doug Pederson said on the sideline, as captured by NFL Films.

"He gotta stop doing that," Jay Ajayi said.

The TD celebration was short-lived as a penalty flag nullified the play, forcing the Eagles back 10 yards. But that wasn't the main reason for concern. Wentz got up slowly and walked gingerly back to the huddle, pointing to his left knee. Two running plays brought the Eagles to the 2-yard line before an incomplete pass forced fourth down. Pederson decided to go for the touchdown—even with a gimpy Wentz.

"I knew something was up," Pederson said. "Didn't know the extent of it, obviously."

Unable to scramble or exert the normal force on his left leg, Wentz stood in the pocket on and found Alshon Jeffery for the go-ahead touchdown.

Wentz had just set a franchise record with 33 touchdowns in a season, breaking Sonny Jurgensen's 1961 record, but he did not celebrate or even smile. He looked stoic as he walked to the sideline. He didn't go over to his fellow quarterbacks to review the drive as he normally would. Instead, he went directly to the medical staff.

It was the last play of Wentz's season.

• • •

The panic started when team doctors brought Wentz into a makeshift blue tent on the sideline for a few minutes before escorting him to the locker room. He walked off the field on his own power, but clearly something was wrong. The team indicated Wentz would not return, but there was no official word about what had happened.

Nick Foles immediately started warming up on the sideline. Zach Ertz, a close friend of Wentz's, did not play against the Rams because of a concussion. Trey Burton, perhaps Wentz's closest friend on the team, suggested that Ertz go to the locker room to check on Wentz. Ertz called their pastor and they prayed together, according to a December *Philadelphia Inquirer* story.

"I figured I was of more use comforting him than try and comfort the guys on the field," Ertz said. "I knew something wasn't right with his knee. He knew something wasn't right with his knee."

Above the field, in the box where the Eagles' executives were watching the game, there was immediate concern. They knew that it couldn't be good if the head trainer and head of security followed Wentz to the locker room. Their initial unofficial diagnosis was a torn anterior cruciate ligament (ACL), but an MRI exam would be needed to confirm. Howie Roseman was notified and told Jeffrey Lurie.

Roseman retreated to the bathroom in a fog. FOX announcer Joe Buck saw Roseman on the way and complimented Roseman on the season the Eagles and Wentz were having.

"Is he serious right now?" Roseman said, remembering the moment in the 3 and Out podcast with John Middlekauff, a former Eagles scout. "And I don't realize, he doesn't know what I know!"

The Eagles players on the sideline didn't know, either. They were in the third quarter of an important late-season game, and knew a win would clinch the NFC East title. They couldn't think about what would happen the rest of the season. They needed to think about the next seventeen minutes.

• • •

The Rams took the lead on their next drive, putting Foles in position to bring the Eagles from behind for the victory. Foles had played mop-up duty in three games when the Eagles had a big lead, but this was his first meaningful action of the season.

He marched the Eagles 52 yards over 10 plays on his first drive, good enough to set up a Jake Elliott field goal to cut the Rams' lead to 35–34 with ten minutes remaining.

Throughout the season, the Eagles defense had created an identity of making big plays when most needed. And on this day, they did it again. With the Rams on their own 35-yard line, Eagles defensive end Chris Long burst around the edge, dove toward Goff, and swiped at his right arm, knocking the ball loose for a strip sack that was recovered by Eagles safety Rodney McLeod. Both Long and McLeod had played for the Rams organization in the past, and now had given the Eagles a chance to beat their old team. The Eagles had the ball at the Rams' 25-yard line. They were already in field goal range.

Foles couldn't lead them to a touchdown, but he didn't the turn the ball, either. Elliott came in and kicked the go-ahead field goal, and the Eagles never relinquished the lead.

"You're just trying to get the win," Foles said. "The defense did an awesome job stepping up when Carson went down. The guys really rallied."

The defense then forced the Rams to punt, giving Foles and the offense the ball back in the final two minutes. Foles's most clutch play of the afternoon came on a third-and-8 from the Eagles' 23-yard line when he hit Nelson Agholor for a 9-yard reception to continue winding down the clock.

When the Eagles finally punted, the Rams got the ball back with one second remaining on the clock. They tried a desperation lateral on the ensuing play, but it resulted in a fumble that Derek Barnett picked up and returned a touchdown, adding an exclamation point on the victory. Eagles' players rushed toward the end zone, celebrating along with a pack of Eagles fans who had made the trip to Los Angeles.

It was official: The Eagles were going to the playoffs. They were the best team in football. And when they returned to the locker room, Wentz stood at the entrance.

• • •

Wentz greeted his teammates and congratulated them. He did not share the initial diagnosis, but many feared something was wrong. They admitted it was a bittersweet celebration, and to a man knew Wentz was their MVP.

The visitor's locker room at the Los Angeles Memorial Coliseum, which opened in 1923, was small and cramped. Pederson stood up on a stool to deliver his postgame speech.

"We said these last couple of weeks that we wanted to take care of business ourselves. It's in our hands! It's in our hands!" Pederson said, as seen on the team website. "That's a heavyweight fight right there, men. Congratulations to all three phases. Offense making plays when we need it. Defense stepping up and making plays when they need it. . . . Hey, greatest team effort we've been a part of all season long!"

Pederson then pointed to the NFC East Champions cap on the head of tackle Halapoulivaati Vaitai.

"Now that we got this out of the way . . . we got three left!" Pederson said. "We're playing for something bigger now, boys. It's going to take every-freakin'-body in the room, everybody in the room to dig in, dig in, dig in for these next few weeks. . . . I'm so proud of you guys. NFC East champs!"

As Malcolm Jenkins watched Pederson speak, he knew he was next and began thinking of what he would say. He knew reporters waited outside of the locker room eager to ask the team about Wentz's injury. He knew what the narrative of the remainder of the season would be if Wentz was out. And being the leader that he is, he decided to acknowledge the elephant in the room directly; there was no fluff required.

"Let's get this s— out of the way, man: Carson being out of this s—, bro, that s— sucks," Jenkins said. "But dig this . . . whoever's in this room, that's who we ride with, man! We said it: 'We all we got, we all we need.' Believe that. . . . Celebrate that s—, know where we're at. But at the end of the day, man, we have bigger goals. So we get back to work, man. You know what's in our minds, bro: Championships, and that's it. Nothing short of that. No excuses. Don't f—ing blink."

Wentz later left the locker room with a division-champs hat on his head and a bulky brace on his left knee, and rode on a cart to the team bus. When he reached the security checkpoint, he got off the cart and limped onto the bus, which took the team to the airport for a long flight back to a city in mourning.

The Eagles lost their star. They didn't lose their season.

LEARNING TO PRACTICE AWAY FROM HOME

Each season's NFL schedule is revealed in two parts. Just after the regular season ends, the league announces each team's home and away opponents for the next season, and a few months later they release the complete schedule with dates and times. When the Eagles saw that they would have three West Coast games in 2017—two in Los Angeles and one in Seattle—they requested that two of them be scheduled in successive weeks so the team could stay out West. The idea was to cut down on the travel and time zone changes, which wear on players' bodies. The NFL granted their request, scheduling the Rams game the week after their trip to Seattle.

The Eagles spent full weeks out West twice under Buddy Ryan in the 1980s, but had not done so since. Pederson compared the process to holding training camp at Lehigh University, which the Eagles used to do before moving it back to Philadelphia in 2013. But with all due respect to Pederson, this was different than training camp, as it came late in the season when everyone was used to a weekly routine. Players were not sleeping in their beds, but rather at a Westin in Costa Mesa, California. They held their meetings there, too. The second and third floors of the hotel turned into offices, meeting rooms, and a training room.

For weightlifting and workouts, they went to a nearby Equinox fitness center instead of the weight room they used every day at the team facility. Practices were held twelve miles away at Angel Stadium of Anaheim, where Major League Baseball's Los Angeles Angels play. At the NovaCare Complex, the team's headquarters in Philadelphia, everything is confined in one space—the locker room, practice field, weight room, training room, meeting rooms, and cafeteria. While in Southern California, they needed to be shuttled from one place to another throughout the day.

"The challenge is just we're trying to eliminate distractions," Pederson said. "It's hard when you've got back-to-back, these West Coast trips like this, to be able to fly back home and practice and then comeback out this way at the end of the week. So we try to keep the week as normal as possible for the guys and for the coaches. We have a great setup here in the hotel. Coaches have offices and work space to get the work done. Players have got everything they need right here from treatment, rehab, doctors, medical facilities, all of that."

To try to preserve a sense of normalcy thousands of miles from home, Pederson maintained the same practice schedule with minor changes—he made the days longer to avoid too much free time as the week progressed. There was also a midnight curfew.

Monday was the off day. The week picked up on Wednesday when practices began. The team bussed over to Angel Stadium, where the Angels had placed a gift in each player's locker stall—a bobblehead of baseball star Mike Trout, a Millville, New Jersey, native and Eagles season-ticket holder. Trout, who is friends with Carson Wentz and Zach Ertz, had gotten married that month and was not in Orange County. Nonetheless, his presence was felt. Nigel Bradham was assigned Trout's corner locker and enjoyed the plush leather couch in the middle of the clubhouse.

That wasn't the only Philadelphia connection made out west. On Friday, before the final practice of the week, Pederson arranged for a special guest speaker to address the team. There are few people who leave professional athletes in awe, but Pederson found one of them. Kobe Bryant, an eighteen-time NBA All-Star and five-time NBA champion, is a native of suburban Philadelphia and a lifelong Eagles fan. He walked into the room with a green No. 8 Eagles jersey over a black T-shirt and spoke to the Eagles about his famous "Mamba Mentality," instructing them to have a killer instinct on the field and make their opponent wish he had become an accountant instead of a professional football player. Pederson said he hoped the message the players took from Bryant was threefold: "Pay attention to details. Do your job. Focus on your assignment."

"To hear the 'Mamba Mentality' in real life was crazy," offensive guard Brandon Brooks said. "To be in the presence of one of the greatest to ever play the sport, it was just incredible. Some of the stuff he was saying really hit home to me. From a mentality standpoint, how he attacked the game, how way he viewed it. Going out there and trying to dominate every play."

The Eagles then went to the stadium for their final full practice. Pederson was pleased with the practice sessions after the Seahawks loss, noting "the guys really embraced the week; no distractions."

That was the objective. But there was an ulterior motive for Pederson, too. He knew that if the Eagles made the Super Bowl, they would spend a week in the host city, and knew from his own experience as a player that it could be helpful.

"It will definitely pay off for us," Pederson said, "hopefully in the near future."

WEEK 15

FOLES IS FINE, DEFENSE IS NOT

GAME DAY: NEW YORK GIANTS :: W 34–29

The Eagles did not need Nick Foles to be Carson Wentz. But in his first start since returning to the Eagles, Foles picked up where Wentz left off.

Foles helped the Eagles to a 34–29 Week 15 victory over the New York Giants to clinch a bye in the first round of the playoffs. He finished 24 of 38 for 237 yards with four touchdowns and no turnovers, albeit against the league's worst-ranked defense. He even brought the Eagles back from a 20–7 deficit, showing the poise that the Eagles valued when they signed Foles as a veteran backup. It was like 2013 all over again.

"It's crazy, if I'm being honest, just wearing the Eagles jersey," Foles said after the Giants game. "To go back to Philly and wear it, I take a lot of pride in that."

There had been speculation all week that Pederson might need to step up the running game so as not to rely too heavily on Foles. However, Pederson called thirteen more passes than running plays against the Giants, proving his faith in his backup QB. There were more conservative, quick passes than deep balls, and Foles spread the ball around to seven different receivers. His two longest completions came on screen passes in which the run after the catch was the key to the play.

"We tailored a couple of things for Nick obviously in the passing game," Pederson said, "but really I wanted to maintain the aggressiveness."

There was even a time when Foles—who is often thought to be a slow, lumbering quarterback—used a pump fake to extend the play. Few would say Foles is as athletic as Wentz, but he showed remarkable agility in this game.

"I channeled my inner Carson Wentz right there," Foles said.

The concern in Philadelphia after the game had less to do with Foles and more with a defense that allowed the Giants a total of 504 yards—208 more than their season average. The Giants converted ten of eighteen third downs—55 percent—against an Eagles defense that had limited its opponents to 30.2 percent on third down conversions before that game. The cornerbacks in particular had a bad day—especially Ronald Darby, who had his worst game with the Eagles despite snagging an interception. The Eagles also committed seven penalties.

"We gave them a lot out there," Nigel Bradham said. "Stuff like that, when you play good teams—real good teams—it's going to put you in a bind to win a game."

Pederson was pleased that the Eagles had now clinched a first-round bye, but he also said that the team "can't play like this and win in the postseason." He wanted his players to be excited about what they had accomplished, but he also needed them to be better prepared for the big games to come.

"I didn't know if we had that dominant swagger today like we normally do, because it didn't show early in this game," Pederson said in the postgame locker room, as captured by the team website. "Now, second half of the game was different. . . . It's hard to win twelve games in this league. It's hard. You guys have done it. Let's just check another box. NFC East? We checked it. First-round bye, playoff game at home? We checked it. Now we're playing for the number-one seed and home field throughout the playoffs. You've got a great opportunity, men. Let's keep this train moving."

The opportunity to clinch home field would come on Christmas against the Oakland Raiders. That game would also bring a new concern for Eagles fans.

JENKINS: FOLLOW THE LEADER

It made sense for Malcolm Jenkins to deliver the speech after Pederson following each game. Jenkins had become one of the NFL's best defensive backs since joining the Eagles. He had also become a team leader, although his leadership qualities were developed decades earlier.

He learned it from Lee and Gwendolyn Jenkins in their home in Piscataway, New Jersey, on Third Street off Rock Ave. Jenkins was the one who always hosted his friends. His father was the one who always drove them to football practice. He was the oldest of three boys and wherever Jenkins went, he led.

"I've always been the guy out front," Jenkins said. "It kind of comes natural to me."

He took that expression literally to earn a college scholarship. As a teenager whose only college interest had come from nearby Rutgers, Jenkins went with his family on a summer vacation to visit his aunt in Columbus, Ohio. While there, Jenkins attended a football camp at Ohio State. Many of the attendees were invited by the coaching staff. And when the top wide receivers in the Midwest were in line to run routes in one-on-one drills, most campers on defense shied away from stepping into coverage. Jenkins jumped to the front of the line. By the end of the camp, Ohio State offered him a scholarship.

Jenkins stood out and led on his team at Piscataway High School, too. His coaches encouraged him to speak up. Jenkins played with three teammates in high school who also went on to play in the NFL, and even they deferred to Jenkins and his leadership style.

"He totally bought into the fact that he could influence and impact what other people do," said Dan Higgins, his high school coach. "He was a natural leader because of that. It wasn't because we said

Malcolm's the captain. It was because Malcolm was the most highly respected guy on the team."

Jenkins is aware that other players don't have the job security he enjoys because he's a prominent player, so he tries to provide a voice for them. Because of Jenkins's comfort with public speaking, he's morphed into a team spokesperson. He considers what his message will be to the team after a game and he chooses his words carefully in public when cameras are on him and recorders are hot. Jenkins said 2017 was his easiest season to lead because of the number of veterans there were on the team. But his leadership extended beyond the locker room, too.

"If you were to ask me at nine, fourteen, nineteen, did I think I was going to be in the NFL, the answer would probably be no," Jenkins said. "But if you were to ask [my parents], would somebody hire me specifically for my leadership skills and the type person I've become, I think they'd say yes."

Jenkins's speech after Wentz's injury proved to be a seminal moment in the Eagles' season. It helped establish the message of the team and bolster Pederson's resolute decree for the postseason. Jenkins stepped in when the locker room was most downtrodden to make it clear the Eagles still had everything in front of them. And though the flight back to Philadelphia from Los Angeles was not nearly as joyous as it would typically be after clinching the NFC East, the locker room in the days after Wentz's injury was not morose.

"I knew all week that we'd hear questions about whether we felt confident enough to move forward, whether our dreams were kind of over with now that we lost our quarterback," Jenkins said. "Before anybody heard it in the media or got to deal with all of those questions, we wanted to let them know, 'Hey, this sucks, but at the end of the day, this changes nothing.' Everything we want to do is in front of us. We'll go about our work like we always do. We've lost people before, important guys in this locker room all year . . . and [found] a way to win. Where we're at in the season right now, there's no time to lick your wounds or feel bad for yourself or take any excuse people try to give you for why you can't win. Because I fully believe we're capable of doing this."

The Eagles had lost Wentz, Jason Peters, Jordan Hicks, Darren Sproles, Chris Maragos, and Caleb Sturgis for the season. They overcame shorter-term injuries to other high-profile players along the way, too. Yet their "next man up" mentality proved to be more than a cliché—it was an effective and winning strategy.

But the Eagles never needed a backup to replace Jenkins. He never missed a game. He barely missed a snap. Jenkins played safety, slot cornerback, and even linebacker depending on what the defense needed in a given game. He defended wide receivers, tight ends, and helped in the running game. The Eagles signed Jenkins in 2014 when the New Orleans Saints, the team that drafted him in 2009, didn't extend an offer to keep him. He had missed time in each of his five seasons with the Saints because of injuries, and his role kept changing while he transitioned from a cornerback at Ohio State to a safety in the NFL.

At the Eagles' facility, there's a long corridor connecting the locker room to the auditorium and cafeteria. The Eagles list all their Pro Bowlers along one of those walls. For two years, Jenkins would tap that wall as a reminder that his name should be there. And after the 2015 season, he finally earned Pro Bowl recognition and got his name added to that wall.

Jenkins's Ohio State coach, Jim Tressel, remembered Jenkins carrying a notebook wherever he walked. He's a diligent note taker who keeps spiral notebooks on every quarterback he's ever faced. Jenkins also keeps a list of his goals on a whiteboard in his locker stall. Among his goals going into the 2017 season were the NFC East title and a second Pro Bowl invitation. Two days after the Eagles clinched the NFC East in Week 15, Jenkins received his second Pro Bowl invite. But he immediately stated that he did not plan to go, because the Pro Bowl is played the week before the Super Bowl and Jenkins fully expected the Eagles to be in Minnesota preparing to play in *that* game—even with Wentz on the sideline. He wanted the players he led to know it.

"If we would have started this year and someone [told] you, 'You've got one game against the Giants to clinch a first-round bye,' you don't care who you have on the field, you'd take those odds," Jenkins said. "Everything we want is in front of us. So we won't let a little bit of adversity, somebody going down, stop us from feeling good about ourselves. Because we're right there."

WEEK 16

|||||||||||||||||||||||||||||||||||||||||||||||||||||||||||||||||||||||||||||||||||||||||||||||||||||||||||||||||||||||||||||||

A MERRY CHRISTMAS,
AN UNCERTAIN NEW YEAR

GAME DAY: OAKLAND RAIDERS :: W 19–10

The stakes were clear for the Eagles when they hosted the Oakland Raiders on Christmas Night. They needed to win to clinch home-field advantage throughout the NFC playoffs, significant for a team that had theretofore been undefeated at home. A win would also render Week 17's game inconsequential, allowing them to rest their starters and start preparing for the playoffs.

The Eagles did go on to beat the Raiders 19–10 to clinch the top seed in the NFC, but the manner of victory gave cause for concern. Most notably, Foles did not look ready for the playoffs. He went 19 of 38 for 163 yards with one touchdown and one interception. He averaged just 4.3 yards per pass attempt and missed a number of open receivers. With a 19-degree wind chill, Foles appeared uncomfortable, especially when throwing downfield. He posed little threat on third down—the "money down" for Carson Wentz—with the Eagles offense converting only one of fourteen in the game.

"I didn't play good enough," Foles said after the game. "I have to play cleaner and, obviously, play better. Third down is a big thing with a quarterback: pin-point accuracy, making good decisions."

Raiders quarterback Derek Carr had a bad outing, too, proof that conditions were difficult for the passers. But Foles refused to use the weather as an excuse. He knew playing late-season games in Philadelphia "is not easy." He also knew that was the same weather the Eagles would likely encounter in the playoffs.

The Eagles were saved by their defense, which rebounded from a forgettable performance against the Giants by forcing five turnovers against the Raiders. The biggest one was an interception by Ronald Darby.

With the score tied 10–10 in the game's final minute, the Raiders had the ball at their own 46-yard line and were driving. On second down, Darby stepped in front of Carr's short pass to Amari Cooper and picked it off, giving the Eagles the ball at their own 48-yard line with 54 seconds on the clock. In one play, Darby renewed the hopes of the Lincoln Financial Field faithful, setting the stage for a Christmas miracle.

"Last week, our offense was carrying us and [the defense was] playing like trash," Darby said. "This week, our offense was making little mistakes and we had to come out there and make some plays. And the end of the day, that's what football is all about."

After infuriating fans throughout the night, Foles completed four short passes to give Jake Elliott a chance to kick a 48-yard, tie-breaking field goal with 27 seconds remaining. It was a difficult kick through frigid air, but Elliott nailed it to give the Eagles the lead. On the final play of the game, the Raiders fumbled a desperation lateral that Derek Barnett scooped up and ran in for the touchdown, sealing the 19–10 victory.

"We're 13–2 and we still have a lot of room to improve," Foles said. "You feel a lot better when you win it. But you're also very humbled. Our defense did an amazing job giving us opportunities at the end to drive the ball down, and Jake made a great kick. But it's something we have to clean up, because we can't go out there and do that."

That was the necessary spin. The Eagles had won and achieved a goal—No. 1 seed in the NFC playoffs—that seemed far-fetched when the season started. It was a reason to celebrate. They would not need to board an airplane until the Super Bowl. The playoffs would come through Lincoln Financial, a venue in which Pederson's team excelled.

"It wasn't pretty, but I don't care about pretty," Pederson told the team in the locker room, as captured by the team website. "Bottom line is you found a way to win the game. . . . Defense, hell of a job in the second half, keeping that offense in there. Offense, we've got to go work. Got to clean it up."

Malcolm Jenkins then wished his teammates a merry Christmas. He reminded them of what he said after Wentz's injury: It wasn't going to be easy and it doesn't need to be pretty. They just need to get the job done.

Outside the locker room, there was growing skepticism about whether they could do it with Foles at quarterback.

ELLIOTT: THE UNEXPECTED KICKER

Jake Elliott's game-winning field goal against the Raiders added to his list of clutch kicks throughout the season. The team-record 61-yard field goal against the Giants in September was many fans' introduction to Elliott, and it was arguably his top highlight of the season. But he was far from a one-kick wonder. In fact, Elliott kicked four game-winners during the season and scored the final three points of the Super Bowl.

The Cincinnati Bengals selected Elliott in the fifth round of the 2017 draft, the first of three kickers selected. Being drafted in the fifth round would usually lead to an automatic roster spot for a kicker, except the Bengals elected to keep a veteran over Elliott, sending the rookie to their practice squad for further seasoning. In the NFL, a practice-squad player is eligible to sign a contract with any of the other thirty-one teams at any time, and after Caleb Sturgis suffered an injury in Week 1, the Eagles signed Elliott as his replacement. Though Elliott appeared shaky in his first game with the Eagles, he turned into an unlikely hero on the team. What was even more improbable was the way Elliott had begun his kicking career a decade earlier.

As a freshman at Lyons Township High School in suburban Chicago in 2009, Elliott attended a pep rally for the football team. He didn't play football at the time—in fact, his main sport was tennis. He watched the Chicago Bears only casually on weekends, and he wouldn't strike an imposing profile in a varsity jacket. During the rally, to get the crowd energized, school officials began randomly picking students from the bleachers to attempt field goals. Elliott was among those chosen.

Elliott had played around with a football in the schoolyard enough to know that he would not embarrass himself in front of his classmates. And avoiding embarrassment was the extent of his ambition when the football was placed 30 yards away from the goalposts and it was his turn to kick. Elliott had no training in kicking, and he barely knew the proper mechanics. But he approached the ball and—boom!—the ball fired off his foot as if he was a top recruit, not a scrawny teenager.

"When the ball comes off [the foot of] someone who knows what they're doing, it makes a very distinctive sound," said Kurt Weinberg, the head football coach at Lyons Township.

After the rally, the head football coach approached Elliott and asked him to come try out for the football team. He flat out refused. He wanted to devote his time to tennis, a sport in which he'd excelled for years. Despite that impressive first kick, Elliott had no idea what he was doing and had no interest in learning at the time. He didn't even tell his father what had happened when he came home from school that day.

"I just went out there and had fun with it," Elliott said, "and called it a day."

Two years passed. At the start of Elliott's junior year, the football team found itself in desperate need of a reliable kicker, and the coaching staff remembered Elliott. An assistant coach walked over to the tennis courts where Elliott was practicing with his team, explained the situation, and asked him to reconsider.

"Why not?" Elliott thought this time. "I'm not doing anything in the fall."

It took only a few practice kicks for the head coach to formalize the offer. Elliott later received the blessing of his family, and suddenly he was a football player.

If Elliott's pep-rally showing was clutch, it was nothing compared to his first homecoming game. With Lyons down by two and with four seconds left on the clock, Coach Weinberg sent Elliott onto the field to attempt a 52-yard field goal. A 52-yard field-goal attempt is not a given for an NFL kicker, let alone a high school junior in his first season. But Elliott made it, Lyons won the big game, and he was the hero.

"That was pretty crazy," Elliott said. "Didn't even know what I was doing out there. No technique, no anything."

This clearly was not luck. Elliott possessed rare kicking talent, however unpolished. He also possessed an even-keeled demeanor that allowed him to remain unperturbed during pressure-packed moments.

"It went from 'Who is this kid and what is he all about?' to 'This kid is supremely talented,'" Weinberg said. "In a heartbeat, really."

Elliott started to take kicking seriously after his junior year. His stepmother found information for a kicking showcase, and the other kickers there asked Elliott who coached him. He didn't have a private coach—just a promising leg. Elliott received a full scholarship offer from the University of Memphis during his senior year. The Big Ten schools in the Midwest, where Elliott otherwise might have attended, only offered the opportunity to try out. Elliott chose Memphis, ultimately turning that random kick at a pep rally into free tuition. He figured that was good enough, and he arrived at Memphis with plans to study marketing, graduate, and land a job on a sales team. Making an NFL team was never part of the plan.

"How often do you think your kid's going to go the pros?" said Bruce Elliott, Jake's father. "That never registered with us."

NFL coaches took notice during Elliott's Memphis career. He earned all-league honors all four years in college, and was also a semi-finalist for the Lou Groza Award, which goes to the top college kicker. As a senior, he made 21 of 26 field goals and all 58 extra points. Going into the 2017 draft, Elliott earned invitations to the Senior Bowl and NFL combine. Clearly the NFL viewed him as one of the top kicking prospects.

The Eagles, though, were not among the teams interested in a kicker during the 2017 draft. Caleb Sturgis was entrenched in that role. But Special Teams Coordinator Dave Fipp still studied all the kickers nonetheless. He rated Elliott as one of the top two kickers in the draft, and considered him a "draftable player who could play in the NFL." That's high praise, because few kickers are drafted each year. When Sturgis went down with an injury, Fipp brought in Elliott and two other kickers for tryouts. While the other two had NFL experience and Elliott didn't, Fipp determined that neither veteran had the leg strength that Elliott possessed, and so they took a chance on him. After Elliott missed a 30-yard field goal in his first game against Kansas City, Fipp recalled that Sturgis had also struggled in his Eagles debut in 2015. One kick would not change the team's commitment.

"If you're going to be that quick to give up on somebody, then you're always going to be looking for somebody," Fipp said. "Obviously, you can't keep missing kicks. There's a point of no return. But I wasn't nervous."

The following week, when Elliott missed his first field-goal attempt against the Giants, his employment seemed tenuous. But after nailing three fourth-quarter field goals, including the 61-yard game-winner, he quieted any concerns. As his confidence grew, Elliott became one of the NFL's most consistent kickers throughout the season. From Week 3 to Week 7, he made twelve consecutive field goals, including four straight from 50-plus yards. By midseason, it was a foregone conclusion that Elliott would be the Eagles' starting kicker. They were not going to activate Sturgis off the injured reserve list.

It all happened so fast for Elliott, who did not have his own place to live when he came to Philadelphia. He crashed at the home of a friend of the fiancé of Elliott's sister. One of Elliott's friends cleaned out his Cincinnati apartment for him. He even returned to Cincinnati during the bye week to settle his lease. Elliott went from star junior tennis player to unlikely high school kicker to college athlete to NFL draftee to practice-squad nobody to Super Bowl champion.

"It's one of those stories that's hard to believe," Weinberg said. "If you did a screenplay and did this story, people . . . would say it's too unbelievable."

WEEK 17

SPUTTERING TO THE FINISH LINE

GAME DAY: DALLAS COWBOYS :: L 0–6

Even with the Eagles' postseason position solidified entering the season finale against Dallas, Doug Pederson elected to play Nick Foles for part of the first half, thinking the offense could use a few series to regain their mojo after a lackluster performance in the Raiders game.

That didn't happen. The Eagles lost 0–6 after pulling most of their starters before halftime. It's common for a team that already clinched its playoff position to lose in Week 17. It's less common for the top seed's fan base to have serious concerns about the quarterback going into the playoffs.

Foles played four uninspiring offensive drives against the Cowboys. He completed 4 of 11 pass attempts for just 39 yards. He threw one interception and no TDs. His quarterback rating was a dreadful 9.3 on a scale of 0 to 158.3. By comparison, during Foles's 2013 season, he set a franchise record with a 119.3 quarterback rating.

"I'm not concerned," Pederson said. "I've still got a lot of confidence in our offense. It's not one person or one guy. There is enough to go around."

However, there is one person more important than the rest. That's why a quarterback bears the credit in good times and blame in bad times. He's the only player to touch the ball every play. And if Foles's last five quarters of the regular season were any indication, there was little reason to be confident in the Eagles' quarterbacking.

"I know who I am as a player," Foles said. "And throughout my career and my life, I haven't always played great games. . . . And the key is you remain confident because you know who you are."

Football is a fickle game. On Foles's opening drive against the Raiders, he started to gather some momentum as the offense moved the first-down chains twice. But when Foles threw a third-down pass to Torrey Smith that would have put the Eagles in field goal range, Smith dropped the ball. The Eagles failed on their fourth-down attempt, and Foles's performance went south from there.

It was another bone-chilling day when the Cowboys came to town, with winds making the 19-degree temperatures feel like 3 degrees at kickoff. One weather-related theory about Foles's two-game slide was that he grew up in Texas and played college ball in Arizona, and so he might not have been suited to play in cold conditions. Then again, nobody said that back in 2013 when Foles led the Eagles to a regular-season victory in a blizzard, or when he exited their home playoff game against the Saints with a lead. In fact, Howie Roseman touted Foles's 10⅝-inch hands as being ideal for Philadelphia winters.

The Eagles had two weeks before their first playoff game to fix the mounting issues with their quarterback. As far as the other fifty-two players were concerned, there wasn't much to fix. The defense excelled for the second consecutive week against Dallas, whose offensive starters didn't score any points until the fourth quarter when the Eagles were fielding reserves. The Eagles' offensive line had established themselves as perhaps the best in the NFL—despite the loss of Jason Peters—with Lane Johnson and Brandon Brooks both earning Pro Bowl invitations and Jason Kelce being named a first-team All-Pro as the NFL's top center.

When the curtain dropped on the regular season, the Eagles were 13–3, the No. 1 seed in the NFC, and tied with the Patriots, Steelers, and Vikings for best record in the NFL.

When Malcolm Jenkins was asked why fans should be confident in the Eagles entering the playoffs, the team leader replied with a quizzical look on his face.

"Why wouldn't they be?" he asked.

The answer seemed obvious. The offense, and Foles in particular, did not inspire much confidence during the previous two games.

"We still won thirteen games. Number-one seed," Jenkins responded. "Everyone's got to come through Philly. I don't care if you were starting at quarterback. We should be confident in that. . . . We win one game, we're in the NFC Championship at home at Philly. So yeah, I don't care who we have at quarterback, who we have at offense, we'd take those odds."

BIRDS OF PRAY

At the end of every Eagles practice, a group of players gather together on one knee and pray. It happens at the end of every game, too. Religion has a place in most every NFL locker room. But it played an especially large role in Philadelphia in 2017.

It was no surprise that shortly after Carson Wentz's injury, he and Zach Ertz sat and prayed together. One year earlier, during a period of mounting criticism, Ertz marveled at how teammates such as Wentz, Trey Burton, and Jordan Matthews remained so even-keeled and unaffected by fans and media. He realized that it was because of their devotion to faith. He then sought a "bigger purpose than football" and was baptized in March, the day before his wedding. He was particularly inspired by Wentz's "Audience of One" message and is part of a growing contingent of Eagles who have found common ground through spiritual devotion.

Since 2016, a number of Eagles—including linebackers Jordan Hicks, Mychal Kendricks, and Kamu Grugier-Hill—were baptized in the team swimming pool in 2016, according to ESPN. Wide receiver Marcus Johnson was baptized at the team hotel in Charlotte the night before October's game against the Carolina Panthers. Players hold a Monday night couples Bible study, a Thursday night team Bible study, and discuss their faith during a separate meeting on Saturdays before the week's game.

Wentz is especially outspoken. He's delivered church sermons and in February 2018 even appeared at the National Prayer Breakfast, an annual event in Washington that has been attended by every president since Dwight Eisenhower. He puts considerable thought into how to present his faith—it's central to his being, yet he also wants to be careful not to conflict with or offend those who aren't like-minded.

"I'm always talking about it with other guys, too, because I never want to be the guy who's beating people over the head with the Bible," Wentz said. "That's not what I'm about. That's not really what Christianity is about. Christianity is all about love and showing that love and that kindness and that grace. You're always walking that fine line without a doubt. I always tell people for example, 'If you love your job, you love your wife, you love what you do, you're going to talk about it.' Well, I love Jesus. That's what I love, so I'm going to talk about it. But I'm not going to force it down your throat, either. It's definitely a fine line that I'm constantly trying to walk and at the end of the day, just kind of how I live and what I'm about hopefully can kind of speak through that."

After Wentz's injury, his first public comments came on social media. He posted a video offering his thoughts on the injury and the recovery. And before he even discussed his confidence in Foles, his confidence in the Eagles' chances, or even his gratitude for the fans' supports, he discussed his faith.

"Obviously, it's been a rough, rough day for me personally," Wentz said on video. "I'm not going to lie. I have a ton of faith in the Lord and in his plan, but at the end of the day, it's still been a tough one. And it will be tough on me for a little bit. But as I just kind of reflect tonight, I just know the Lord's working through it. I know Jesus has a plan through it. I know he's trying to grow me in[to] something, teach me something, use me somehow, some way, this is just going to be a great testimony as I go forward. Maybe not all of you out there are Christians or followers of Jesus, but I can say with one-hundred percent confidence, as a follower of Jesus, I have the utmost confidence in his plan. His plan is perfect. If we got everything we wanted in life, it would be a disaster. I know Jesus is up there looking down and he knows what he's doing. So I'm just going to surrender that to him and trust him in that."

In an interview before the season, Wentz explained that he wanted to use his platform to spread his beliefs, and social media was one way to do it. And if there are those who do not like it, "maybe they shouldn't follow me on social media."

Like Wentz, Nick Foles speaks often about his faith. During his first tenure with the Eagles, he explained that "faith is my most important thing" and that he reads the Bible every morning. That continued through his second stint as the Eagles' starting quarterback. In between, when Foles's career derailed and he contemplated retirement, he leaned on his faith and even enrolled in seminary classes.

In the minutes after the Super Bowl, with the confetti falling down on the Eagles, a group of players gathered for prayer led by offensive lineman Stefen Wisniewski. The prayer circle was videotaped by Sports Spectrum and showed some of the highest-profile Eagles, at the pinnacle of their career, bowing their heads and offering thanks.

"You gave us the talent, you gave us the strength!" Wisniewski said. "This team had so many injuries. We had no business being here! . . . When God is for you, no one can be against you! God, thank you for being for us! Take all the glory!"

PART 3

SUPER BOWL RUN

Postseason

PICKING ON NICK

The Eagles finished the regular season on a Sunday, and Doug Pederson gave the players a couple days off to rest their bodies and minds, and to recharge their batteries. They would reconvene on Wednesday to begin playoff preparations.

Nick Foles enjoyed a few rare mornings at home. He allowed his wife to sleep late as he took care of their six-month-old daughter, reading children's books to her while he sipped his morning coffee. "Those little things reenergize you," Foles said.

The Eagles would not know their first postseason opponent until the wild card playoff games were played. So Foles thought the early portion of the bye week would give him time to scout his own recent performances and determine what had gone wrong the last two weeks. He had completed just 46.9 percent of his passes and threw two interceptions with only one touchdown. There was no spin possible to rationalize those performances.

"Obviously on Sunday [against Dallas] and the week before, that's now how I want to play," Foles said. "But if anyone's ever played a sport, you can't sit here and say, 'OK, that's what it is.' I've had games like that and I've come back and played at a higher level."

Foles sheltered himself as best he could from the national media attention that was building around him. He had arrived in Los Angeles a few weeks earlier as a season-long backup, and returned home as the starting quarterback on a Super Bowl contender. He wasn't afforded much time to process and reflect until the bye week. And while he used the time to evaluate himself, he avoided taking stock of his outside approval rating. It wasn't good.

In fact, Pederson was asked in his press conference if he was sticking with Foles, or if he considered going with third-stringer Nate Sudfeld instead. The second-year quarterback, who was cut by Washington and picked up by the Eagles just prior to Week 1, had never taken an NFL snap until the starters left the game in Week 17. Pederson confirmed that Foles would start, but some in the football media interpreted his answer to mean that he was open to making an in-game switch if Foles struggled. Pederson tried to confirm in no uncertain terms that Foles is the Eagles' quarterback. The fact that there was even a question as to Foles's status illustrated the level of panic surrounding the Eagles.

By now, the psychoanalysis of Foles had become a cottage industry. Time and time again he was asked if he'd lost his confidence, and he repeatedly insisted that he had not. The same question was asked of the coaching staff and Foles's teammates, none of whom wavered in their confidence for the quarterback. At some point, Foles just locked into football and started leaving calls and text messages unanswered. He would answer them on the field.

"You're always going to have criticism. I know that," Foles said. "And I think the big thing is I feel good and I'm in the moment."

Pederson's message to Foles was simple: "Let's go be Nick." Pederson did not need to magnify the moment. Foles did not need to consider the outside criticism. He just needed to have fun and play football like he had done since he was a kid in Texas. And when he sat down to watch the film of the last three games, he noticed he wasn't doing that. It became obvious to him that he had been overthinking it.

"Sometimes, the hardest things are the simplest things," Foles said. "Basically, get out of your own head and go play the game you know how to play."

Frank Reich, the Eagles' offensive coordinator who played fourteen seasons in the NFL, had grown close with Foles. Reich was a career backup quarterback who famously replaced injured Hall of Famer Jim Kelly in the last game of the 1992 season, then led the Buffalo Bills back from a 35–3 deficit against the Houston Oilers to win the wild card game 41–38 in overtime. After Reich's playing career, he became a pastor—just as Foles planned to do. Reich did not want Foles's last five quarters to sink him. He told Foles to "maintain your confidence and aggressiveness," and he was convinced that Foles's past would give him all the confidence he needed.

"First because of the length and breadth of his career," Reich said. "There's enough substance behind his career that merits having confidence. . . . I've seen the best quarterbacks in the world have a bad game or two in a row. I mean, the best. It happens."

Foles's past success was often referenced by his teammates, especially those who were in Philadelphia a few years prior when Foles was at his best. Jason Kelce reminded skeptics that "he's got a set of cleats in the Hall of Fame"—a reference to Foles's seven-touchdown performance in 2013—and that "he's been pretty darn good in Philadelphia before."

After Wentz went down and Foles stepped in, Pederson said he did not plan to change much of the offense. During the bye week, Pederson went back and studied the film from Foles's first stint with the Eagles, including his rookie year in 2012, his record-breaking campaign in 2013, and even Foles's last play-off appearance with the Eagles in January 2014. Foles watched every one of his pass completions of 15 yards or longer from 2013 and 2014, allowing him to "rediscover who I truly was as a quarterback," Foles wrote in his book, *Believe It*. Pederson then tailored the play-calling to what Foles does best, but it was still essentially the same Eagles' offense.

"The quick throw was there, a little play-action pass, the shotgun stuff," Pederson said. "Those are all things that are in our system. We might just have to dust a few more off and get that ready to go. But that's kind of what this [bye] week is for: to get some of those ideas and thoughts down on paper and execute them this week in practice."

Pederson considered mixing in elements of the up-tempo offense that Foles flourished in under Chip Kelly, particularly the run-pass option (RPO) where the quarterback makes the decision to run or pass based on what the defense presents after the ball is snapped. The Eagles had used it often with Wentz, too, so the entire offense was already on board, and Pederson knew he could use it to Foles's advantage.

The bottom line was that regardless of their specific game plan, the Eagles desperately needed the "good version" of Foles to show up. His career to that point had been marked by inconsistency, with a wide variance between excellent and awful. One week, he could look like a star. The next week, he could look like a journeyman. Foles had had fourteen career starts with a passer rating better than 100, sixteen starts with a passer rating lower than 80, and only nine starts with a passer rating between 80 and 100. There wasn't much "in-between" with Foles.

Eagles fans would soon learn which Foles showed up for the playoffs.

RENEWING THEIR FOCUS

Late in the regular season, with the players' bodies battered from more than four months of football, Doug Pederson started scaling back practices. This is customary in the NFL, and typically involves staging walkthroughs of plays without wearing pads or engaging in brutally physical drills. Pederson intended to reserve the players' energy for the playoffs, and more importantly, to avoid injury.

During the regular season, Pederson met every Tuesday with his leadership council—a group comprised of the five captains plus other respected veterans such as Brent Celek and Jason Kelce—to allow players to voice their concerns and to gauge the mood of the locker room. During their bye-week version of the meeting, the council asked Pederson for more intense practices. They wanted to wear pads again. Pederson was on board—it was time to take it up a notch.

"This is something that the players want," Pederson said when asked about his unusual decision. "It's not a punishment thing; it's not coming directly from me. . . . I think they understand that there is a sense of physicality that we have to get back to. I'm not saying we're not there, because obviously football is a physical game, but I think there is a sense over the course of a few weeks [with lighter practices] intensity sometimes can be minimized."

Pederson didn't have the players going hard every day, but instead worked in a few more physical practice sessions to help set the tone. Malcolm Jenkins explained that some aspects of football are difficult to prepare for without wearing pads. He reiterated Pederson's message that the players wanted this, that they welcomed the work.

"We understand the significance of the situation we're in and we want to take advantage of all the time we have," Jenkins said. "Guys didn't want to be off for the whole week. We wanted to get better."

Another change in preparation was pitting the first-team offense against the first-team defense in practice during the bye week. In a regular-season practice week, when they know their upcoming opponent, the starters practice against a "scout team" comprised of reserves and practice-squad players who simulate what the opponent might do on Sunday. Without an opponent to prepare for during the bye, and with the starters practicing against each other, the players compared it to a training camp. It was, in a sense, like August in January.

The physicality was also important in terms of applying Pederson's stated postseason formula: "Play great defense and be able to run the football." That was interpreted by some as a means to overcome Nick Foles's shortcomings, and there may have been some truth to that. Jenkins suggested that it was a time-tested game plan for playoff teams without an elite quarterback. But for Pederson, it was less about the quarterback and more about his own experiences in what it took to win playoff games, including ones with Hall of Famer Brett Favre under center.

• • •

The Eagles' road to the Super Bowl would run through Philadelphia. Which meant the games were going to be played in cold weather, and they would have a raucous home-field advantage. The defense allowed 13.4 points in eight home games during the regular season—ten points fewer than in their eight road games. Defensive coordinator Jim Schwartz said the "fans in the stands are going to mean an awful lot" to winning at home in the playoffs. And Pederson pledged to make a "conscious effort to stay dedicated to the run game," which would also help Foles on third downs. Third down had been Wentz's time to shine, but after Foles's three games at QB, Pederson identified it as an "Achilles Heel."

"I think that's a formula," Pederson said. "Especially now outside, January-type games, the weather can be bad. I think you have to be able to do that and keep yourself on the field and keep your defense rested. But somewhere in there you're going to have to make a play in the passing game, too, whether it be on a third down or maybe a first-down shot or something like that."

In team meetings, Pederson called on veterans with Super Bowl experience and playoff experience to address the team. He wanted the younger players to learn "what it takes to prepare themselves for not only divisional games, but hopefully games after this." One message that resonated came from someone who had never been to the Super Bowl. Brent Celek, who made it to the NFC Championship game in his second year and had never won a playoff game since, urged his teammates not to waste this opportunity.

The Eagles' opponent for the divisional round of the playoffs was decided when the Atlanta Falcons upset the Los Angeles Rams on January 6, sending Atlanta to Philadelphia the following week. Even though the Falcons finished 10–6 during the regular season and needed to win in Week 17 just to make the playoffs, they were the defending NFC champions and profiled as a formidable foe. That was confirmed by Las Vegas bookmakers when the Falcons opened as three-point favorites over the Eagles. It was the first time since 1970 that the No. 1 seed was an underdog in the divisional round of the playoffs.

In Pederson's first news conference to kick off the divisional round week, the coach was noticeably terse. He was in playoff mode. There was little elaboration in his answers, and he would not discuss injuries. He didn't expound on matchups. It was the closest Pederson came all year to delivering a Bill Belichick–like news conference—gruff, monosyllabic, and lacking information. A football coach's news conference can sometimes be staged theater—they're not speaking to the reporters in the room as much as they are to the fans watching from home and, perhaps even more, to the players in the locker room. Pederson explained that "sometimes the outside, whether it be the media, the fans, can make [the game] bigger than it really is."

One of the popular narratives leading up to the game was the Eagles' underdog status. The players were not yet engaging publicly in this storyline, but behind the scenes the coaching staff made it known to them that they were not expected—by almost anyone—to beat Atlanta. In their team meeting the night before the game, the Eagles watched a video reinforcing the "nobody-believes-in-you" message. Players bought in, saying they were being overlooked and deserved more respect after securing the top seed. But they also dispelled the notion that the underdog status was being used for motivation.

"What would it sound like if I stood here and was like . . . 'Man, I wasn't that motivated for this playoff game, but I just found out we're underdogs and nobody picked us on ESPN so now I'm more motivated,'" Chris Long said to Bleacher Report. "I mean, it's just not the way we think."

Lane Johnson's Amazon shopping cart would prove otherwise.

FIRST, THE FALCONS

GAME DAY: **NFC DIVISIONAL: ATLANTA FALCONS :: W 15–10**

Malcolm Jenkins gathered his teammates together before the Falcons game. For two weeks, all the Eagles heard about was their unheard-of underdog status as top seeds, and whether their remarkable regular season would end without a playoff win. On a Saturday night in January, they prepared to answer those questions.

"Hey, respect is all you got in this league, man!" Jenkins hollered to his teammates, as captured by NFL Films. "Don't nobody respect us, but guess what? For the next four hours, those motherf—ers are locked here! They can't go home until we're done with them!"

The Falcons had star power at quarterback (former MVP Matt Ryan) and wide receiver (All-Pro Julio Jones), and their running back combination was one of the best in the NFL. The Eagles knew they would need their defense and running game to help control the clock. Pederson remained committed to the run, especially early in the game. The defense pressured Atlanta all night and kept the Falcons scoreless in the second half. Fletcher Cox was the best player on the field. The entire Eagles defense came through in the clutch, instilling the Eagles with the momentum needed for a Super Bowl run.

On a fourteen-play, 86-yard scoring driving in the second quarter, the Eagles rushed nine times. One of those was a surprising hand-off to Nelson Agholor on a third down that netted 21 yards and brought the Eagles deep into the red zone. It's not typical that there's a running play to a receiver, so the play caught the Falcons off guard. He was waiting for the right situation, and a key third down in the postseason was it.

Down 3–0, Pederson was faced with a fourth-and-goal from the 1-yard line. A field goal would have been the safer—and more expected—call, but Pederson decided to try for the touchdown. It was a bold decision in a low-scoring game where points were at a premium. But that was the way Pederson coached all season.

"There's a difference between playing football to tie the game and playing football to win," analyst Mike Quick said on the Eagles' radio broadcast. "That's playing football to win the game."

The Eagles didn't even line a receiver out wide, fully intending to run the ball. They put eight players on the line of scrimmage, with Trey Burton as the fullback blocking for LeGarrette Blount. Watching from the sideline, Jenkins remarked that this was a "playoff play."

"Who's going to move who?" he asked.

Foles handed the ball to Blount, who raced to the outside. The blockers kept bodies out of his way in the middle of the field and Burton made a perfect cut block on the edge, allowing Blount to gallop into the end zone for the touchdown. After Elliott's extra point attempt hit the upright, the Eagles led 6–3.

The Eagles defense held the Falcons on their next possession, forcing a punt. But a strong winter wind knocked the punted ball out of midair like a dead duck, dropping it shorter than expected and into a crowd of Eagles blockers. The ball deflected off an unaware Bryan Braman and was recovered by the Falcons at the Eagles' 19-yard line, giving Atlanta renewed life. Ryan quickly made the Eagles pay, flicking a third-down pass to Devonta Freeman for a touchdown and a 10–6 lead.

It takes a dose of luck to win in the playoffs, and the Eagles got their own break just before halftime. With twenty-two seconds remaining in the half and the Eagles backed up on their own 30-yard line, Foles threw an ill-advised pass 20 yards downfield into a gaggle of Falcons. Safety Keanu Neal looked poised for a sure interception, but the ball ricocheted off his knee and bounced high into the air. Eagles' receiver Torrey Smith alertly sprinted under it, reeled it in, and ran forward for a 20-yard gain. At midfield with twelve seconds remaining and no time-outs, the Eagles were close to field goal range. Foles would have to hit a receiver on the sideline in order to gain enough yards and also get out of bounds to stop the clock. In a virtual replay of the first Giants game, Wentz once again hit Alshon Jeffery along the sideline with just enough yards gained and with one second remaining on the clock. Elliott calmly boomed a 53-yard field goal through the uprights to cut the Falcons' halftime lead to 10–9.

"That was huge," Pederson said afterward.

The success of the running game in the first half helped Foles in the second half, when Atlanta's defense loaded the line of scrimmage in an attempt to stop the run. The Eagles offense also kept third-and-long situations to a minimum the rest of the game. The key to Foles's game is to find a "rhythm," and he did just that in the third quarter. He completed 6 of 8 pass attempts in the quarter, and on a late scoring drive hit 5 straight. Pederson went with an up-tempo offense after big gains, using multiple run-pass options to put Foles in his comfort zone. The combo proved effective.

"Nick played his butt off; he made the throws when he had to," tight end Zach Ertz said. "We ran the ball efficiently so we weren't facing a ton of third-and-longs, which was huge. . . . That's going to be the way we can continue to do this thing, is not having those third-and-long situations."

The Eagles defense continued to stonewall the Falcons in the third quarter, and a late 37-yard field goal by Elliott sent the Eagles into the fourth with a slim 12–10 lead. The Eagles defense forced a Falcons' three-and-out to start the final quarter, giving their offense the ball with just under fourteen minutes remaining. On their most critical offensive possession of the season to date, they sustained a fourteen-play drive with three third-down conversions, taking the ball all the way to the 3-yard line with 6:05 left on the clock. It was again decision time for Pederson on a fourth-and-1 at the Falcons' 3-yard line. Pederson used a timeout to consider his options. He had been so aggressive on fourth down all season, and a touchdown would make it a two-possession game. But discretion is the better part of valor. Pederson knew that if the Eagles failed to convert on fourth down, the Falcons would only need a field goal to take the lead.

"I was really considering . . . going for it," Pederson said. ". . . Obviously [with] the kick, you're up five and you're putting it back in your defense's hands, which is a positive, because I felt like they were playing extremely well at that time. But I also knew that if we do go for it and make it at that point, [the] game could be over at that time."

Considering how well the defense played all game, Pederson decided to send Elliott out to try to take a five-point lead and force Atlanta to score a touchdown. Elliott's 21-yard kick sailed through the uprights and gave the Eagles a 15–10 lead. After the ensuing kickoff, Atlanta took possession at their own 24-yard line with just under six minutes on the clock.

"It's on us, man," Bradham said. "That's all that was said. It was on us and we wouldn't want it any other way. That's how you feel when you're on [defense] and you feel like we lead this team. We set the tone for this team and we set the pace for this team."

After containing Ryan throughout the game, the defense could not get him off the field during Atlanta's final drive. On fourth-and-6 with 3:30 left and the ball at his own 42-yard line, Ryan connected with Julio Jones for a first down to extend the drive. A few plays later, Jones made his ninth catch of the game on a third-and-goal from the Eagles' 9-yard line with 1:05 left on the clock. Ronald Darby tackled Jones at the 2-yard line, making it fourth-and-goal from the 2. If the Falcons scored, they would take the lead. If the Eagles made the stop, they would win.

"That's what you want as a defender," Jalen Mills said. "That's what you dream of."

The Eagles called a timeout to discuss their defense. When they returned to the field, Jenkins made sure everyone knew the stakes.

"Hey, this is the season," Jenkins screamed, as captured by NFL Films. "This is it, right here! Let's go! This is the season right here!"

Sitting up in the broadcast boost, play-by-play announcer Merrill Reese told the radio audience that it would be the "biggest play in the ages."

In the Falcons' huddle, there appeared to be little question who they would target.

"How you feeling on this one?" Ryan asked Jones. "Give you height on it?"

"Just let me . . . go up and get it," Jones said.

The Falcons lined up with a fullback split wide, a running back in the backfield with Ryan, a tight end in motion, and their top two receivers on the right side of the formation.

"They're not going to run it! They're not going to run it!" Jenkins screamed. "Be ready for the pass!"

The Eagles had studied the Falcons all week and had a sense of the play. They expected that Ryan would sprint to his right side to try to connect with Jones or Mohamed Sanu, Atlanta's No. 2 receiver. One was supposed to go to the front pylon and the other to the back corner of the end zone. Jenkins and Rodney McLeod alerted the cornerbacks to their coverage, and linebacker Nigel Bradham knew his job was to rush toward Ryan.

The ball was snapped and the Eagles guessed correctly. Ryan went to his right, but his receivers couldn't get open. Jones stumbled to the ground fighting for leverage on Mills and Sanu was bracketed in the back of the end zone. As Bradham closed in on Ryan and forced him to backpedal to buy time, Jones got back to his feet and finally gave his quarterback a target. Ryan threw a desperation pass toward Jones, but the All Pro receiver jumped a second early, Mills got position in front of him, and the ball sailed through Jones's hands and out of bounds. The Eagles took over on downs. Pandemonium erupted from the Eagles sideline to the entire crowd. After getting one final first down and running out the clock, the Eagles escaped with their first playoff win since January 2009.

"As a competitor, you always want to be the guy to make to make that play," Mills said. "You've got to live and die by it."

The defense came through again, holding the Falcons to only ten points. It was a matter of pride for the unit, and not just because they generally outplayed a normally potent offense. They knew their intense preparation during the week paid off on the game's most important play.

"We recognized the formation as soon as they lined up and were able to take away the first two reads on the sprint out," Jenkins said. "He tossed it up into coverage, and we move on."

Once the clock hit zero in the 15–10 win, Lane Johnson ran to the sideline and retrieved a pair of realistic-looking German shepherd masks that he had purchased earlier that week. He and Chris Long replaced their helmets with the masks and ran back onto the field for all to see, giving birth to the Eagles' underdog image that would define their playoff run. The team's road to victory stretched out before them and they would ride it at least one more week. In the postgame locker room, Pederson emphasized that the Eagles were not finished yet.

"I'm so fricking proud of every one of you men. I can't believe it!" Pederson said, as captured by the Eagles website. "Well, I can believe it. . . . One week from tomorrow, we come back together and we shock the world again!"

Team owner Jeffrey Lurie then joined the locker room celebration, taking center stage with an impromptu dance as everyone cheered him on. It was the perfect ending to the first leg of their playoff journey.

UNDERDOG CITY

On the night before the Eagles-Falcons game, a group of five Eagles gathered for a pregame meal. Jason Kelce couldn't keep a straight face as he looked at Zach Ertz and Brent Celek, who could tell something was up. Lane Johnson, one of the boldest and funniest players on the team, appeared ready for mischief.

"Lane, tell 'em," Kelce said, according to an article Ertz wrote for the *Players' Tribune*. "Tell 'em what we ordered."

"You know how everyone keeps saying we're underdogs? Even though we're the No. 1 seed?" Johnson responded. "Well . . . we were on Amazon last night, and we ordered these dog masks."

Ertz didn't know what Johnson meant, figuring they were puppy masks that a kid might wear for Halloween.

"No, man. German shepherds," Johnson said. "They're creepy. Real creepy. Two-day shipping. They're coming tomorrow. . . . And when we win, because we're gonna freaking win, we're going to do everything in the masks. Media. Postgame. Everything. Dogs."

Johnson and Chris Long hatched the idea during lunch earlier in the week. Sure enough, when the Eagles beat Atlanta, Johnson and Chris Long donned the masks and paraded around the field barking like dogs with their latex tongues wagging and ears pinned back. And when they sat down to give their postgame media interviews, the masks stayed on, at least at first.

"People are terrified," Long told reporters after the game. "It was bigtime to win the game, but we really wanted to put the masks on. So that was an added bonus."

The masks became an instant phenomenon in Philadelphia as fans rushed to Amazon to buy them. Across the globe in Dongguan, China, a representative from Amazon retailer CreepyParty, which typically sold ten masks a day, awoke Sunday morning to find that his entire inventory of 230 masks had sold out overnight, according to *Sports Illustrated*. Resourceful Eagles fans started buying their other breeds of dog masks and turned Lincoln Financial Field into a veritable kennel. The company rushed to make more, and those sold out, too.

"I would hope it's like *The Purge*, minus the violence," said Long, referencing the 2013 horror movie featuring gangs of masked killers.

Long joked that neither he nor Johnson received a cut of the mask profits from Amazon, which ended up proving "bad business." Johnson made up for it by selling a T-shirt that read "Home Dogs Gonna Eat" over an image of Johnson and Long in their Eagles gear and dog masks. All proceeds went to Philadelphia schools.

As much as the Eagles tried touting the company line forwarded by Pederson—that it didn't bother them to be seen as the underdogs—it clearly rankled them. They thought they deserved more respect. It's become a trope in professional sports to say "Nobody believes in us," and even favorites sometimes break it out. But the Eagles had good reason to believe that no one did, in fact, believe in them—that's all they heard since Wentz's injury. The masks were a fun but meaningful way of stuffing their noses—or latex dog tongues, in this case—in the faces of the naysayers.

"When did Carson go down?" Pederson asked in his postgame news conference. "Since that point, no one has given us a chance. Nobody has given us a chance. And I understand, Carson's a great player. But every week, our guys are hearing the same thing, that now we are all of a sudden not good enough. We're 13–3 and have the best record in football, we've got home-field advantage throughout. . . . I mean, the guys are going to motivate themselves just based on what they have done and heard for the last month of football. Listen, it really doesn't matter what you guys talk about because that locker room in there is united, and I'll go to bat for every one of those guys, and I'll go to war with every one of those guys in that dressing room."

The underdog story only added to this team's allure, as the city of Philadelphia and all its sports teams always seemed more comfortable in that role. There's a reason why there's a statue of Rocky at the Art Museum, and why Vince Papale, the home-grown inspiration for the movie *Invincible*, is so beloved in Philadelphia. So many residents in the region derive their identity from their sports teams. They had watched all their division rivals win multiple Super Bowls each—from Dallas to New York to Washington. The Eagles were the only NFC East team without a ring. Eagles fans have fallen in love with many Eagles teams since the franchise's inception in the 1930s, but there was something especially endearing about this 2017 group. They were historic underdogs who lost so many key players to injury but survived with a resilience and a toughness that engendered a new height of pride among the fans.

"I think we embody what our city is," Malcolm Jenkins said. "We're a bunch of guys [that] don't care about the glitz and glamour. Very blue collar. We enjoy a fight. We talk a little trash. And we fly around and hit people. We don't really care about the big plays. We enjoy the scrap. We don't want everyone to hype us up. We want to prove it every time we step on the field."

They didn't need anyone else to believe in them. Before games, when Jenkins tried to rally his teammates, he ended his pregame talk the same way Brian Dawkins once did. Jenkins called out, "One, two, three," and his teammates responded, "We all we got!" Jenkins followed with "four, five, six," and his teammates concluded, "We all we need!" This rallying cry became more than just another cheer for the Eagles. It defined their ethos.

"From the beginning, we didn't feel like anybody gave us a chance. We felt like we were underdogs," Jenkins said. "The questions were, is this a rebuilding year or a building year? What's [quarterback] Carson going to be? What is the defense going to be? So we always focused on the guys we had in the huddle. So I think that mentality . . . [has] been handy for us all year. Losing the amount of guys that we've lost and facing a lot the adversity that we have, to have that mentality that we are sufficient, that the guys we have in this room can get it done, no matter what's in front of us, has kind of been the storyline of this team. Obviously, I think everybody has kind of embraced that mentality."

COX: A MAN ON A MISSION

The day that changed Fletcher Cox's career—and changed the way he would be viewed around the NFL—came in June 2016. Cox was under the hood of a race car in Yazoo City, Mississippi, when he got a phone call from his agent to discuss a contract extension with the Eagles. Cox, who grew up in a three-bedroom trailer with his mother and three siblings, agreed to a six-year, $103-million contract with $63 million guaranteed—the biggest ever for a nonquarterback in franchise history. He was twenty-five years old and already viewed as one of the league's best defensive linemen. This contract cemented that status. It also raised the stakes.

"He's got a chance to be a great player in the history of this franchise," Howie Roseman said when Cox signed the contract.

Before the 2016 season, the Eagles released a promotional video featuring images of the franchise's most storied defensive players. It showed Chuck Bednarik standing over Frank Gifford, Reggie White with a halo around his head, and Brian Dawkins flexing his biceps. Then, in the final cutaway, it showed Cox . This was the company Cox could join, but he still had a ways to go to earn his place.

Teammate Brandon Graham knew what Cox was capable of

accomplishing with the Eagles. "To be a Hall of Famer," he said. "And win a championship, so we can be known forever in Philly."

• • •

Before football camp began every sweltering summer at Yazoo City High School, Coach Tony Woolfolk gathered his players to deliver his annual message: "You got to get out of here."

A similar message was given to students who visited the office of Christy Cader, the school guidance counselor, whose stated objective was to help them try to find a way "out of Yazoo City."

Cox heard the same sentiment from his older brother, Shaddrick, who died in January 2015. Shaddrick fixed cars and helped look after Fletcher. He always told his younger brother to find a career, not a job, and to learn about the world beyond the confines of Yazoo's Haley Barbour Parkway and Jerry Clower Boulevard.

"I just wanted to make sure he had what I didn't have," Shaddrick said in 2012. "For him to come from a small town like this, a lot of kids don't get a chance."

Yazoo City is a small town of about eleven-thousand people one hour from Jackson, Mississippi. It has a charming Main Street, with storefronts painted blue, yellow, orange, green, and pink. But cross the bridge to Jonestown, where Cox lived, and it was a different story. On a Wednesday afternoon in October 2012, Woolfolk found teenagers skipping school, shuffling past boarded-up homes. He saw former high school football players who now sell drugs.

"This is where Bug is from," Woolfolk said, referring to Cox's nickname of Bug Eye in Yazoo City.

Woolfolk passed vacant sheds on Martin Luther King Jr. Avenue and pointed to a small bridge. No loitering is allowed on the bridge, but that's where Woolfolk often found "Two-Two," a one-time player of his who had stood 6-foot-7 and 300 pounds a few years earlier in high school. Woolfolk once imagined Two-Two playing for Ole Miss or Mississippi State, but the kid never graduated high school, and instead became Woolfolk's cautionary tale. Woolfolk told his players they could become another Cox, or they could become another Two-Two.

There's a federal prison near Yazoo City that's one of the area's biggest employers. Job candidates must pass a drug test and have a good credit score to gain employment—both often disqualifications for many whom Woolfolk knew in Yazoo City.

"There's nothing here for [Cox]," Woolfolk said. "There's no industry. You just get caught up and get lost in the shuffle. He can come back, like he comes back now, and they love him."

Of course, Cox possessed rare ability. At his first practice as a freshman at Yazoo City High School, Woolfolk turned to an assistant coach and said, "Everybody in the country is going to want this kid!" Though Cox wasn't the only one who was big and fast, others didn't share his resolve.

"Fletcher got himself where he is today," Cader said. "He had people behind him and supporting him and helping him, but I didn't do for him what I wouldn't have done for any of them. But he just listened."

Cox is not much of a talker. He is a listener. It was his advice to students at a May 2012 banquet in Yazoo City. Cader kept a newspaper clipping on the wall in her office from Cox's draft day with the Eagles. She wanted that to be an example for her students.

"A lot of these kids don't have a ticket out of here," Cader said. "We all saw [football] as [Cox's] ticket out."

• • •

Cox earned his contract extension with the Eagles because he played defensive tackle better than almost anyone else in the world, not because he possessed rare leadership ability or acted as the face of the franchise. However, the best players—and highest-paid players—are often thrust into leadership roles whether they have that natural ability or not. Cox endured criticism from some reporters when he skipped voluntary workouts during the spring of 2017, the argument being that he had a responsibility to attend given his stature on the team.

Those debates were long forgotten by January 2018, when Cox played like the $103-million man. In the Falcons game, Cox played 90 percent of the snaps and finished with one sack, two quarterback hits, and two tackles that resulted in lost yards. Those statistics, while good, did not do his performance justice. Afterward, Doug Pederson called Cox "a man on a mission." Graham said it was "the best I've ever seen him play." Stats aside, Cox often draws a double-team which helps the linemen next to him be more effective. When he penetrates from an interior spot, the quarterback does not have space to step up into the pocket, and the defensive ends have an easier path to him. The linebackers behind Cox can run free whenever Cox occupies multiple blockers, which is often. The secondary benefits from the quarterback throwing the ball early because of Cox's pressure. Those plays never show up on the box score for Cox. But when the defense thrives, it's often because Cox dominates.

"It sparks a fire under their ass," Cox said. "When you got the big dog up front playing at a really high level, I think it's contagious. You saw it. You had everyone making plays."

Jim Schwartz countered that Cox played that way all season; the bigger stage just drew more attention. Like Graham said two years earlier, Cox had the potential to become a Hall of Famer and help bring Philadelphia a championship. He achieved the championship, but he didn't have to say much to do it. He just needed to play.

"I said to myself, 'Go out and take over this game, and everybody else will follow,'" Cox said. "I think it kind of rubbed off."

THE FOLES-KEENUM CONNECTION

One night after the Eagles' last-minute goal line stand against Atlanta, they would all watch the other NFC divisional round playoff game: the New Orleans Saints versus the Minnesota Vikings. The winner of that game would visit Lincoln Financial Field one week later to play the Eagles for the NFC Championship.

It appeared that the Saints had the game won until the Vikings pulled it out in dramatic fashion. Out of timeouts at his own 39-yard line with ten seconds left, Vikings quarterback Case Keenum hurled a last-ditch pass to wide receiver Stefon Diggs who was supposed to get out of bounds quickly to set up a field goal attempt. But when the Saints defender whiffed on the tackle, Diggs turned upfield and ran along the sideline all the way to the end zone for a walk-off touchdown. The Vikings were coming to Philly. And if they could beat the Eagles, they would become the first team ever to play the Super Bowl in their home stadium.

Doug Pederson watched the Vikings-Saints game from his office. Most Eagles players watched from home and exchanged text messages. Once their opponent was set, the Eagles planned to regroup and find a way to channel the emotion from the Falcons win into another productive week.

"That's the challenge, in probably our case and in the Vikings' case, is coming off these emotional, close victories, and then having to turn around and do it again," Pederson said. "I've just got to make sure that I continue to stay aggressive with the week of practice and prepare the guys just like we have the last couple of weeks, and just try to stay in our lane and try to block out some of the noise."

The Vikings were installed as the favorites, with the initial spread set at 3½ points. The Eagles certainly took that as disrespect, yet again, although there were more believers in them now than one week earlier. In addition to the spread, oddsmakers set the over-under for the game at thirty-eight points, supporting the expectation that the game would be a defensive slugfest. While the Vikings had the NFL's top-ranked defense, the Eagles had the fourth-ranked defense but were significantly better at home.

The biggest challenge for the Eagles would be converting third downs. The Vikings held opponents to 25.2 percent on the "money down"—the best percentage since the NFL started keeping track in 1991. The Eagles, who needed long drives to score against Atlanta, would likely have a harder time going on those fourteen-play, run-heavy, clock-bleeding possessions against Minnesota. They knew they'd need the passing game to step up, too.

"That's the challenge [in] going up against one of the better defenses in the league," Frank Reich said. "And so I think . . . we have to . . . [find] ways to make a few chunk plays here and there."

The Vikings' offense, which ranked No. 11 in the NFL, was also going to present a challenge. Like the Eagles, they were led by a backup quarterback in Case Keenum. Besides the similarity of sending second-stringers to the penultimate game of the season, the teams' quarterback situations were connected in other ways, too.

• • •

When Chip Kelly traded Foles to the St. Louis Rams for Sam Bradford in March 2015, the Rams hoped Foles would become their franchise quarterback. His backup on the Rams was Case Keenum.

Foles didn't even last a full season as the Rams' starter, getting benched and replaced by Keenum before Week 11. But the Rams weren't sold on either of them, and traded up to the No. 1 pick in the 2016 draft to acquire Jared Goff. Keenum started the 2016 season for the Rams until Goff was ready to take over in November.

In Philadelphia, Pederson liked Bradford but did not view him as the team's quarterback of the future. That would be Carson Wentz. Bradford was supposed to be Philadelphia's placeholder quarterback throughout the 2016 season, but when the Minnesota Vikings' starting quarterback Teddy Bridgewater suffered a gruesome injury one week before the 2016 season began, the Vikings needed a quarterback and traded for Bradford. Wentz became the Eagles opening-day starter, and the Eagles brought in Foles one year later as Wentz's backup.

Bradford had solidified himself as the starting quarterback for the Vikings entering the 2017 season. With Bridgewater still on the mend, the Vikings signed Keenum as Bradford's backup. After Bradford reinjured his knee in September, Keenum took over as the starter. When the Vikings kept winning with Keenum, they didn't make a change. And of course, three months after Keenum took over for the Vikings, Foles replaced the injured Wentz as the Eagles' starter.

"I know this is what all you guys predicted back in the day, was a Foles vs. Keenum NFC Championship," Keenum joked with reporters. "So good job to all you guys who predicted that."

Keenum called Foles one of his best friends, and they remained in contact throughout the season to discuss common opponents and their families. They're both from Texas and are around the same age—Keenum is eleven months older than Foles—and they both believed they could be starting quarterbacks even when the league seemed to insist otherwise. Foles said the lesson from their matchup was that "no matter what happens, you've just got to keep believing in yourself."

But in all honesty, they never could have guessed they would reunite as unexpected starters facing off in the NFC championship game.

"Life is crazy, this game is crazy," Foles said. "All the parallels that are going on . . . just shows why everyone loves this game. It's not just the playing, but all the moving pieces and everything. It's been pretty wild to look at it that way."

VIKING QUEST

In the moments before the first NFC Championship game in Philadelphia since January 2005, Malcolm Jenkins told his teammates not to think about their opponent. This game was not about the Vikings, a formidable foe with their top-ranked defense and miraculous victory one week earlier.

"It's all about us!" Jenkins screamed in the pregame huddle, as captured by the Eagles website. "I don't know if you all realize, but this is the last time this team . . . is going to play on this field together. This team won't ever be the same now. So this is our last chance! The disrespect will not be tolerated! All year they told you what you couldn't do, what you couldn't be. We're four quarters away from being a . . . legendary team! . . . We're four quarters from being up there! Being up there in those rafters where they can't take us down!"

A Super Bowl bid was on the line. The Eagles could make history. But you wouldn't know it by the way the game started.

• • •

The Vikings drove 75 yards over nine plays on their opening drive to take a quick 7–0 lead. If the Vikings were going to score with such ease, it would be a long day for the Eagles. And those fears only grew when the Eagles were forced to punt after four plays on their opening possession, giving the ball right back to Minnesota.

After making one third-down conversion, the Vikings faced another—a third-and-8—from their 41-yard line. The Eagles defense was built on their pass rush, and on obvious passing downs they would often bounce Brandon Graham from defensive end to defensive tackle in place of Tim Jernigan, and insert Chris Long into the game where Graham typically plays.

"If you need me, I'll come under," Long told Graham before the third-down pass rush, as heard on NFL Films. "But I'm gonna try to get up the field."

When Keenum received the snap, Long sprinted past the right tackle, rushed deep into the pocket behind the quarterback, extended his right arm toward Keenum and made enough contact to disrupt the pass, which whimpered in the air well short of its intended target.

"Oh man," Patrick Robinson thought, "it's going to be an easy pick."

Robinson camped under the ball at midfield, secured the interception, and then took off running. He called for blocks as his fellow defensive backs tried to clear space. Two hours before the game, Robinson told himself, "If I get a pick, I'm not going out of bounds." That thought entered his mind during the return as he crossed the width of the field and raced into the end zone for a touchdown. After the extra point, the game was tied at 7–7 and the crowd came alive. Howie Roseman's two signings at the league meeting in March proved invaluable on that momentum-changing play. In fact, every touchdown and forced turnover during the NFC Championship game involved a player Roseman acquired during the 2017 off-season.

"When you get a pick-six like that and get yourself back into the game, yeah, guys begin to feed off that and feed off the crowd," Pederson said after the game.

The fans didn't sit down after the defense forced a three-and-out on the Vikings' next possession, and they erupted when LeGarrette Blount rushed for an 11-yard touchdown early in the second quarter to give the Eagles their first lead of the game at 14–7.

Down by seven, Minnesota drove to the Eagles' 17-yard line late in the second quarter, threatening to tie it back up. But on third-and-5, rookie defensive end Derek Barnett—whom the Eagles drafted with the first-round pick they acquired from Minnesota in the Sam Bradford trade—pummeled Keenum from behind and knocked the ball onto the ground, and Long immediately pounced on it to recover the fumble. Minnesota didn't score, and the Eagles made them pay.

"We're about to go up 21–7 right now," Graham said on the sideline. "Then it's our game."

On a third-and-10 from the Eagles' 47-yard line, with Foles under duress, Alshon Jeffery broke through coverage and ran free down the field. Foles spotted him and hurled a deep pass into the hands of the Eagles' top receiver, who caught it unimpeded and jogged into the end zone.

"It was sort of a broken play where they thought they probably had a sack," Foles said. "I was able to get out and Alshon made an amazing play. He saw the coverage and he sort of approached it like a scramble drill."

Jake Elliott added a 38-yard field goal as the first half clock expired to bring the score to 24–7. The fans were confident that the Eagles were on the road to victory, but the team wanted more. Running backs coach Duce Staley shouted on the sideline, "Just don't be satisfied where we are right now!" Pederson wasn't. On the opening drive of the second half, the head coach called a play he hadn't used all season.

With the ball at the Vikings' 41-yard line and the Eagles starting a fresh set of downs, Foles was surprised to hear the call—flea flicker!—that came through his helmet speaker. He tried not to smile as he relayed the play in the huddle. Foles took the snap and handed the ball to Corey Clement, who pitched it right back to Foles. Torrey Smith ran past the cornerback along the left sideline as Foles hurled the ball deep and high toward the goal-line pylon. It was as perfect a pass a quarterback could throw, placed where only his receiver could catch it. Smith secured the ball and fell into the end zone to give the Eagles a 31–7 lead. Foles had never run a flea-flicker in a game before. The Eagles practiced it a few times, but Pederson waited for the right moment to call it.

"I wasn't saving it," Pederson said. "You don't just pull them out and think, 'I'm going to run it this week.' There's got to be a reason for running a gadget play. And I just felt that as I game-planned this week and studied our formations and some of the things that we did, I felt like we'd get an opportunity to at least attempt the play."

The rout was on. The Vikings had not allowed more than thirty-one points all season. Yet the Eagles reached that number with more than twenty-five minutes left to play.

"We ain't done bombing on their ass either!" wide receiver Mack Hollins said on the sideline, as captured by NFL Films.

Everything was falling in the Eagles' direction. On their next drive, the Vikings thought they had scored a touchdown on a fourth down, but an official review determined the pass was incomplete. Instead of getting points, the Vikings turned the ball over on downs. Foles responded by leading the Eagles on another touchdown drive, once again finding Alshon Jeffery for yet another third-down score against the NFL's best third-down defense. After their opening-drive touchdown, the Vikings did not score again. When the game ended with a final score of 38–7, the party was already starting in Philadelphia. Chants could be heard throughout the stadium: "Super Bowl! Super Bowl!"

It was a dominant performance. Foles, who was a cause for concern just two weeks earlier, finished 26 of 33 for 352 yards and three touchdowns. His 141.3 quarterback rating was the third-best all-time in a championship game.

"That's the way to shut their ass up!" Kenjon Barner said to Foles on the sideline. "What they gonna say now?"

"I'm so proud of you, bro!" Long told Foles. "I always believed in you."

Brent Celek, then the longest-tenured Eagle, embraced Pederson. "Can you believe it?" he screamed. Pederson nodded.

"I can, too!" Celek said.

Graham turned to Long and exclaimed, "This is the moment we've been waiting on!"

"It only gets better," Long replied.

• • •

Once the clock struck zero and cameramen rushed onto the field, Keenum sprinted toward Foles. He knew everything that Foles had gone through to reach this point.

"You don't know how happy I am for you," Keenum said to Foles. "Dude, nobody deserves this more than you."

Confetti fell from the sky at Lincoln Financial Field. All the fans stayed at their seats, though few sat in them. A makeshift podium was set up for the trophy presentation. FOX analyst Terry Bradshaw started a stadium-wide rendition of the Eagles' fight song.

"Fly, Eagles Fly! On the road to victory!"

Bradshaw then presented the George Halas Trophy to Jeffrey Lurie. It was the second time Lurie ever hoisted that hardware that is given annually to the NFC champion.

"The resilience this group of men has is unequaled," Lurie said over the stadium's speakers. "What we've gone through, I've never seen anything like it. This group of men wants to win so badly for Philadelphia. These fans are the most passionate fans in sports. And by the way, we're not only going to Minneapolis—we have something to do in Minneapolis. One more win!"

The team rushed into the locker room and cranked up their unofficial anthem—Meek Mill's "Dreams and Nightmare"—to maximum volume. Music pulsated through the air as players danced and sang along. Lurie danced again, too, just as he did one week earlier. Pederson came into the room and gathered his team together, waiting for the music to die down to address the group.

"We're going to the Super Bowl, boys!" he said.

The players started chanted, "We goin' to the 'ship!" in response.

"From the bottom of my heart, I love every one of you—coaches, players, personnel—in the entire organization," Pederson said, as captured by the Eagles website. "The amount of work that has gone into what you have accomplished this season, and guess what? We are not done . . ."

"Yet!" the players replied in unison.

"We've got one more football game to play this season," Pederson continued. "We play this game to play on the world's biggest stage."

Jenkins followed Pederson, as he always does. And he wanted to make sure his teammates knew this was not just about reaching the Super Bowl.

"We ain't just going. We're going to win," Jenkins said with his teammates huddled around him. "We don't put in all this work just to get here and celebrate. We're going to win. Everybody in this world that talked bad about us and doubted us, all we did was stick together, love each other, and have fun playing."

When the locker room opened to reporters, the players still danced and sang. There was a great joy that came from achieving something so elusive, especially being so disrespected along the way. But they also knew the season was not yet finished. There were two weeks left and one more game to play.

"We're going to the stinking Super Bowl, and that's all we need to know," Pederson said. "I was just so proud of them for the season so far. We still have some unfinished business, obviously. But we're going to pack our bags and head to Minneapolis."

ROBINSON AND LONG: REWARDS FROM MARCH

Back in March, when the Eagles signed Chris Long and Patrick Robinson on the same day at the league meeting in Phoenix, the moves did not do much to move the needle. They were nice veteran signings, but didn't appear to be the type of transactions that could tilt a playoff game.

As it turned out, that was one of the most important days in the Eagles' roster-building efforts. Both Long and Robinson became key players for the Eagles throughout the season, and were both especially clutch in the NFC Championship game against the Vikings.

• • •

Long, the No. 2 overall draft pick in 2008, played the first eight years of his career for the St. Louis Rams. He never made the playoffs with them, and, in fact, they never even finished with a winning record. He was a productive player for the Rams and signed two lucrative contracts with them, but he was ultimately released in 2016. He then signed a one-year contract with the New England Patriots and was a contributor on their 2016 Super Bowl team.

The only downside to Long's New England experience was that the defensive scheme did not maximize his skill set, and he believed he was a better player than what the film revealed. He appreciated his time in New England, but had reached a career crossroads. He was thirty-two. He had earned a fortune. He had won a Super Bowl. What remained for Long was to find a better football fit, and so he decided preemptively not to re-sign with New England. As he wrote on Instragram at the time, "This has zero to do with money. . . . I want to get back to being the player I was before. . . . I'm itching to do what I do best."

With Long still available a few weeks into free agency, and the Eagles needing defensive-line depth after releasing Connor Barwin, Long phoned Howie Roseman looking for an opportunity to play in Philadelphia, according to ESPN.

"It wasn't about anything other than getting back to the player I was, or as close as you can be to that, and that's something I'm driven to do," Long said when he signed.

And that's exactly what happened. Long was a key part of the Eagles defense, totaling five sacks and four forced fumbles during the regular season and raising his play in the postseason. He did not start, but rather played a situational role in the defensive end rotation, which allowed him to remain fresh and most effective. He felt like himself again on the field, and it showed in his performance. But that wasn't enough; he wanted to be more than just a football player.

Long's life changed in the winter of 2013. After completing his fifth season in the NFL, Long traveled to Tanzania to climb Mount Kilimanjaro with teammate James Hall. He wanted to experience "something out of my comfort zone."

"I really enjoyed that," Long said, "but what I saw was an opportunity to really improve the world."

At the hotel bar after the climb, Long heard a voice behind him call his name. Who could possibly know him at a Tanzania bar? He turned around to see sportscaster Joe Buck standing with Doug Pitt, brother of Brad Pitt and U.S. Goodwill Ambassador to Tanzania. Buck made introductions all around, and before he knew it Long was engaged in an extended conversation about water-borne illness in Africa. Pitt happened to be there overseeing the construction of a sustainable well, and Buck was along to assist.

"It hit me that water would be as good a way to change the world as any cause that I encountered," Long said.

Upon returning home, Long began to think about what he could do to help, and in 2015 he started the Waterboys Initiative to bring clean water to rural communities in East Africa. To date, the organization has installed forty deep-bore wells that serve more than 150,000 people. Long hosted a fundraiser during the 2017 season at Del Frisco's restaurant in Center City, Philadelphia, that raised $80,000. Some of his teammates attended the event to support Long, who quickly became a popular figure in the locker room.

While many Eagles fans do not know of Long's work in Africa, they all know of his commitment to donate his entire $1 million salary in 2017 for educational equity in the three cities he's played in, plus his hometown of Charlottesville. This caught the attention of former President Barack Obama, who tweeted out the story of Long's decision. Long was among the Eagles who met with lawmakers to discuss criminal justice reform, and he's also met with NFL leadership to discuss broader social justice initiatives.

"He's someone who walks the walk," Malcolm Jenkins said. "For all the endeavors he's in, it's really impressive. And even the things he might not be involved in, he's willing to listen and learn. The amount of empathy he's able to give is something that's missing right now in society. I haven't had a teammate quite like him."

Long's outlook on how to use his platform changed throughout his career. The son of NFL Hall of Famer Howie Long, a longtime supporter of the Boys & Girls Clubs of America, Chris saw the benefits of philanthropy from a young age. Chris's determination to stimulate change began as a high school student in Charlottesville, Virginia, where he mentored underprivileged kids. For years he squirmed at the notion of seeking publicity for his philanthropic endeavors, until he realized how he could leverage the publicity to greater support them.

"I almost resented it when people did things publicly," Long said. "But then I kind of started to see the value of getting more of a return on your investment in whatever your cause is in involving fans and using your platform."

Long engaged fans and players in Philly and across the league to match his game-check donations with pledges of their own, creating a healthy competition that helped raise more than $1 million for educational equity. By Long's sixth season in the NFL, he realized he was getting older and that his platform would only last for so long.

"I've been lucky," Long told reporters. "This isn't a heroic effort. I just really believe my platform is going to shrink from here on out. If I'm not playing football in a couple of years and I do this, it's not going to have the same effect. It's evidenced by the fans that have gotten behind it and the money we're going to be able to raise."

Long's off-field profile had never been bigger. Even though it was his first year in Philadelphia, Long quickly became a high-profile player with the fan base. He achieved his desire to be known as "more than a football player," and he owes his advocacy to a chance encounter in a Tanzania bar.

"As a young player in the league, he was very mindful of wanting to not only impact his community, but impact the world," Howie Long said. "Climbing Kilimanjaro . . . is a metaphor for his life. What's the next mountain to climb?"

• • •

Patrick Robinson spends idle hours at home watching football videos on repeat. He flips through footage of other cornerbacks looking for any tendency that could help him improve his own game. He watches until his eyes get heavy and he loses focus, then drifts asleep for the night. In addition to watching film to enhance his play, he could often be found at his locker after practice with an electrical stimulation device wired to his leg muscles to enhance his health and avoid nagging injuries.

Robinson, who turned thirty during Week 1 of the 2017 season, was a 2010 first-round pick. But by the time he joined the Eagles, it was his fourth team in four years. He had become the definition of a journeyman, and he signed a modest contract in hopes of proving to the league—and to himself—that he could find the consistency that had eluded him. He did just that in 2017, and he credited his success to two pieces of advice he wished someone had given his younger self.

"Make sure you take care of your body," Robinson said, "and make sure you watch film."

During the summer, it appeared Robinson might not even make the team. He struggled in training camp as an outside cornerback. But the August trade for Ronald Darby meant Robinson no longer had a starting job on the outside. Coordinator Jim Schwartz then moved him to the slot, where he had played sporadically throughout his career. When he was able to focus entirely on that position, he thrived. He ended up playing the position better than the Eagles could have imagined, giving the defense high-level production at a crucial position and allowing Jenkins to take on a more versatile role. Robinson played 69 percent of the defensive snaps in the regular season, and 70 percent in the postseason. His achievement with the Eagles validated his standing around the NFL going forward.

"I try not to think about the past," Robinson said. "I try to focus on the now. When you start thinking about other things, that clouds your mind about doing your job right now. . . . Don't worry about too much.

Just do my job. Execute everything they ask of me. And I'll be fine."

So Robinson's routine never changed. He watched game film daily, and he focused on treating his body after every game and practice. He played in all sixteen games for just the third time in his eight-year career. And he played three more games in the postseason, too.

"If you're not available, they can't use you," Robinson said. "If they can't use you, they don't need you. It's as simple as that."

CRISCO CELEBRATIONS

A group of Philadelphia police officers were given a new nickname on January 21: "Crisco Cops." These were the officers tasked with slathering Crisco, the popular cooking grease, onto light poles in Center City, Philadelphia, on the morning of the Eagles-Vikings game in an attempt to keep fans from climbing them in celebration. Of course, it didn't dissuade fans from doing just that during the postgame celebrations—it just raised the level of difficulty. Many determined fanatics made their way up the poles on that euphoric night in Philadelphia.

An estimated 5,000 to 10,000 people flooded Center City, with thousands more filling other pockets in the city and its suburbs. Broad Street, the major North-South arterial road in Philadelphia, was closed for five blocks while fans covered the road. Open container rules were suspended, and the police allowed the fans to party with little intervention.

The city's subway trains overflowed with fans carrying the party from the stadium back into Center City and beyond. Chants of "Super Bowl! Super Bowl!" echoed from the subway entrances. At the Ellsworth-Federal station, one fan wearing a Brian Dawkins jersey tried to pump up subway riders while running alongside a departing train. He was so focused on the fans inside the train that he did not see the support pillar in front of him, leading to a head-on collision that dropped him like a brick. The video went viral.

Eagles fever quickly spread throughout the city. There would be two weeks of growing excitement. The underdogs had captivated the region. And if they could win one more game, it would prompt the biggest party Philadelphia had ever seen.

• • •

While the city partied in the streets after the Vikings game, Eagles center Jason Kelce went home, sat in the shower, and burst into tears. He reflected on various points in his life when he had reached a crossroads and needed to overcome an obstacle. He didn't receive a college scholarship out of high school in the Cleveland area, but instead walked onto the team at the University of Cincinnati. He was a sixth-round draft pick who turned himself into one of the Eagles' longest-tenured players and one of Philadelphia's most beloved athletes. And at one point, he had faced the real possibility that he might need to play elsewhere.

By his own admission, Kelce had a poor season in 2016. He had been a starter on the Eagles since 2011 and developed into one of the best centers in the league. But after his subpar 2016, for the first time in his career, doubt crept into Kelce's mind. He experienced the unsettling feeling of not knowing whether he can play well enough to keep his job. Throughout the 2017 off-season, there were rumors that Kelce could be released or traded. But the Eagles kept him, and Kelce had the best season of his career in 2017. So after the Eagles won the NFC Championship and secured a spot in the Super Bowl, he thought about all it took for him to reach that point. He knew his teammates shared similar stories, and he thought about them, too.

He also thought about the fans. For seven years, whenever someone met Kelce, all he heard was, "Just get us that one. We've been waiting forever."

They would need to wait only two more weeks. And then, Kelce would give them a rallying cry for the rest of their lives.

PART 4

PHILLY SPECIAL

The Super Bowl

PLAYING GOLIATH

Hours before the Eagles dominated the Vikings, the New England Patriots punched their ticket to the Super Bowl with a second-half comeback over the Jacksonville Jaguars. What else was new? The Patriots are a 21st-century dynasty in American sports, having made seven consecutive AFC championship games; three Super Bowls in four years; and eight Super Bowls since the 2000 season—five of which they won.

The Super Bowl had almost become a February tradition for the Pats, but it was far from routine for the Birds. But the newcomers had plenty of time to prepare, with two weeks between the championship weekend and the Super Bowl. They spent the first week in Philadelphia, then flew to Minnesota a week before the game. League-mandated events were scheduled each day that disrupted their typical schedule, but the coaching staff was prepared to mitigate the distractions.

"Of all the things we've been through this season, the ups and downs, the highs and lows, and sitting here right now, you're two weeks away from playing in the Super Bowl," Doug Pederson said in the first team meeting during the Super Bowl bye week, as captured by the team website. "It's one thing to be excited about playing in this game. 'Oh, we can take a breath, we've arrived.' But no, no. We're going up there to win the game. We're in the Super Bowl, but you're not playing the Super Bowl. You're playing the damn New England Patriots. Another faceless opponent. So I need everybody's attention today and the next eleven days until we play this game. We focus on the New England Patriots. One more game. And you don't make it any bigger than that."

Pederson often spoke to his team about the concept of a "faceless opponent." The idea was to prevent his players from focusing on the reputations and win-loss records of the upcoming opponents. Whether it's a dynasty or a perennial loser, Pederson wanted the same level of focus from his own squad. That's harder to do against the Patriots, whose consistent success could affect the psyche of even the most confident group. Pederson admitted that dealing with the Patriots mystique was a "real issue," knowing the Patriots have "been there" and "done it." But he did not harp on the Patriots with his players. Instead, he did the opposite.

"If I make this all about them, we're in trouble," Pederson said in his first news conference during the Super Bowl practice week. "Everything is going to be written about it. Everything has been written about it, talked about it, discussed, debated. And it's about us. And I'll keep saying that. It's what we do and how well we execute. I can't worry about that."

Patriots quarterback Tom Brady and Head Coach Bill Belichick are the best quarterback-coach combination in NFL history. During quiet moments, Pederson allowed his mind to drift and wonder whether he and Carson Wentz could one day enter that discussion. The consistency and dominance of Brady and Belichick were something Pederson hoped to emulate. Brady was forty years old and an eighteen-year NFL veteran, yet he had one of his finest seasons in 2017. It was good enough, in fact, for Brady to be named the league's MVP for the third time. Wentz might have won the award if he had remained healthy, and the argument could be made that it should have gone to Wentz anyway.

Malcolm Jenkins's collection of notebooks included "pretty detailed" information about Brady from the three games he faced the quarterback. What stood out most to Jenkins was the way Brady and the Patriots adjusted during the game. He knew that if the Eagles defense used an effective strategy, Brady could make changes "middrive" and "midquarter" to turn the table and exploit favorable matchups elsewhere.

"So everything that my book might say going into the game, three drives in, you've got to throw it out because they've all been changed," Jenkins said. "You have to have that flexibility on defense [against Brady]."

The Eagles defense believed they had the personnel and the plan to do so. Defensive Coordinator Jim Schwartz often mixed personnel groupings on defense depending on the opposing offense. In the four games leading up to the Super Bowl, the Eagles' defense limited opponents to 8.25 points per game.

Of course, all four of those games were at home. It would be a different dynamic in Minneapolis. Neutral-site games—especially the Super Bowl—are difficult to predict since so much of the crowd is there for the experience and not necessarily to cheer their hearts out for either team. Both Philadelphia and Boston are among the NFL's most passionate sports cities. However, New England fans had ample opportunities in recent years to spend a lot of money to travel to watch their team play in the Super Bowl.

This was not the case for Eagles fans who had waited more than a decade to see their team in the big game again, and had waited forever to see them win it. After the NFC Championship, airfare from Philadelphia to Minneapolis skyrocketed. When flights filled up, additional flights were added in an effort to accommodate the growing throng of Eagles fans. An airline ticket that normally cost a few hundred dollars was now going for four figures. Ironically, fans were spending that kind of money to visit Minnesota in February, when temperatures there often dipped below 0 degrees. The Eagles wanted to use the crowd to their advantage, as they had done on the road a couple of times throughout the season. Schwartz in particular hoped that the crowd would lean toward the Eagles, as defenses benefit the most from crowd noise when offensive players can't hear their quarterback.

"I think that the fans that are able to make it to Minneapolis, just like the fans that made it to Los Angeles and so many other places along the way for us, they will turn it into a home crowd for us," Schwartz said. "Our Eagles fans travel. It's tough travel. The Super Bowl's a tough ticket. But I think that we're going to see a lot of green and we're going to hear a lot of people singing our fight song, as opposed [to the Patriots' fight song]. So, I'm hoping that it's not a neutral site."

Despite the Patriots' credentials, the Eagles were not intimidated. In fact, they wanted to play Goliath. What better way to become the champs than to beat the defending champs?

"Tom Brady, pretty boy Tom Brady—he's, hey, the best quarterback of all time," Lane Johnson told reporters. "Nothing more I would like than to dethrone that guy."

FROM WENTZ WE CAME

Carson Wentz walked off the field after the NFC championship with a cane in his right hand. He still celebrated on the field with his teammates, hoisting the championship trophy and hugging Nick Foles and slapping hands with Mike Trout. But he was not the star of this show. Wentz admitted he wished he was the one out there. That's natural for a quarterback. But he also emphasized it did not detract from the way he felt about Foles or his teammates.

"As humans, we all want to be the competitors that we are and be out there on the field," Wentz said. "Every time the offense runs out on the field on Sundays, it's tough. It hits me a little bit. But then I'm in it because I love these guys and I'm a part of this team just as much as anybody else. I get involved in the game and then it all kind of goes away."

Wentz would have been the story of the Super Bowl had he played. His potential would have been juxtaposed against Tom Brady, the standard-bearer for NFL quarterbacks and one Wentz long admired. The game would be played just across the state line from Wentz's native North Dakota. It's hard to go from star to spectator, and Wentz knew the world would be watching how he handled it.

"To me, one of the greatest things about a person that you can say is when you see him celebrating somebody else's success," offensive coordinator Frank Reich said. "Human nature tells you that's hard to do, and it's been fun to see those two do that. It's fun to see Carson have the maturity to truly celebrate Nick's success and understanding how he's helping this team, and also with the frustration knowing that he wants to be in there."

Wentz maintained a behind-the-scenes role leading up to the Super Bowl. He still attended the 6 a.m. quarterback meetings alongside Foles and Nate Sudfeld. Although Doug Pederson adjusted the offense to accentuate Foles's strengths, Wentz still prepared each week as if he was the starting quarterback. He offered input on the game plan. Wentz also attended the full-team meeting each morning, but missed the installation meetings while rehabbing. He noted that he's not the coach and only voiced his opinion in "small pieces." But he still made sure he was at the facility each day, never allowing his presence to be missed. And during games, he listened over the headset to the play calls and met with Foles after each possession. Teammates admitted that injured players can sometimes check out, and in the NFL, out of sight usually means out of mind. Wentz did not allow that to happen.

"Just the way he's handled it has been amazing," Foles said. "His support for this team, for me personally, whether it's in our meeting rooms, at walk-throughs, at practice, during the game, it's been outstanding."

There was an interesting tightrope that the quarterbacks walked. The starting quarterback takes on an alpha-dog quality in the locker room, and that mentality always came naturally to Wentz. But there he was, on the day before the Eagles departed for Minneapolis, explaining how Foles is "the guy." And Foles was always sensitive about the label knowing Wentz's role in the organization.

"This is Carson's team," Foles said after Wentz's injury. "I get, 'You're the guy,' but that's how I am: I respect Carson Wentz. I love that guy. I work with him every day and I'm going to give him that respect because he is the franchise quarterback. My job right now as the starting quarterback is to lead these guys on the field, and I'm going to do that. I've been here, I've done that. I know what it entails, I know the responsibility. But this is Carson Wentz's team, and I respect him too much to make that statement."

Tight end Trey Burton, a close friend of Wentz, acknowledged that "in a sense, it's harder to see [the team] succeed not being there, because you always want to have value, you always want to have worth." In his next breath, he pointed out that Wentz is "as happy as can be."

The friendship between the quarterbacks helped. Wentz also knew what Foles had gone through in his career, making it even sweeter to see Foles's success. But teammates and coaches did not want that success to diminish what Wentz had accomplished in 2017. In the waning minutes of the championship game win over Minnesota, Reich looked for Wentz and reiterated the "incredibly important role that he's played in everything, most particularly the fact that that game was played on our turf." The Eagles might not have reached the Super Bowl if they didn't secure home-field advantage. Wentz's MVP-caliber season was the reason they had the best record in the NFC.

And Wentz was only twenty-five. "You've got next year," Alshon Jeffery told him at the practice facility during the Super Bowl bye week. Other teammates also pointed out that Wentz will be in Philadelphia for years to come, and that the organizational standard was now reaching the Super Bowl. Wentz nodded in agreement, adding that the Eagles are "wired for success for a long time." But the only Super Bowl that was a given was this year's, and it was Foles's chance to play hero.

IN FOLES WE TRUST

Leading up to the Super Bowl, Nick Foles used some variation of the same answer when describing the gravity of the game and his journey to reach it: "Live in the moment."

This was how he maintained the necessary equilibrium despite starting the season as a backup and now facing off against the formidable Tom Brady, all just two years after contemplating retirement.

"Just live in the moment," Foles said. "Especially since what I've gone through the last few years, what I've seen. My perspective's changed. . . . I'm really just enjoying the moment, grateful for the moment."

Foles maintains a consistent game-day routine. He wakes up and reads the Bible and writes his thoughts in a journal. He'll feel the game-day butterflies, but knows they'll calm down once the game starts. He takes the first bus to the stadium and goes through a pregame stretching and throwing routine. This became imperative after Foles missed time in the summer due to his elbow injury. Before he steps onto the field, Foles takes a deep breath. It's showtime.

"It slows down. You're just in tune," Foles said. "You don't really see the environment around you. It's probably hard to understand unless you've been there."

Nobody knew how Foles would play in the Super Bowl, his biggest stage yet. In high school, he played in the Texas state championship game at the Alamodome in San Antonio against Carroll High School, Texas's version of the Patriots. He played in big-time college bowl games. In the NFL, he played in Dallas's AT&T Stadium with the NFC East title on the line in 2013. He started three NFL playoff games. There was always a bigger stage. But there was nothing bigger than the one Foles was about to encounter.

Yet Foles also carried a unique perspective. He had nearly left football for good. He would have been happy watching the Super Bowl at his Newport Beach, California, home with his wife and daughter. He had envisioned a life without this, so he was going to enjoy his life with it.

"A lot of people look at this moment and say, 'Wow, aren't you excited you [didn't retire] and are in the Super Bowl?'" Foles said. "I'm grateful to be up here. . . . But at the same time, if I would have made the other decision, my life wouldn't have been a loss."

DOUG PEDERSON'S TIME TO LEAD

Doug Pederson prepared to coach in the Super Bowl against perhaps the greatest coach in NFL history. It was a rapid ascent for someone who was coaching high school football less than ten years earlier.

Soon after Pederson retired from playing in the NFL, he became the head coach at Calvary Baptist Academy in Shreveport, Louisiana, where he had made his off-season home. He coached at Calvary for four years, going 40–11 and twice reaching the state semifinals. He had been on the NFL radar as a potential coach—Andy Reid saw coaching in Pederson's future even during Pederson's playing days—but Pederson didn't plan to make it a quick stop. During his first year at Calvary, the San Francisco 49ers offered Pederson a job. Johnny Booty, Calvary's athletic director and Pederson's boss, didn't want a revolving door in his football program.

"Doug, I don't want to hire you if you'll be gone next year or next week," Booty said.

"I'm only going to take one job if I get an offer," Pederson said. "If Andy Reid calls me, I'm gone."

The job was a great learning experience for Pederson. It put him in the mindset of a coach and taught him how to work with different people who have different interests, from the players to the student body to the teachers to the parents to the administrators. On the field, Pederson needed to realize these were not NFL players he was dealing with. He simplified his concepts. At one point, an assistant coach discussed running a curl-flat play on consecutive downs because it had been working. Pederson said he cannot keep calling the same play. But why not, the assistant asked, if the other team couldn't stop it?

"I think by his second year, he found a good balance of giving us what we could handle, and then backing off a little bit," said Colton Derrick, who played wide receiver for Pederson for four years at Cavalry. "We all knew he was going to go on to do bigger and better things and end up in the pros one day, so it was just a matter of time. But he had to learn how to put it on our knowledge level, and he did a good job of that."

More than Pederson's schemes, his Calvary players remembered the way he could connect with them. He knew what buttons to push, how to rally his players. Calvary trailed by three touchdowns in a game they needed to win in 2007, and starting quarterback Jack Booty (Johnny's son) came back to the sideline after throwing an interception. Describing that pivotal moment, Booty wrote in a text message, "He always had this look when you did something wrong where his chin hits his neck and he tilts his head and looks at you through the corner of his eyes. He stared at me, and I looked back. Then he smiled real big and said, 'Let me know when you're ready to show up.'"

Calvary came from behind to win by twenty-three points, and a week later won the district championship in a game they were expected to lose. The players on the team mentioned Pederson as the difference. He offered an advantage, but they knew it wasn't going to last for long.

In 2009, Reid offered Pederson a quality-control job on the Eagles' staff. When Pederson entered Johnny Booty's office, little needed to be said.

"I got the call, Johnny," Pederson told him.

"Brother, go for it," Booty said.

• • •

By 2017, Pederson had erased any doubts that Philly fans and sports commentators had about him, especially the skepticism about his play-calling and decision-making. In fact, Pederson's play-calling creativity had become an asset for the Eagles. Pederson and offensive coordinator Frank Reich met for ninety minutes the night before games to discuss the play-call sheet. Pederson also explains his emphasis for a given game. In the NFC Championship, Pederson pledged to be aggressive, keep the Vikings off balance, and focus on the unexpected.

Pederson's play-calling style as a head coach was unique and ever-evolving. Reich noted how Pederson's play-calling was "unorthodox, in a good way" because he was willing to defy convention. Throughout 2017, that unorthodox style often paid off. Pederson's coaching staff included two former NFL offensive coordinators, but he did not want to cede the play-calling responsibilities. He wanted to be in control of the game. That's the quarterback in him.

"I think you either have it or you don't," Pederson said. "If you just look at what I've done in two years, you'd probably call me unorthodox with some of the decisions I've made on fourth downs and going for it, two-point conversions, things like that. . . . Sometimes you just don't do the norm, just don't do what everybody expects you to do and sometimes that can help you."

Pederson wanted to be aggressive when he became a head coach, believing that such an approach could resonate with players. But the organization also wanted to make data-based decisions, using analytics to help gain an advantage. The Eagles went for it on twenty-six fourth downs throughout the 2017 regular season; only Green Bay attempted more. In the playoffs, they went for it on three fourth downs—and converted all three. A year earlier, in Pederson's first season, they led the NFL with twenty-seven fourth-down attempts. While some of the fourth-down decisions seemed to defy conventional wisdom, Pederson didn't make the decisions based on a whim—he used data.

"It's all [decided] in the off-season, done with mathematics. It's not based on any form of instinct," owner Jeffrey Lurie said, explaining how they play the percentages. "If it's going to be 50/50 . . . then a coach is going to have their instinctual predilections. But what we found is there's been so many decisions over time that are too conservative for the odds of maximizing your chance to win at the opportunity. You've seen certain coaches that are deemed more aggressive [and it's] because the math leads them there. That's all it is. So any decision hopefully any coach of ours makes is based on maximizing the chances to win. . . . When you do the math, you really want to try to be a lot more aggressive than the public would normally anticipate. So I think the smarter teams do it that way."

During games, Pederson's headset connects him to Ryan Paganetti, an assistant coach who relays the data in real time. Coaches need to make split-second decisions, so there's not much time for discussion. On fourth downs, the percentages often suggest whether they should go for it, consider it, or punt the ball. Pederson and Paganetti talk every day during the week about potential situations, and throughout each offensive drive Paganetti offers input to Pederson about what to prepare for in upcoming plays.

"When we get into those situations, those areas of the field where it might be a go-for-it situation or it might be a, 'Hey, let's get the points here, let's do "this,"' whatever it might be, we have those conversations early actually in the series," Pederson said.

The analytics department is overseen by Alec Halaby, the vice president of football operations and strategy. A Harvard alumnus, Halaby started with the Eagles as an intern during his sophomore year of college. Roseman promoted him to a bigger role after the 2016 regime change.

When Pederson interviewed for the head coaching job in January 2016, the use of analytics came up with Lurie, Roseman, and team president Don Smolenski. Pederson was on board. Lurie said Pederson wanted "all the information he could get" and expressed interest in knowing the "odds on everything." Lurie tried to dispel the notion that Pederson is merely pushing buttons called for him, explaining it as a collaborative effort. But entering the 2017 season, Pederson pledged to gain an even better understanding of data. He realized that although it was a different approach than he had learned as a player, "the numbers prove that you should do it a certain way." Now his public comments are infused with percentage probabilities.

Andy Reid was Pederson's most notable NFL coaching influence, but he's also learned from Mike Holmgren and Mike Sherman in Green Bay and hasn't been shy about incorporating concepts from past colleagues. He learned about run-pass options in Kansas City and continued developing that knowledge from assistants who remained from Chip Kelly's staff in Philly. In the Super Bowl, Pederson used a play that Sam Bradford introduced to him from his time with Kelly. Reich also offered ideas from his past, as did DeFilippo and wide receivers coach Mike Groh. Although Pederson built an offense that was uniquely his own, he always wanted to hear new ideas. He even had his coaches mine film from other teams in the NFL and college to look for plays, and this effort paid off in a big way in the Super Bowl.

In addition to compiling an impressive arsenal of offensive weapons, Pederson is always considering how to best deploy them. He is especially shrewd in the way he saves certain plays—for weeks or even months—to call in just the right moment. No play illustrated Pederson's gutsy, intelligent play-calling more than the Philly Special in the second quarter of the Super Bowl—a call that will go down as one of the best in Super Bowl history.

"Nothing just comes out of thin air, just off the top of my head," Pederson said. "Everything's out of the game plan, everything is things we've repped during the week. And it just comes down to film study, just like the players, and I'm no different. I've got to study the tape and understand situations, understand down and distance, and what the defense might be trying to accomplish and try to put our players, offensively, in the best position on that particular play to be successful."

• • •

Pederson's brilliance throughout 2017 was not just about his prowess with Xs and Os, but also about his expert management of the players in the locker room. He always had his finger on the pulse, starting in the off-season and continuing through the season and playoffs. His guidance in this regard was a big part of the resilience the Eagles displayed. Pederson implemented the "next man up" mentality that the team often discussed, and he paid close attention to the tone he set each week. That was most evident after Carson Wentz's injury, an event that would have sunk most teams. Pederson wanted the burden on his shoulders. He knew his players would look to him. And he wouldn't flinch.

"I'm going to lead this football team," Pederson said shortly after Wentz's injury. "It falls more on my shoulders than it does these players. That's why they need to stay encouraged. That's why they need to stay excited about this opportunity we have in front of us."

Pederson admitted that he allowed himself a brief moment of frustration, but he kept that to himself. He would never project concern about Wentz's injury to his team or to the public. Messaging mattered with him. He believes the game is about the players. He needs his players to be loose, to be confident, and to be free to do what they do best. And he knows it starts with him. During an offensive meeting after Wentz's injury, according to the *Philadelphia Inquirer*, Pederson walked into the room, and angrily kicked over a trash can. He purposely kept a serious look on his face as the players sat there on edge. And then Pederson started to laugh, breaking up the room. One day earlier, Jason Kelce had kicked a trash can at practice after he had been stepped on. Pederson wanted to lighten the mood, and knew what button to push that day.

In stark contrast to his Super Bowl counterpart, Pederson encourages his players to show their personality. He doesn't mind when they dance and celebrate. He wants them to enjoy coming to work. On the night before every game, Pederson ends his final team meeting by saying that it's time to go eat ice cream, which is always waiting for them in an adjacent room. His reason? Well, for one, he likes ice cream—Pederson grabbed his belly when explaining this in a moment of self-deprecation. But in terms of practicality, he doesn't want to speak so long that the ice cream melts.

"Doug Pederson is just himself," Jeffrey Lurie said. "And at times, that's very humble, and at times, it's just very real. At times, that's very bright. At times, it's tough. But he does it in a true, genuine way and I think players really respond to that in today's world."

SUPER BOWL LII

The Eagles tried to take advantage of the practice week in Philadelphia before heading to Minneapolis. They approached the Super Bowl bye week as if the game was on Sunday, practicing with pads and installing their game plan. The players tried to sort through their families' travel arrangements that week, too, so they could be unencumbered upon arriving in Minneapolis.

Doug Pederson said the Eagles were not going on vacation to Minnesota, but he had less control of the schedule once there. The team arrived on the Sunday before the Super Bowl, but they did not hit the practice field until Wednesday. They stayed at the Radisson Blu Hotel attached to the Mall of America in Bloomington, Minnesota, far removed from downtown Minneapolis. The Patriots came one day later, on Monday.

"I wanted our team to get here and kind of get settled in, get used to the hotel, get set up, get our meetings room set up, and let our guys unwind," Pederson said.

Players could be seen roaming the mall early in the week. That became less frequent as the game approached. By the end of the week, you couldn't walk anywhere without encountering Eagles fans. The E-A-G-L-E-S Eagles! chant became an ongoing soundtrack, as did the fight song. If they were on the road to victory, it included the Mall of America. There was heavy security surrounding their hotel. No one could enter without team credentials or without getting signed in by a team employee. There were few places more secure that week than the Radisson.

The Eagles practiced at the University of Minnesota while at the Super Bowl.

Their first full session came on Wednesday, although the Eagles were not in pads. Pederson decided they had their intense physical practices the week before; these practices were meant to keep the players sharp mentally.

Pederson added an interesting wrinkle to the session that would only apply in the week before a Super Bowl. The Eagles were in the middle of an effective practice, with music ranging from Nirvana to James Brown blaring over the speakers. Midway through the workout, the music stopped. Practice was halted as players and coaches left the facility. They were simulating a Super Bowl halftime, which is twice as long as a typical halftime. Teams unfamiliar with the halftime length could struggle in the second half of the game, and Pederson did not want to leave anything to chance. It was useful preparation, because the Eagles were not nearly as efficient when they returned from the mock halftime. Pederson addressed it with the team leaders and wanted to see improvements on Thursday.

"It wasn't get the team together, get the coaches together, and then start browbeating everybody," said Pederson, who celebrated his fiftieth birthday that day. "We're so late in the season now that we understand how to practice. Just making sure that we understand the importance. . . . That's why I did the break, was to put us in that situation. Now we understand it. It was a very teachable moment for our guys, our coaches for how to prepare for the second half of a football game."

Pederson saw the desired improvements in Thursday's practice. The pre-snap mistakes were fixed. Nick Foles was sharp. They were closing in on gameday. By Friday, the Eagles were ready. They went over their red-zone plays and tied up loose ends. After 80 minutes, Pederson called the team together and gave them a pep talk, emphasizing the importance of seizing the moment and having fun. On Saturday morning, NFL Hall of Famer Brett Favre spoke to the team. Favre and Pederson were longtime teammates and close friends. It was Pederson who broke the news to Favre that Favre's father died. Favre told the team that these two weeks would be the longest of their lives—and especially the last 24 hours before the game. But once the game arrives, it will slow down. The Eagles held one final walkthrough on Saturday at U.S. Bank Stadium, giving them a sense of the venue before arriving the next day. Then, it was just a matter of watching the clock and getting ready to play.

By this point, families and team employees were in Minnesota. It was an unusual Super Bowl destination, too cold for most visitors to spend time outdoors. But this was a business trip for the Eagles. Jeffrey Lurie didn't need an alarm clock in his Radisson hotel room. His obsessive quest for a Super Bowl was near complete, and it was coming against his favorite childhood team—and one that he once tried to purchase. The Patriots beat Lurie's Eagles 13 years earlier, and it still stung. Lurie wanted a ring, period. But for it to come against New England would be even more personal and gratifying.

Lurie awoke at 4:45 a.m. on Wednesday morning worried about Patriots receiver Brandin Cooks drawing pass interference penalties with his deep speed. He's up at this hour often with a question about the Eagles vexing him. There are times in June when he might phone Howie Roseman wondering about the nickel defense. He believed in Nick Foles, was bullish about how the Eagles' offensive line matched up against New England, and was encouraged by the offense. But those beliefs didn't wake him up in the morning.

"I don't think about those things; those are all true," Lurie said. "But I worry about what are we going to do with up-tempo on [Tom] Brady's part. Will we be able to counteract that? Things like that. Are we going to step up in the A-gap and put pressure on him so he can't step forward? Those are the crazy obsessions, but they're real. And that's life."

Lurie admitted he's thought too often about No. 12 on the Patriots. The quest for a Super Bowl dominated his life. He questioned every day whether the Eagles were doing what was needed for their best chance to win. He was 60 minutes away from finding out.

GAME DAY: SUPER BOWL LII: NEW ENGLAND PATRIOTS
W 41–33

Finally, game day arrived. Bill Belichick found Doug Pederson on the field before the game to shake Pederson's hand. Belichick, as venerable a foe as Pederson could encounter, congratulated Pederson on the season the Eagles had to date.

"I tried to find a game where you're behind," Belichick told him, as captured by NFL Films. "I couldn't find one."

"There's plenty," Pederson responded, although that was false modesty. The Eagles played with a lead throughout most games during the season.

"Hell of a year," Belichick said.

Belichick knew how to handle the Super Bowl Week—it had become almost an annual sojurn for him. But for Pederson, this was all new.

"I'll tell you what, you get through this week, you're like, 'Finally!'" Pederson said. "There's a game somewhere in here."

Belichick almost cracked a smile. "Great to be here," he told Pederson.

The players tried to find the balance between being focused and loose during pregame warm-ups. Jenkins spotted NBA star Steph Curry supporting the Patriots. "See, I knew I didn't like Steph Curry," Jenkins said.

The Eagles gathered in a huddle on the field one final time before heading into the locker room. Jenkins stood in the middle, offering his final speech to his teammates. He implored them not to make the game any bigger than it already was.

"You all want to be world champs? You all want to be world champs?" Jenkins screamed.

"Hell yeah!" they replied together.

"Well, guess what? All it takes is to give everything you've got! Everything that you've got for sixty minutes!" Jenkins huffed. "That's all that stands between you and immortality. We've been the best team in the league from start to finish. They're just finding out! So show the whole world today, man."

This was what many dreamed about as children, what they had worked toward all season. The world was watching. Philadelphia was waiting. And it was all in the hands of the players in the midnight green jerseys.

"One, two three!" Jenkins screamed.

"We all we got!" his teammates responded.

"Four, five, six!" Jenkins continued.

"We all we need!" they answered.

Pink sang the national anthem. Nobody kneeled. The United States Air Force Heritage Flight soared over the domed stadium. The Eagles sent their five captains to midfield for the opening coin toss, including injured leaders Jason Peters and Chris Maragos. Fletcher Cox and Nick Foles joined them as additional gameday captains. Sixteen recipients of the Medal of Honor stood between the Eagles and Patriots. The coin was tossed by Hershel Woodrow "Woody" Williams, who won the Medal of Honor for valor during the Battle of Iwo Jima in World War II. It had the Super Bowl 52 logo on one side as heads and team logos on the other side as tails. Brandon Graham called tails. The coin landed on the Super Bowl logo, giving the Patriots the choice of how to start the game. They deferred to take the ball in the second half. The Eagles would send their offense onto the field first.

Carson Wentz, wearing a sweat suit and a headset, stood with Nick Foles, who was in uniform and a helmet. That was supposed to be Wentz leading the Eagles onto the field. Instead, Philadelphia's hopes were now with Foles.

"Be great tonight," Wentz told Foles. "You're made for this. Enjoy it."

FIRST HALF

From the opening drive, the Eagles' offense was in sync. They converted two third downs and drove all the way to the Patriots' 2-yard line before the drive stalled. They settled for a 25-yard field goal, which was a small consolation for Pederson. He knew the Eagles needed touchdowns, not field goals. He told his assistant coaches as much. On the other sideline, the field goal was a small victory for New England, whose coaches congratulated their defense for holding the Eagles to three points on the drive.

The Patriots quickly tied the score by settling for a field goal of their own, and the Eagles' coaching staff reacted in the same manner. "We know we've got to be good in the red zone," defensive line coach Chris Wilson told his players. "Keep getting these f—ing field goals as long as you can, and we'll get us the stop."

In his headset, Pederson said it was time for the offense to go down the field and score. His players quickly obliged, needing just three plays to find the end zone. Foles hit Nelson Agholor for a 7-yard gain, then handed the ball off to LeGarrette Blount who barreled through the defense for a 36-yard gain to the Patriots' 34-yard line. On the next play, Foles faked a handoff to Blount and looked deep to Alshon Jeffery, who was tightly covered by cornerback Eric Rowe. Jeffery made an adjustment on the ball as it descended through the air, pushing off the cornerback and contorting his body in midair to haul in a spectacular touchdown while falling backward. It was the exact type of play the Eagles envisioned when they signed Jeffery in March, and here he was making it in the Super Bowl. The Eagles had scored the first touchdown of the game, while the Patriots' personnel decision at cornerback set off a minor controversy.

The Eagles had drafted Eric Rowe in the second round in 2015 when Chip Kelly was in charge. After the regime change in 2016, Rowe dropped in the depth chart and Roseman dealt him to New England. Rowe was pushed into extended action in the Super Bowl after the Patriots' usual starting cornerback, Malcolm Butler, was inexplicably benched by Belichick. The move was questioned by NBC announcers Al Michaels and Cris Collinsworth a few times throughout the game, and by others later. The Eagles did not take long to capitalize on the Jeffery vs. Rowe mismatch.

"They're going to have deal with it all game!" Blount said to Jeffery.

"What's up, GOAT?" Chris Long shouted to Foles, referring to the acronym for "Greatest of All Time"—a label often reserved for Tom Brady.

Elliott missed the extra point, and the Eagles settled for a 9–3 lead. Foles immediately found Elliott on the sideline and told him they'll be fine, and that Elliott will have more opportunities later in the game.

"We'll give you a bunch of them," Foles said.

That proved true, as New England had trouble stopping the Eagles all night. The big-play offense that was a staple throughout the season seemed to escape the Eagles after Foles first took over for Wentz, but it made a reappearance against the Vikings and then came out firing in the Super Bowl.

"We ain't even close to done!" Celek said on the sideline. "They can't stop us."

Brady needed to keep pace with the Eagles. But he's done it so often before, and his frequent heroics had already earned him the "GOAT" nickname. He said in the huddle that it was going to be a "dogfight," which the Patriots expected. The underdogs weren't going to be an easy opponent.

Using a no-huddle offense, the Patriots had no trouble moving the ball against the Eagles until they got to the red zone, where the Eagles clamped down. On a third-and-2 from the Eagles' 9-yard line, Brady handed the ball to Brandin Cooks on an end around, but safety Rodney McLeod sniffed out the play and slid over to make the tackle. Cooks tried to leap over McLeod to gain the first-down line, but it didn't work. McLeod upended Cooks in dramatic fashion, forcing the Patriots to attempt a field goal.

What should have been an easy 26-yard chip shot proved to be anything but. A bad snap led to a mishandled hold, causing Patriots' kicker Stephen Gostkowski to bang the kick off the left upright for the miss. The Eagles preserved their six-point lead.

After the Eagles punted on their next possession—the only punt of the game—New England took over at their own 37. On the first play of their drive, Brady hit Cooks on a comeback route at the Eagles' 40, and with no defenders around him, Cooks ran in a half circle looking for daylight upfield. He never saw Malcolm Jenkins coming from behind him, and the safety laid the biggest hit of the game on Cooks, pummeling him to the ground where he lay motionless for a good ten seconds. He would leave the game and not return. It was a hard but clean hit, and there was no penalty on the play. Lurie's early-morning worries would no longer apply.

Two plays later, the Patriots attempted a trick play that would foreshadow a trick play by the Eagles later in the quarter. Brady handed the ball off to a running back, who pitched the ball to a wide receiver, who then threw to Brady streaking down the sideline. A pass to a quarterback? That takes gumption in a Super Bowl. But Brady, wide open, failed to bring the ball in as it sailed right through his fingertips. The play fooled the Eagles, but the Patriots failed to execute on the trickery.

"C'mon, Tom! C'mon, Tom!" Jenkins yelled to Brady moments after the crucial drop, slapping the quarterback on the backside.

The Patriots failed to convert on their fourth down attempt, giving the Eagles the ball back on their own 35. After a couple of short runs, Foles hit Ertz and Jeffery on 19- and 22-yard receptions, respectively, setting up a first-and-10 from the Patriots' 21-yard line. On the next play, Blount took the handoff and found an enormous hole behind the Eagles' offensive line, scampering virtually untouched into the end zone. It was the third consecutive postseason game Blount scored for the Eagles. The Eagles failed on their two-point conversion attempt, keeping the score at 15–3.

"I ain't going to lie, I'm kind of impressed," Eagles' running back Kenjon Barner said to Blount on the sideline.

After a Patriots field goal cut the Eagles' lead to 15–6, the Eagles were driving again when Foles tried another deep pass to Jeffery inside the Patriots' 10-yard line. By now, the Patriots had put cornerback Stephon Gilmore on Jeffery instead of Rowe. Gilmore, who was Jeffery's roommate at South Carolina, had tight coverage and forced Jeffery to jump over him to get to the ball one-handed. For a moment, Jeffery had the ball pressed against his shoulder just a couple of strides from the end zone, but it bounced free and ricocheted up into the air, where the Patriots' interceptions leader Duron Harmon snagged the ball at the 2-yard line, then ran it out to the 10 before Jeffery tackled him.

Turnovers are often momentum changers, but the Eagles were far from demoralized. "Great punt, we straight," Jeffery said to Foles after the play, suggesting that a deep interception is as good as a punt. That was an optimistic way to look at it.

"Unfortunate," Wentz said to Foles on the sideline.

"Hey, part of the game," Foles said.

"Keep giving him a chance," Wentz responded. "He had that."

"We don't have to play the second-guessing game," Nate Sudfeld said to Foles. "You're playing phenomenally."

The Patriots answered with a 90-yard touchdown drive, turning what was nearly a 22–6 Eagles lead into a 15–12 score after they missed the extra point. After the Patriots kicked off, the Eagles had the ball on their own 30-yard line with 1:59 left on the first half clock.

"Let's go right down and put this thing in there," Foles said when he joined the huddle.

The Eagles gained 7 yards on their first two plays, setting up a crucial third-and-3. The offense didn't want to give the ball back, knowing that the Patriots specialized in scoring before halftime in these situations, and that New England would start the second half with the ball.

"Hey, Nick. I'm not [messing] around here," Pederson told Foles in the headset. He called a play that would send running back Corey Clement on a wheel route.

When the Eagles signed the undrafted rookie less than a year ago, he was an unproven pass catcher. But on this third down, he was a matchup problem. Foles took the shotgun snap and floated a pass out to Clement who caught the ball beyond the first down marker, ran it inside, broke a tackle, and raced for 55 yards to the 8-yard line.

Two Clement rushes later and the Eagles had a third-and-goal from the 1-yard line. When Foles couldn't connect with Jeffery for the touchdown, it was fourth down. All eyes were on Pederson. A field goal would make it a six-point lead going into the half, and would have been the most practical decision.

"That's a no-brainer," Patriots running back Dion Lewis said on the sideline. "He ain't going for it."

Pederson was resolute. He didn't want to settle for a field goal when a touchdown was possible. He was aggressive on fourth downs all season. They won the Falcons game, in part, because of that aggressiveness.

"Hold on, hold on," Pederson said in his headset as he deliberated. "We're going for it right here!"

The coach called a timeout to discuss the play call. Foles jogged over to Pederson on the sideline.

"You want Philly Philly?" Foles asked.

Pederson paused for a moment to think. He looked Foles in the eyes, and neither man flinched.

"Yeah, let's do it," Pederson said.

The offense took the field with Clement as the only running back. Blount, who scored the short-yardage rush against Atlanta, did not raise a fuss with his coach. But he was curious.

"What we got, Dougie?" Blount asked Pederson.

Pederson showed Blount his play sheet.

"Philly Special!" Blount said.

• • •

With ten players looking at him in the huddle, Foles read off the play call: "Philly Special. Philly Special."

Alshon Jeffery split wide to the right side of the line. Torrey Smith, Zach Ertz, and Trey Burton lined up tight on the left. Corey Clement initially set up to the right of Nick Foles, who stood in shotgun formation. Foles waved his hands down, trying to quiet the crowd. He gestured to Clement to slide in directly behind him. Then he walked up to the line and put on the best acting job of his career, pretending that he was changing the play.

"Easy, easy!" he shouted. "Kill, kill!"

Foles took two steps to his right, tapped Lane Johnson on the rear end, and called out, "Lane! Lane!" The Patriots thought Foles was signaling Johnson, but, in fact, that was the cue for Jason Kelce to snap the ball. With Foles away from the center, the snap went directly to Clement, who took the ball and sprinted to his left. Tight end Burton, who was once a quarterback at Florida, took the pitch from Clement and saw Foles running wide open toward the end zone. Burton took a couple of steps, positioned the ball in his hand for a throw, and lobbed a perfect pass to Foles, who looked back and reached up for the ball with his massive hands. Unlike Brady earlier in the quarter, Foles caught the pass. It was a touchdown, and one that Philadelphia will never forget.

The Eagles sideline erupted. They saw the play in practice and Pederson had talked about using it, but there's a difference between running a gadget play in practice and calling it in a critical moment on the biggest stage.

"Hell of a call!" Duce Staley said to Pederson.

"This play call has a chance to be remembered as one of the all-time greats," analyst Cris Collinsworth said on the NBC telecast.

"They brought it out in the Super Bowl?!" Jenkins said.

"Everything today!" Blount told Foles. "Catch them and throw them!"

"That was a dime, baby!" Celek said to Burton.

"Hey, Foles, why were you so open?" Burton asked Foles.

"I sold it!" Foles answered. "I did some acting!"

• • •

The play design for the "Philly Special" came from quality control coach Press Taylor. One of his jobs is to study film from around the league to look for trick plays. He saw the Chicago Bears run the identical play in a game the year before, and as it turns out, the Bears had copped it from Clemson, who ran it in 2012.

The Eagles had practiced the play for three weeks and inserted it into the game plan for the NFC Championship against Minnesota, but never got the opportunity to use it. In the week before the Super Bowl, they did a walk-through of the play in a ballroom at the Radisson to keep it under wraps. And the night before the Super Bowl, Pederson and offensive coordinator Frank Reich discussed the play during their routine review of the play sheet.

But what they couldn't practice or discuss was exactly when the play would be used, and it was the timing that stood out the most to Reich. It's one thing to call such a play on a third down in the middle of the field, but to call it on a crucial fourth down at the goal line demonstrated just how "gutsy" Pederson is.

"A quarterback going out on a route?" Foles said after the game. "That's probably the best it has looked. So, we hit it at the right time."

Foles always caught the ball in practice. The Eagles' coaching staff maintained that Foles was an underrated athlete, and although he had never caught a pass in the NFL, they believed in him in that moment. They also felt confident in Burton passing the ball, even though he had never thrown a pass in the NFL. Reich said the coaches had discussed finding a way for Burton to throw the ball all year long.

"I've been dreaming of throwing a touchdown pass since college," Burton said. "I still don't believe it. Guys said, 'You just threw a touchdown pass in the Super Bowl.' It's something that I'll never forget and my kids will never forget. It's special."

ERTZ SO GOOD

Since arriving in Philadelphia in 2013, Zach Ertz had been talked about more for his potential than for his achievements. Even though his career statistics through 2016 ranked among the top tight ends in the NFL, and though he had already inked a five-year $42-million contract extension, there were unending questions about whether Ertz was poised for a "breakout" campaign.

Part of that could be interpreted as complimentary. He was viewed as having the skills of a Pro Bowl player, even though he had not yet reached that status. But criticism reached a crescendo after one particular play in 2016 when Ertz did not block a defender on a Carson Wentz scramble against Cincinnati. His toughness was questioned, and it was not the first time. At times, his impressive statistics were rationalized as coming when the Eagles were out of contention. Fair or not, Ertz heard the criticism.

"I was in the dumps a little bit," Ertz said. "That definitely put things in perspective."

Ertz pointed to that day as a turning point in his career. He intended to ensure that his toughness was never questioned again. He also learned how to disregard public scrutiny and remain as even-keeled as other teammates he admired. He was no longer a young up-and-coming player adjusting from his school career in Northern California to the pros in Philadelphia. He was a second-contract NFL player in the prime of his career whose performance was essential to the team's postseason ambitions. He entered the 2017 season a stronger person and player, and he finally achieved the Pro Bowl status that eluded him during his first four seasons.

"Early in my career, if I didn't get the ball or if something would happen, or the media would say something [negative], I'd take it personally," Ertz said. "But now I know what I am. I'm very confident in my abilities."

• • •

Lisa Ertz never envisioned her son would be an NFL player. In fact, she didn't even let Zach choose where to attend college. Once Stanford offered him a football scholarship, that's where he would go. Stanford would provide the best education, and as far as his mom was concerned, that was the objective.

He didn't start taking football seriously until he was in high school in Danville, California. He had always wanted to play college basketball instead. More importantly, he wanted to be an admirable older brother. A child of divorce, Ertz became the man of the household as a teenager and wanted to help guide his three younger brothers. He was also fortunate to find someone who would help guide him: former San Francisco 49ers tight end Brent Jones. Jones's daughters went to high school with Ertz. The football coach told Jones the school had a junior tight end with potential. For a three-time all-Pro like Jones, "potential" was a relative term. Jones came to practice and saw Ertz's hand-eye coordination and hands, and also learned that Ertz was still growing. It took him about a week until he was convinced Ertz could excel at football, and he tried to persuade Ertz to give up his basketball ambition.

"We don't need another 6'6" white guy in the NBA," Jones told him. "You're a tight end. Not only can you play in college, you can play in the pros."

For the next year, Jones worked closely with Ertz to help him learn how to move defenders with his eyes, use his body to his advantage, and generally grow in the position. Off the field, Ertz studied the NFL's top tight ends and was especially mesmerized by Jason Witten. Jones promoted Ertz to his friend Jim Harbaugh, the head coach of Stanford. After Jones sent Harbaugh game film of Ertz's junior season, Harbaugh offered him a full ride.

Ertz exceled at Stanford and developed into a an NFL prospect, eventually being selected by the Eagles in the second round of the 2013 draft. But his maturity would be tested upon moving to Philadelphia. Ertz went to high school in the relatively laid back region of Northern California, and attended college a short drive from his hometown. Not only did he move to a much grittier city in Philadelphia, but he joined a team with an established starting tight end in Brent Celek. Adding to the culture shock and positional competition, he faced a rabid media corps and even more rabid fan base that would hold him to a higher standard than he'd ever faced.

"The cliché is there—I was a boy, and now I'm a man," Ertz said in 2017. "That first season was tough."

• • •

In his fifth season, Ertz felt a sense of self-satisfaction that eluded him earlier in his Eagles career. When he split time with Brent Celek as a younger player, Ertz had a harder time shaking off a mistake. By his fifth season, Ertz was entrenched as the starter and knew he didn't need to look toward the sideline to see if he would stay in the game. A newfound devotion to his faith provided a spiritual center that he lacked in previous years. And his marriage to soccer star Julie

Johnston, whom he dated since college, rounded out his life. He also adjusted his off-season training regime to avoid soft-tissue issues that could disrupt his season, working with his Stanford trainer back on campus.

The result in the 2017 season was seventy-four catches for 824 yards and a career-high eight touchdowns. He earned his first Pro Bowl appearance. And no one accused him of piling up stats when games were out of reach; he was routinely clutch when it mattered most. All eight of his touchdowns during the regular season came in the red zone, and thirteen of his sixteen third-down catches went for first downs. In the playoffs, he caught a team-high nine third-down conversions.

"Red zone, third down, I want to be the guy who gets the number called," Ertz said. "I put a lot of pride into what I do as a receiver in those situations—using my body when we need to make a play."

Ertz made that statement early in the playoffs. He validated it in the Super Bowl in the biggest moment of his professional life.

SECOND HALF

The Eagles were prepared for the long halftime, knowing what to expect while Justin Timberlake performed on the field. But what they didn't know was how Belichick and the Patriots would adjust, which is one of the hallmarks of their success.

"We've got to come out swinging!" Celek said when the Eagles returned to the sideline.

"Thirty minutes!" Graham screamed.

"That's all we've got," Jenkins answered. "That's all we need, too."

"Let's rock and roll," Pederson said.

The biggest adjustment the Patriots made in the second half was targeting star tight end Rob Gronkowski down the seams of the field. Gronkowski caught only one pass in the first half. To start the second half, Brady looked in his direction on the first three downs and on five of eight plays on the drive. Gronkowski caught four of those passes, including a 5-yard touchdown pass just minutes into the second half, cutting the Eagles' lead to 22–19. The Patriots looked like a machine on the drive. The Eagles had no answer for Gronkowski. Veteran safety Corey Graham was tasked with covering the big tight end, but no one player can cover Gronkowski downfield. Schwartz uttered an expletive to himself on the sideline.

"They can't cover you, man," a Patriots assistant told Gronkowski.

"We've got to go answer," Pederson said in the headset.

The offense had the answer. Foles found Agholor and Ertz on third downs to extend the drive, and on a third-and-6 from the 22-yard line, Foles needed to do it again. Pressure surrounded him as his top options were covered. He saw a sliver of space open in the back of the end zone where Clement would complete his route, and fired the ball over the helmets of Patriots in coverage, dropping a perfect pass into his receiver's hands. Clement reeled it in, then got knocked into a couple of cameramen, but came up with the ball. The referees both signaled for a touchdown.

"That's nasty, bro!" Jenkins said. "Over three of them!"

"Not how we drew it up," Foles said to Pederson, "but it worked!"

"Great throw," Pederson replied.

The Eagles' celebration was short-lived as the referees decided to review the play; it was unclear whether Clement maintained possession throughout the catch. The NFL's definition of a catch was ambiguous, so much so that the official definition would be revised a month after the Super Bowl. On the Eagles sideline, however, they were convinced Clement had scored.

"If you don't have enough evidence, you can't overturn it," Foles said while watching the replay.

On the other sideline, Brady waved his arms in a cross-cut motion to suggest "no catch."

Finally, the head referee turned on his microphone to give his decision.

"After review, the ruling on the field stands," the official said over the stadium speakers. It was a touchdown. The Eagles answered. They had reclaimed their ten-point lead, 29–19.

One problem: Tom Brady was on the other sideline, and the Eagles couldn't stop him. Brady completed four consecutive passes on the next drive, including a 26-yard touchdown throw to Chris Hogan. It was officially a shootout in Minnesota.

"Hey, we good," Jenkins said on the sideline. "We're just searching for one stop. That's it! Don't let it frustrate you."

"They're not stopping our offense," Maragos said.

But then, they did. Forced into a fourth-and-11 from the Patriots' 24-yard line, Pederson had no bold fourth-down decision to make this time. He needed to settle for a 42-yard field goal by Elliott, which he got. It was better than leaving the possession with no points, but the Eagles' lead was now only 32–26. The Patriots could take their first lead of the game with a touchdown.

To no one's surprise, that's what happened. For the third consecutive drive, Brady drove the Patriots down the field and into the end zone with relative ease. He hit Gronkowski for a 4-yard score with 9:22 left in the game, and after making the extra point, the Patriots took a 33–32 lead. Everyone had seen this movie before. The Eagles needed to write a different ending.

"Just keep playing ball," Foles said while warming up on the sideline.

"They cannot stop us," Ertz said to Foles.

"No, they can't," Foles said.

On the Patriots sideline, players implored each other to play nine minutes of their best football.

Foles ran to his huddle, looked at his teammates, and gave them their directive.

"I love you guys, first off," Foles said. "Let's put this thing in the end zone."

Foles brought the Eagles 20 yards forward, but on a third-and-one screen pass to Torrey Smith, the Patriots stopped him for no gain. The Eagles and Doug Pederson were staring down a fourth-and-1 at their own 45-yard line with 5:39 remaining in the game. This was a season-defining decision, if not a franchise-defining one. Pederson could punt it deep and trust his defense, but they hadn't stopped Brady all night.

"Let's go for it right here!" he called out.

It was another gutsy call by Pederson. If the Eagles missed, New England had a short field to the end zone. Pederson wasn't about to wilt in fear in the Super Bowl.

Foles took the snap and was immediately forced to sidestep interior pressure. Falling backward, Foles flicked a short pass to Ertz. The Eagles' tight end hauled in the catch a yard past the first-down marker and was driven backward, but the referee gave him forward progress and the Eagles lived to see another set of downs.

"We got it when we need it," Jenkins said on the sideline.

After securing the first down at midfield, the Eagles set their sights on getting a touchdown. But they had another problem to worry about—the clock. After a 1-yard rush from Blount, Foles completed three passes to move the ball to the Patriots' 14-yard line with 2:37 left on the clock. They were now in position to take the lead, but if they scored too soon, Brady would get the ball back with a chance to do what he has done so often—lead his team to a comeback victory. On the Eagles side-line, there was a sense that they needed to chew away the clock.

After a 1-yard gain by Blount, the Patriots called a time-out.

Foles approached his coach on the sideline. "What's your thought process right now?" he asked.

"We're going to score a touchdown," Pederson answered.

Celek found Ertz during the time-out and told him the Eagles needed him right now.

Back in the huddle, Foles said they must put the ball in the end zone. After an incomplete pass to Jeffery in the end zone, the Eagles faced a third-and-7 from the 11-yard line with 2:25 left. It would be the fourteenth play of the drive. Foles listened to the play call in his helmet, and looked down at his wristband. "Gun trey left, open buster star motion . . . 383 X follow Y slant," Foles called out, according to *Sports Illustrated*.

The Eagles isolated Ertz out wide left, where he was covered one-on-one by Patriots free safety Devin McCourty. The Patriots expected the pass to go to Ertz, and sent safety Duron Harmon over to help. But before the ball was snapped, Foles motioned Clement to sprint from his set spot in the backfield toward the right sideline, and Harmon sprinted after him, leaving Ertz one-on-one with his man. On the snap, Ertz ran 3 yards straight toward the end zone before cutting hard inside. McCourty bought the initial go route and when he tried to cut with Ertz, he stumbled. Ertz gained a clear inside position and was sprinting across the middle of the field when Foles released the ball. Foles never looked at anyone else. His pass hit Ertz in stride at the 6-yard line, Ertz pulled it in, broke through contact, and dove forward to break the plane of the goal line. The ball popped loose when he hit the ground, and once again, the referees went to the video review booth.

"Biggest replay in Eagles history," Merrill Reese said on the radio broadcast.

"It's a touchdown," Foles said while watching the replay. "He was past the line!"

Ertz could not imagine would what happen in Philadelphia if the play was overturned. But it was a possibility. There had been plays in recent years when apparent touchdowns were nullified because the league rule required the receiver to "survive the ground." It happened at the end of a Patriots game against the Pittsburgh Steelers in Week 15, helping the Patriots to a victory and giving them home field advantage in the playoffs.

A few tense minutes passed, and the referee turned on his microphone to make the call.

"After review, the receiver possesses the football, becomes a runner, [and] breaks the plane of the goal line. The ruling on the field is confirmed."

The Eagles took the lead. And they never gave it back.

Any previous criticism that Ertz endured was nullified with this one play. He made the clutch catch, fought for the hard yards, and would not be denied the go-ahead touchdown. And he did it on a play that was added to the playbook just a few days before the Super Bowl, according to *Sports Illustrated*. The coaching staff found the play while scouring through film and saw something in the formation that they believed would work against New England. And Ertz was the one they trusted in that moment.

"I mean, he had to run a slant, he had to get physical on the route, he did it, got open, and made the catch and then dove over the dude," Brent Celek said after the game. "Ertz is one of the top two tight ends in the NFL, in my opinion. You know they got Gronk over there, he's really good. But Ertz is the man, dude, and I'm so happy for him. I'm so honored to be in the same tight-end room with him."

When the big plays from the Super Bowl are remembered, the Philly Special will rank at the top of the list. But Ertz's touchdown deserves its own place in history as well. At the time, Ertz thought the Eagles would need to score again. He did not think it would remain the game-winning score.

"It hasn't really hit me that that play is going to have a lasting impact on my legacy," Ertz said two months later. "It's just something that it was, third-and-7 on the 11-yard line. That's the situation that I put a lot of pride in, all the work up to the point was for a situation like that. You've heard me say it all the time: Third down and in the red zone, I want to be the guy. That situation was third down and the red zone. I got my number called and I tried to make the most of it."

• • •

There were still two minutes and twenty-one seconds remaining in the game. The Eagles held a 38–33 lead, but the Patriots had the ball. And they had Tom Brady, who led eleven career game-winning drives in the postseason, including all five of his Super Bowl victories. Many football fans watching the game, maybe even those in Philadelphia, believed there was too much time left on the clock to feel safe with Brady holding the ball. Cris Collinsworth stated as much on the NBC broadcast, and Al Michaels agreed.

On the Eagles sideline, the message was clear: One stop. They spoke throughout the game about hitting Brady, and they continued to push that message. There were no sacks yet, but the Eagles had come close. One big hit could seal the game.

"Funny thing is, somebody on defense is about to be a superhero," Jenkins said to Darren Sproles on the sideline. "Whoever makes the play, somebody's going to be a hero."

Foles walked passed Long and screamed, "Strip him!"

Pederson turned to Brandon Graham and said, "Everything you've got!"

Graham took it to heart. On the second play of the Patriots' drive, Graham made the biggest play of his career. He lined up as a defensive tackle on the left side of the line, pushed through the Patriots offensive line, found a hole, and dove toward Brady with his left arm stretched to its limit. Just before Brady started his passing motion, Graham's hand slapped down on the ball and pushed it out of Brady's grasp.

"Fumble!" Foles screamed from the sideline. "Get it! Get it! Get it!"

Derek Barnett immediately spotted the loose ball in the air and moved toward it. Fumbles often take unpredictable bounces. This one caromed off of Barnett's leg, onto the ground, and up into his hands in the space of a second. On the Eagles sideline, players and coaches erupted.

"We got the ball!" Pederson said, with as much relief as joy in his voice.

Brady sat on the turf in disbelief. It felt like the moment Ivan Drago started to bleed in *Rocky IV*. David's slingshot found its mark.

The Eagles sent their offense onto the field at the Patriots' 31-yard line with 2:09 on the clock. They could begin to taste a victory.

"I love you guys, first off," Foles said in the huddle. "Second, let's blow them off the ball, get a first down, and finish this thing."

The offense couldn't score a touchdown. But they took seventy seconds off the clock and set up a 46-yard field goal for Elliott. He had been clutch all year. He was clutch again.

"The kick is [. . .] goooooooooood!" Merrill Reese said on the radio.

Elliott's field goal sailed through the uprights to give the Eagles an eight-point lead at 41–33. The Patriots still had time to tie the game—with 0:58 left on the clock—but a tie was the best they could do. Their players and coaches encouraged each other on the sideline, saying that the game was not over. On the Eagles sideline, though, they knew what it would take to finish it.

"One drive, let's go!" Wentz said to Cox. "Finish this thing, and you're world champs!"

On Jenkins's way onto the field, he walked past Foles. The quarterback screamed "Finish it!" Jenkins stopped, turned around, and slapped Foles's hand. "We got you," he said.

Schwartz told Pederson he was going to be aggressive with the defensive calls. The defense would either seal the game or get the ball back for the offense. But the offense already did its job, and they were so close.

"You've been playing your balls off, brother," Jason Kelce said to Foles. "I'm so happy for you."

Foles just wanted to "finish it." That was the complete focus. He told Sudfeld he had been praying all game. Those prayers were so close to being answered.

After Brady converted a desperation fourth and 10 deep in Patriots' territory, he rattled off three completions to bring the Patriots to midfield with nine seconds remaining. That would give Brady at least one chance at the end zone. Howie Roseman watched nervously from a box above the field, as seen on the NBC broadcast. This was it.

"Hey, this has got to go to the end zone!" Jenkins said to the defense, making sure they were deep. "If they go vertical, snatch them as they come out."

On the final play of the game, Brady avoided a sack by Graham and hurled a Hail Mary pass to the end zone. He released it just before Cox pummeled Brady to the ground for the first time all game. Brady had already thrown for 505 yards and three touchdowns during the game, but there was no more magic left. Three Eagles defenders surrounded Gronkowski at the goal line, as several others secured the perimeter. The ball was batted around before Patrick Robinson knocked it to the ground.

The clock read 0:00. With 41 points to the Patriots' 33, the Eagles—yes, the Philadelphia Eagles—won the Super Bowl.

• • •

Foles put two hands on the brim of his cap in disbelief. Sudfeld told him the game was over. Some players sprinted onto the field. Others stood in place and cried. Jenkins fell to the ground, buried his head down for a moment, and looked up to the sky with a huge smile on his face. He laughed out loud. It really happened.

Pederson turned to Chris Wilson and gave him a big hug, uttering "World champs." After the Eagles' first win of the season, Kamu Grugier-Hill and Steven Means poured Gatorade on Pederson. When the clock expired in U.S. Bank Stadium, those same two players showered him once again. Pederson shook Belichick's hand at midfield and then found Foles. They hugged each other. Green, black, and white confetti shaped like the Lombardi Trophy fell from above them.

"We did it, man!" Foles said.

"We did it," Pederson said. "Congratulations, man. Hell of a job."

Pederson bumped into Jason Peters and told the injured future Hall of Famer that he was a "world champ."

"Thank you, Doug!" said Peters, choking up while holding his coach in a long embrace. Peters found Foles and told him he's "a legend."

Wentz, holding a newspaper with Foles on the cover, had tears pouring from his eyes. He found Foles and hugged the player who stepped up when he went down.

"You deserve this, brother!" he said.

Those conversations happened all over the field. Grown men cried and told each other they loved them.

"Can you believe this, bro? Can you believe it?" Foles said to Kelce.

"You played your ass off!" Kelce said.

"We're world champions forever!" Roseman said to Foles. "Nobody can take this away from us."

Foles found his wife and gave her a kiss. He held his daughter onstage during the trophy ceremony, giving her headphones to block out the noise.

The Lombardi Trophy was escorted to the podium by Hall of Fame corner-back Darrell Green. Players touched the top of the trophy as it passed them.

Some had their cell phones out to record the moment. NFL Commissioner Roger Goodell stood with Jeffrey Lurie and his wife, Pederson and his family, along with Foles, Ertz, Roseman, and Don Smolenski. After twenty-four years of owning the Eagles, Lurie was finally able to hoist the Lombardi Trophy over his head, dedicating the trophy to Eagles fans, and to his parents. He touched his lips to the Lombardi, waiting more than two decades for the first kiss.

"If there's a word called 'everything,' that's what it means to Eagles fans everywhere," Lurie said. "For Eagles fans everywhere, this is for them."

GRAHAM: NOT A BUST

Brandon Graham's production at defensive end was one of the keys to the Eagles' Super Bowl season, and that sentence would have shocked anyone who read it just a few years earlier. Nelson Agholor might have come close to the "bust label," but Graham actually lived it.

The Eagles traded up in the first round of the 2010 draft to acquire Graham, a pass rusher from Michigan. When they made the trade, fans thought the Eagles would select Earl Thomas—a safety from Texas who would have replaced Brian Dawkins. After passing on Thomas, the Eagles watched him develop into one of the NFL's best players and lead Seattle to the Super Bowl. Meanwhile, Graham struggled with injuries and scheme changes early in his career and totaled only eleven-and-a-half sacks through his first four seasons while starting only twelve games.

Graham knew fans thought he was a bust. He never stopped hearing about Thomas. The Eagles moved him to outside linebacker under Chip Kelly, who ran a defensive alignment with four linebackers, and Graham flashed potential. But it didn't seem to warrant his draft slot, which he could never escape the criticism.

"For me, I started focusing on myself and not worrying about what people [were] saying—that he's not living up to [being a] first-rounder," Graham said in December 2014 before playing Thomas. "I mean, I got hurt. I was starting to feel real good and then I got hurt and I had to work from the ground up."

Graham had the option to leave during the 2015 off-season. He was a free agent and could have signed elsewhere, charting a new beginning in a place where he was not considered a bust. Yet Graham decided to stay. He liked Philadelphia and he was encouraged by the promise he showed at the end of the 2014 season in a reserve role.

The Eagles had a starting spot ready for Graham. He signed a four-year, $26-million contract, looking for redemption in Philadelphia.

When the Eagles hired Jim Schwartz in 2016 and moved to an attacking, 4–3 defensive scheme, it best fit Graham's skill set. He excelled under Schwartz, starting all sixteen games while recording five-and-a-half sacks and applying consistent pressure on the quarterback. His statistics did not tell the entire story. The game film revealed just how productive Graham had become. He earned second-team All-Pro honors, validation of how well he played. His reputation in Philadelphia underwent transformation.

"All it did was put a big chip on my shoulder that's going to carry me through my career," Graham told the *Philadelphia Inquirer* before the Super Bowl.

By 2017, Graham was recognized as one of the Eagles' best players. He finished the season with career-high nine-and-a-half sacks. He combined with Fletcher Cox to lead the Eagles defensive line, the strength of the defense. In the Super Bowl, he made a memorable, fourth-quarter play that will be remembered as one of the greatest in Eagles history. And Graham never forgot those early years.

PART 5

CHAMPIONS AT LAST

FINALLY PHILLY

The moment Philadelphia fans had waited a lifetime to experience had finally come. And the celebration, by all reports, dwarfed what took place two weeks earlier after the NFC Championship. There weren't enough cans of Crisco to stop Eagles fans. In fact, the city had upgraded to hydraulic fluid to try to keep fans off the poles. The epicenter of the celebration was outside of City Hall in Center City, where Broad Street filled with thousands of fans for the first time that week—but not the last. Fireworks exploded in the air. Eagles chants continued all night. There was dancing in the streets.

And yes, there was light-pole climbing, among other things. A dozen fans climbed on top of the entrance awning outside of the Ritz-Carlton, causing it to collapse. And while there were a few cases of looting and vandalism, it was mostly fans reveling in the unadulterated joy of a euphoria long overdue. There were hugs and tears and endless singing. They cheered Nick Foles. They jeered Tom Brady. And the celebration spread throughout the city and beyond—in South Philly, in the Northeast, at Temple University, in the suburbs. Even while celebrating in the Eagles locker room, players checked their phones to see what was happening back home. It wasn't just a celebration for the Eagles. It was a celebration for an entire city.

The cover of the *Philadelphia Inquirer* on the morning after the game read "AT LAST!" The *Daily News* read "WON FOR THE AGES." And the game story in those pages explained just why there was so much joy in Philadelphia:

This night will be remembered for decades in Philadelphia, when old friends reminisce about where they were on Feb. 4, 2018, and parents tell their children about the moment the Eagles won their first Super Bowl. They'll remember when Doug Pederson called the trick play at the goal line, when Zach Ertz dove into the end zone in the fourth quarter, when Brandon Graham stripped Tom Brady of the ball, and when the greatest dynasty in

NFL history fell to an improbable champion from Philadelphia.

[. . .]

This moment is bigger than what happened during 60 minutes on Sunday. Try nearly 60 years, generations of Eagles fans waiting since 1960 for this type of celebration. There were all those autumn Sundays, from the Franklin Field bleachers to the 700 Level at Veteran Stadium to pristine Lincoln Financial Field. There were seasons that started with championship promise and all finished with the bitter disappointment of the city's desire going unfulfilled. And it would renew each year, from the draft to training camp to the preseason into the regular season, with every weekend serving as a referendum and the Monday-morning mood throughout the region dictated by the final score the day before. If the fans were lucky, they had postseason football. But the last game was never a victory.

"DON'T BE AFRAID TO FAIL"

On the morning after the Super Bowl, with the moment still surreal, Nick Foles accepted his MVP trophy. He had thrown for 373 yards and three touchdowns. He caught a touchdown, too. Someone who Philadelphia had known for six years became an overnight sensation around the world. It was not just because of the way he played on the biggest stage, but all that had come before. Foles thought he would retire during that fishing trip in 2016. He had been near the top of the game, fell to the bottom, and climbed back to the top. So when Foles was asked what can be learned from his story, he put thought into the answer.

"I think the big thing is don't be afraid to fail," Foles said. "I think in our society today, Instagram, Twitter—it's a highlight reel. It's all the good things. And then when you look at it, you think 'Wow,' when you're having a rough day or your life is not as good as that, and you're failing. But failure's a part of life. That's a part of building character, growing. Without failure, who would you be? I wouldn't be up here if I hadn't fallen thousands of times, making mistakes. We're all human; we all have weaknesses."

In fact, Foles viewed the Super Bowl as a chance to share his story. When he first arrived in Philadelphia, he was reluctant to discuss much beyond football. But during the Super Bowl run, he was willing to share his story with the world. He wanted to be transparent, knowing that it would resonate with fans. After the Super Bowl, he appeared on talk shows. He wrote a memoir. He was a household name.

"I might be in the NFL and we might have just won the Super Bowl, but we still have daily struggles, I still have daily struggles," Foles said. "That's where my faith comes in. That's where my family comes in. And I think when you look at a struggle in your life, just know that's just opportunity for your character to grow. If something's going on in your life and you're struggling, embrace it, because you're growing."

A similar lesson could be learned from the Eagles' season. They were a model of resiliency. Much of evaluating a football player is tangible—How big is he? How fast is he? How well does he throw, catch, block, tackle?—but there are intangible characteristics that make a team. The underdog story captivated the nation, but the Eagles shouldn't have been underdogs. Their talent was underrated all along. In fact, they were the more talented team throughout the season, especially the Super Bowl. And part of that was because of a component of the team that was never understood, because it was intangible. They were a tough-minded team who did not let adversity swallow them, and each player embraced his role. They had a strong locker room and genuinely liked each other, developing a chemistry that made them want to play for each other. They were not afraid to work—across the roster, players had improved because of the work they put in. And they performed when it mattered most.

The margin for error in the NFL is so thin. What if Jake Elliott's field goal in Week 3 against the Giants landed a yard shorter? What if Julio Jones caught that ball in the divisional round playoff game against Atlanta? What if Chris Long never forced the fumble against Minnesota? What if Foles dropped the pass on the Philly Special or Derek Barnett did not recover the fumble Brandon Graham forced in the fourth quarter of the Super Bowl? Every team has these "what ifs." The difference between hoisting the Lombardi Trophy and waiting another year is performing in those moments. That was why the Eagles are champions.

COMING HOME CHAMPIONS

The Eagles' party did not stop in the locker room. It went straight through to the Renaissance Depot in downtown Minneapolis, where the Eagles held a victory celebration for players, coaches, team employees, family, and friends. They danced with the trophy, capturing the nightclub-like scene on social media. Jeffrey Lurie reveled in the moment with his ninety-year-old mother, who stayed awake until hours usually reserved for those a fraction of her age. Diplo, a popular DJ, controlled the music. Cardi B performed. There was no curfew on this night—just a flight home to catch in the morning. The Eagles boarded American Airlines Flight No. 9475 at 11 a.m. in Minneapolis. The Super Bowl champions touched down in Philadelphia at 1:54 p.m.

"It's our pleasure to welcome the world champion Eagles back to Philadelphia," an air traffic controller said to the flight's pilot, as heard on the flight's audio record.

Adoring fans waited outside the airport's fences to welcome home their heroes. While the plane taxied on the runway, a loud rendition of the Eagles fight song could be heard from the television cameras chronicling the arrival.

"[. . .] On the road to victory! E-A-G-L-E-S, Eagles!"

Lurie was the first person off the plane, with his wife, Tina. He held the Lombardi Trophy high into the air, marking the first time it could call Philadelphia home. Howie Roseman's cell phone, used to acquire so many of these players, turned into a video camera capturing the celebration. The team walked over to the fence near the throng of fans to show off the trophy. More phones came out. Usually, it's the players and coaches who are in the lens. On this day, they wanted to remember their fans' adulation.

The players and coaches then boarded buses and headed to the NovaCare Complex. They turned off I-95 at the South Broad Street exit, made a left turn on Pattison Avenue, and saw a mass of fans waiting there, too. Green and white balloons lined the barricade holding fans back. The cheers reverberated through the February air. Fans wearing Kelly green jerseys from generations earlier held signs high while the buses honked. The fight song was on repeat.

Many players didn't go home to rest. Nick Foles flew to Disney World, where a parade was thrown in his honor as the MVP. Jay Ajayi and Corey Clement went to Los Angeles after the game to appear on *Jimmy Kimmel Live!* Zach Ertz, Alshon Jeffery, Nelson Agholor, Chris Long, and Jalen Mills flew to New York City to appear on *The Tonight Show starring Jimmy Fallon* on Tuesday. Fallon's band, the Roots, is from Philadelphia and played the "Fly, Eagles Fly" fight song on air that night. Malcolm Jenkins appeared on *Late Night with Seth Meyers*.

Doug Pederson went out to dinner with his wife at Barone's in Moorestown, New Jersey, on the Tuesday after the Super Bowl. Fans kept flocking to his table to congratulate him. This was his new normal, and that's a term Pederson thought about often. On Wednesday morning, the players reported to the NovaCare Complex. They cleaned out their lockers and had exit interviews. Pederson held one final team meeting to put a bow on the 2017 season.

"Get used to this," Pederson told his team. "This is the new norm in Philadelphia."

With that, their season was complete. They returned the next day for the parade they will never forget.

END OF THE ROAD

The biggest celebration of all came on February 8. The parade was scheduled to begin at Broad Street and Pattison Avenue at 11 a.m., when the Eagles would ride buses three miles up Broad Street and around City Hall, then a mile and a half up Benjamin Franklin Parkway to the Rocky Steps at the Art Museum for an afternoon ceremony—the same spot where the 2017 draft was held months earlier. Fans started to line the streets the night before to get into prime location to see the buses drive by and hear the speeches. Schools and city offices were closed. Many fans took off from work. The city never released an official attendance count, but they expected up to three million fans. The Manchester Metropolitan University in England studied bird's-eye view photos and estimated to the *Inquirer* and *Daily News* that 700,000 were in attendance, a number that caused furor among those present who insisted that number was too low. Whatever the number, there was undoubtedly a mass of fans that was difficult to navigate. An attempt to walk up the Parkway on the day of the parade, well before the buses even approached the end of the route, proved a challenge. Fans packed close enough to smell whatever deodorant they were wearing, beverage they were drinking, or substance they were smoking.

The players were ready for a party. Jason Kelce arrived in a Mummer's outfit, looking like a green-and-purple bedazzled leprechaun, albeit one who is 6-foot-3 and 295 pounds. And he wasn't the only one dressed for the occasion. Chris Long's (faux) fur coat covered an Allen Iverson jersey. A few Eagles paid homage to past Eagles greats—Brent Celek wore a Harold Carmichael jersey, Jason Peters wore a Brian Dawkins jersey, Fletcher Cox wore a Reggie White jersey, and Rodney McLeod wore a Randall Cunningham jersey.

The Lombardi Trophy was passed around to different players atop the buses. Players occasionally stepped off the buses to celebrate and dance with fans. Those fans threw beers to the players on the bus—the promise to Lane Johnson was fulfilled—and ticker tape floated through the air. A skywriting plane spelled out "Philly Philly, Dilly Dilly" above the parade route, another homage to the Philly Special play (and the free Bud Lights given out that day). Along the parade route, a teammate came up to Kelce with ashes in their hand.

"I don't know what to do, somebody just poured their grandfather's ashes in my hands," the teammate said to Kelce.

"I don't know what to do, either!" Kelce said.

After the parade, there were multiple stories about fans who scattered ashes of deceased family members at the parade. It showed just how long fans waited and just how much it meant.

"The thing that's hit home so much has been that this fan base has really been waiting for this for a long time, and it's really a part of their families," Kelce said. "It's ingrained in father-son relationships, ingrained in brother relationships. . . . There's been so many heartfelt stories, 'watching games every single Sunday with my father and he never got to see it,' and those emotions come into it, and thanking [the Eagles] for finally getting it done. Or people whose parents just held on a little bit to see the . . . championship."

When the Eagles finally reached the Rocky Steps, the ceremony commenced. And it was epic. It started with Jeffrey Lurie, who said the Eagles "epitomized what this great city and what this great country can be at its best," honored the Eagles alumni, and dropped the mic at the end to punctuate the speech. Doug Pederson followed, and he emphasized that the Eagles were not finished. Like he told the players, this was "the new norm." Howie Roseman came after Pederson and asked Philly if "this is what heaven's like." Then came the players: Nick Foles, Peters, Chris Maragos, Celek, Johnson and Long together, Brandon Graham, Carson Wentz, Alshon Jeffery, Kelce, Zach Ertz, and Malcolm Jenkins all spoke. They touched on their connection with each other, their passion for the fans, and how much fun the parade had been for them. Libations bolstered some of the speeches.

Ask anyone watching, and they will say one speech was most memorable. Jason Kelce lay awake the night before thinking about what he would say, and it was ultimately a speech he started in the shower after the NFC Championship win against the Vikings. His speech will be remembered as the highlight of the parade, as it explained, at times explicitly, the 2017 Eagles and their connection with the fans:

> *[. . .] I'm going to take a second to talk to you about underdogs. I know Lane and Chris just talked about this, but I don't think it's been beat home enough.*
>
> *Howie Roseman, a few years ago, was relinquished of all control pretty much in this organization. . . . He was put in the side of the building where*

I didn't see him for over a year. Two years ago, when they made a decision, he came out of there a different man. He came out of there with a purpose and a drive to make this possible. And I saw a different Howie Roseman. An underdog!

Doug Pederson. When Doug Pederson was hired, he was rated as the worst coaching hire by a lot of freaking analysts out there in the media. This past off-season, some clown named Mike Lombardi told him that he was the least-qualified head coach in the NFL. You saw a driven Doug Pederson, a man who went for it on fourth down, went for it on fourth down . . . in the Super Bowl with a trick play. He wasn't playing just to go mediocre! He's playing for a Super Bowl!

And it don't stop with him. It does not stop with him!

Jason Peters was told he was too old, didn't have it anymore. Before he got hurt, he was the best freaking tackle in the NFL! Big V was told he didn't have it. Stefen Wisniewski ain't good enough. Jason Kelce is too small.

Lane Johnson can't lay off the juice. Brandon Brooks has anxiety!

Carson Wentz didn't go to a Division I school. Nick Foles don't got it. Corey Clement's too slow. LeGarrette Blount ain't got it anymore. Jay Ajayi can't stay healthy. Torrey Smith can't catch. Nelson Agholor can't catch. Zach Ertz can't block. Brent Celek's too old. Brandon Graham was drafted too high. Vinny Curry ain't got it. Beau Allen can't fit the scheme. Mychal Kendricks can't fit the scheme. Nigel Bradham can't catch. Jalen Mills can't cover. Patrick Robinson can't cover.

It's the whole team! It's the whole team!

This entire organization, with a bunch of driven men who accomplished something. We were a bunch of underdogs. And you know what an underdog is? It's a hungry dog! And [offensive line coach] Jeff Stoutland has had this in our building for five years—it's a quote in the O-line room that has stood on the wall for the last five years: "Hungry dogs run faster. " And that's this team!

Bottom line is, we wanted it more. All the players. All the coaches. The front office. Jeffrey Lurie. Everybody wanted it more. And that's why we're up here today. And that's why we're the first team in Eagles history to hold that freaking trophy!

Any of you know who the biggest underdog is? It's y'all, Philadelphia. For fifty-two years, y'all have been waiting for this. You want to talk about an underdog? You want to talk about a hungry dog? For fifty-two years, you've been starved of this championship! Everybody wonders why we're so mean. Everybody wonders why the Philadelphia Eagles aren't the nicest fans. If I don't eat breakfast, I'm f—ing pissed off!

No one wanted us! No one liked this team! No analyst liked this team to win the Super Bowl and nobody likes our fans. And you know what? I just heard one of the best chants this past day, and it's one of my favorites and it's new, and I hope y'all learn it, because I'm about to drop it right now.

You know what I got to say to all those people who doubted us, all those people that counted us out, and everybody who said we couldn't get it done? What my man Jay Ajayi just said: "F— you!"

No one likes us! No one likes us! No one likes us! We don't care! We're from Philly, f—ing Philly, no one likes us, we don't care! No one likes us! No one likes us! No one likes us! We don't care! We're from Philly, f—ing Philly, no one likes us, we don't care! E-A-G-L-E-S, Eagles!

• • •

Nothing else needed to be said. Kelce summed up the team's emotional, historic season. They were unlikely champions that satisfied a starving city's hunger. The parade started by the practice facility and stadium in South Philadelphia. It finished on the Rocky Steps, where the Eagles were celebrated as Philadelphia's most beloved underdogs. In between, Broad Street and the Benjamin Franklin Parkway were packed with generations of adoring Eagles fans. The memorable lyric from the Eagles' fight song never seemed more appropriate. This was their road to victory.

ACKNOWLEDGMENTS

I never quite knew the importance of this section in books until 4:51 p.m. on May 15, 2018, when I clicked "send" on the final part of the manuscript. While walking home from a coffee shop, I realized that this book could not be completed by myself alone.

I'm appreciative of Running Press for giving me this opportunity and trusting me to tell the story. In particular, Jess Fromm has been outstanding to work with, and this project relied on her editing, vision, and oversight. She was patient and supportive from the first interaction. Greg Jones was extraordinarily valuable during the editing process, too, and the book improved with his help and guidance. Thank you also to Josh McDonnell for the great cover and design, and to Susan Hom for her close read.

Larry Kane, Marc Brownstein, Todd Zolecki, and Mike Sielski were incredibly helpful in kicking off this project. I'm indebted to Larry for his guidance throughout the process, always making time.

Norman Rosenthal offered the first set of eyes for every word. I could never explain how valuable his feedback became.

There was no one better to write the foreword for this book than Merrill Reese. I'm ever grateful that he agreed—his kindness rivals his voice.

This is a compilation of six years covering the Eagles. The media relations office has been helpful during that period, and my reporting relied on their accommodations throughout the years. The players, coaches, and executives have been professional to deal with, and I never took for granted their time and insight. Many of their voices are heard in this book. Many are not, but interviews with them nonetheless shaped and contextualized this story.

Almost all of my Eagles reporting took place for the *Philadelphia Inquirer*, and I appreciate Pat McLoone and Stan Wischnowski for allowing me to turn it into a book. Even more, I'm grateful that they allow me to do this every day. John Quinn first trusted me with this job. Gary Potosky followed and I continue to benefit from his oversight.

I'm privileged to have the colleagues I do. Jeff McLane has been a tremendous partner on the beat for six years, and I'm fortunate that Les Bowen and

Paul Domowitch are now colleagues and not competitors. The other members of the Eagles beat make me better. I read them each morning and enjoy their companionship every day.

My first teammates were at the *Daily Orange*. They're now lifelong friends. Matt Gelb and Zach Schonbrun were instrumental in this book taking place. Matt planted the seed in my head, and Zach was invaluable in explaining and guiding me through the process from the beginning. Both were critical sounding boards all the way through.

I've learned from colleagues and editors at every place I've worked since—from the *Washington Post* to the *Newark Star-Ledger* to *Philadelphia Daily News* to the few months contributing for the *New York Times*. I'm also lucky to have formed relationships with so many people that I admire in this business. Greg Bishop and Seth Wickersham have been beyond helpful with my reporting.

My work takes up most of my time. But nothing is more important than my family—to aunts, uncles, cousins, and in-laws, I'm extremely grateful. I'm fortunate to have such involved and loving grandparents. My grandfather always pushed me to do something like this. I hope you're as proud as I am appreciative.

My brothers and sister (and their spouses) are my best friends and have seen me go from the person reading these books to the person writing these books. It wouldn't have happened without them.

My mother first encouraged me to join the high school newspaper and has been right about everything ever since. Her encouragement and support has been a critical foundation for everything I've ever done. I'm a lucky son. My father is my role model, and his character and wisdom remain a guiding light and a constant presence in my life, including the work that went into writing this book.

Finally, the only thing I enjoy more than writing and reading is being married to Emily and being the father to Reid. Thank you for everything, Emily—your patience, support, love, and understanding of how much I enjoy this. It never went unnoticed.

And Reid—one day, I hope you read this and like it half as much as *Little Blue Truck*.

ABOUT THE AUTHOR

Zach Berman covers the Philadelphia Eagles for the *Philadelphia Inquirer* and *Philadelphia Daily News*. He previously wrote for the *Washington Post* and *Newark Star-Ledger*, and was a contributor for the *New York Times*. He also makes regular television appearances on NBC Sports Philadelphia. Zach is a graduate of Syracuse University's S.I. Newhouse School of Public Communications and lives in Philadelphia with his wife, Emily, and son, Reid.